Reimagining *To Kill a Mockingbird*

REIMAGINING
To Kill a Mockingbird

FAMILY, COMMUNITY,
AND THE POSSIBILITY
OF EQUAL JUSTICE
UNDER LAW

EDITED BY
Austin Sarat
AND
Martha Merrill Umphrey

University of Massachusetts Press
Amherst & Boston

Copyright © 2013 by University of Massachusetts Press

All rights reserved

Printed in the United States of America

ISBN 978-1-62534-016-0 (paper); 015-3 (hardcover)

Designed by Jack Harrison

Set in Adobe Caslon Pro

Printed and bound by Thomson-Shore

Library of Congress Cataloging-in-Publication Data

Reimagining To Kill a Mockingbird : family, community, and the possibility of equal justice under law / edited by Austin Sarat and Martha Merrill Umphrey.

    pages cm

Includes bibliographical references and index.

ISBN 978-1-62534-016-0 (pbk. : alk. paper) — ISBN 978-1-62534-015-3 (hardcover : alk. paper)

1. Lee, Harper. To kill a mockingbird.   2. Law in literature.

I. Sarat, Austin, editor of compilation.   II. Umphrey, Martha Merrill, editor of compilation.

PS3562.E353T654 2013

813'.54—dc23

2013001344

British Library Cataloguing-in-Publication Data

A catalogue record for this book is available from the British Library.

To Ben, with love and hope (A. S.)
For my family (M. U.)

CONTENTS

ACKNOWLEDGMENTS

The essays in this book were first presented at a conference held at Amherst College on September 23–24, 2011. We are grateful for the generous support provided by Amherst College's Charles Hamilton Houston Forum on Law and Social Change and by the Dean of the Faculty, Greg Call. We thank Heather Richard for her skilled research assistance and Megan Estes for her good work in organizing the conference.

An earlier version of chapter 1 was previously published as Austin Sarat and Martha Merrill Umphrey, "Temporal Horizons: On the Possibilities of Law and Fatherhood in *To Kill a Mockingbird*," *Cultural Studies*, www.tandfonline.com/doi/full/10.1080/09502386.2012.722295.

Reimagining *To Kill a Mockingbird*

Reimagining *To Kill a Mockingbird*
An Introduction

MARTHA MERRILL UMPHREY & AUSTIN SARAT

The year 2012 marked the fiftieth anniversary of the release of *To Kill a Mockingbird*, the film remake of Harper Lee's acclaimed novel.[1] In taking note of that milestone, this volume looks at the film, a classic and canonical text in legal scholarship, with fresh eyes. The chapters that follow revisit and examine Atticus, Scout, and Jem Finch, their community, and the events that occur there through the interdisciplinary prism of law and humanities scholarship—work that brings a distinctive interpretive framework to the study of law.

The film and novel are of course widely available and have taken on both a mythical and a pedagogical role in American culture (and beyond). Earnest teachers have for generations urged schoolchildren to understand Atticus Finch's defense of Tom Robinson as a linchpin moment in the nation's narrative of racial progress. Indeed on one standard reading, *To Kill a Mockingbird* is a profoundly pedagogical text, one that strives to teach us ways of overcoming prejudice and to live with one another in a better and more just world. That rendering of the film situates it in a past moment that has been overcome, and conjures Atticus Finch as a hero who, while failing in the narrative space of the film, nevertheless paves a path to a better future through his work and his children.

The readings of the film offered in this volume complicate without fully rejecting that mythologizing interpretation. They peel back the film's visual representation of Maycomb, Alabama's many-layered social world, offering sometimes counterintuitive rereadings through the prism of a number of provocative contemporary theoretical and interpretive questions. What, they ask, is the relationship between the subtle subversion of social norms and the doing of justice or injustice? How does one come to belong to, even to be recognized as "human," within this community? Through what narrative and visual devices are some social hierarchies destabilized while others remain hegemonic? How should we understand the sacrifices characters make and are asked to make in the name of justice and comprehend their failures in achieving it? Asking such questions casts light on the film's eccentricities and internal contradictions and suggests the possibility of new interpretations of a culturally iconic text.

The Film as a Cultural Icon

Five decades after its first screening, *To Kill a Mockingbird* retains a central place in the American cultural imaginary.[2] Indeed it seems to transcend its historical moment and to be a refracting mirror in which we view ourselves and our relation to the legacy of a racist past. Its continuing and powerful resonance signals what Naomi Mezey would view as an act of translation that produces a text's "afterlife"—"not what happens after death but what allows a work (or event or idea) to go on living and to evolve over time and place and iteration."[3] Part of this film's afterlife is, we think, produced by its layered temporal framework, the way in which it looks both backward and forward at once.[4] It begins, hauntingly, with an image of a cigar box full of old toys, trinkets, and crayons, a little girl humming and laughing in the background. The film then cuts to a street in Macomb as we hear a voice-over—the voice of a mature woman recalling the world of this town in the 1930s from the unlocated vantage point of the 1960s. She reflects back on the slow pace of everyday life in the depression-era summers of her childhood. Scout Finch thus provides the film with a doubled narrative presence, both embedded in childhood and a child's relation to her family and community and overlaid with the passage of time and the perspective it offers.

Scout's tone is nostalgic; and yet as a number of the contributors to this volume note, the family and community she describes are more eccentric than easily romanticized, riven beneath the surface by individual loss and social fragmentation.[5] Atticus is a widower raising the insistently tomboyish Scout and her brother, Jem, with the help of Calpurnia, their African

American maid. Their friend Dill has no apparent family at all (beyond the invisible aunt whom he is visiting). Across the street lives Miss Maudie, a single woman and friend of Atticus's who might, but never quite, takes up a motherly role toward Scout and Jem. Nearby Boo Radley lurks, an unseen madman in a frightening house—and yet one who leaves small gifts for Jem and ultimately saves his life. Down the road sits Mrs. Dubose, spitefully chiding the children who run wild in the neighborhood, until she is mollified by Atticus's courtly manners. And somewhere past the edge of town and essentially offscreen live three families: the Robinsons, a poor but respectable African American extended family; Walter Cunningham's family, impoverished farmers in debt to Atticus; and the Ewells, "white trash" who spit and lie and embody the ever-present threat of racist violence.

When Bob Ewell accuses Tom Robinson of raping his daughter Mayella, Atticus takes up Tom's defense, breaking the implicit social compact undergirding southern white supremacy and releasing ominous clouds of looming violence—in the schoolyard, where Scout fights children who insult her father; in the town square, where a mob gathers to lynch Robinson; and in the woods, where Ewell attacks Scout and Jem. Atticus counters that violence by asserting the supremacy of the law, grounded in principles of formal equality and individual dignity. His stirring and canny defense of Robinson in court fails, but we as spectators, reflecting back with the adult Scout, see Robinson's conviction through the lens of a future in the process of overcoming that past. Atticus, with his faith in law, is not strong enough to overcome Ewell or to protect his children from him. But Boo Radley's heroism in killing Ewell and rescuing Jem bodes well for a future in which community can be reimagined as inclusive and bound by ties of affection that overcome barriers of race and difference. The film situates us, as contemporary spectators, in that imagined future, encouraged to reflect on the ways in which the United States has taken up the mantle of progress and bestowed it so hopefully on us.[6]

Legal Imaginings and Contestations

To Kill a Mockingbird is not only a resonant cultural text but also a classic text in American cultural-legal studies. Scout Finch's voice-over recounts her memories of both the town and Tom Robinson's trial. It echoes through the decades in ways that affect our judgments about law's current entanglements over racial justice. Indeed the film, as a trial film, demands just that spectatorial stance. As Carol Clover suggests, "the trial movie . . . positions us not as passive spectators, but as active ones, viewers with a job to do."[7] Even as it situates us to condemn the inanity and injustice of depression-era racism in the South, it also invites our continuing assessment of Atticus Finch's failures and speculations about the ultimate, beyond-the-frame trajectory of his principles.

Legal scholarship on *To Kill a Mockingbird* tends to focus thematically on the ways in which characters embody and negotiate the ideological conflict between liberal egalitarianism and a pernicious social caste system. The film vividly captures the manner in which racism confounds the connection between the constitutional principle of equality and a town's local legal processes, and follows the path of Atticus Finch, who vindicates the former—not in the film's courtroom but in the courtroom of spectatorial opinion. It offers in Atticus a hero who, as Stephen Lubet suggests, is popular culture's most important embodiment of lawyerly virtue.[8] In a well-known article capturing this celebratory strain of scholarship, Thomas L. Shaffer views Finch as a hero because of his role as truth teller in the community.[9] Shaffer conjures Finch as a redemptive figure whose defense of Tom Robinson preserves his own integrity, reminds Maycomb of its better self, and points to a future freed of racism and its violence. In Lubet's apt (if ultimately arch) characterization, Atticus Finch "saves us by providing a moral archetype, by reflecting nobility upon us, and by having the courage to meet the standards that we set for ourselves but can seldom attain."[10]

And yet these encomiums have their dissenters. One recent exemplar is Malcolm Gladwell, who echoes a long line of commentators critical of Atticus Finch's essentially conservative approach to obtaining racial justice.[11] Equating Finch with the populist Alabama governor James (Big Jim) Folsom, who held office on and off from 1947 to 1959, Gladwell writes, "What it meant to be a racial moderate, in that context, was to push for an informal accommodation between black and white." All politics being local, both Folsom and Finch put personal ties above principle in order to accommodate, but not reform, southern white society. "If Finch were a civil rights hero," Gladwell writes, "he would be brimming with rage at the unjust verdict. But he isn't. . . . [H]e could not grasp that those frailties were more than personal—that racism had a structural dimension."[12] To argue that such a position unfairly wrenches Atticus Finch out of his own time and space is only to underscore, as Marjorie Garber has argued about the cultural life of another racialized film, *Inherit the Wind*, that "the political valence of an incident or an argument cannot be detached from its cultural context. . . . [I]deas and events are read differently in different cultural domains."[13]

This continuing fascination with the successes, failures, and ambivalences of Atticus Finch and of Maycomb, Alabama, occupies an important place in this volume. Distinctively, though, a number of the contributors consider the ways in which these issues are expressed not just thematically but visually. Indeed in focusing on the film version of *To Kill a Mockingbird*, we wish to emphasize how its visual dimension shapes the presentation of ideological conflict.

This visual dimension is important, too, in understanding how the film departs from the novel, compressing or eliminating certain themes and expanding others. Gone is any mention of Finch's Landing, Atticus's ancestral home; gone is any thick depiction of the African American community; gone is Aunt Alexandra, Atticus's sister, the stern enforcer of southern gender norms. Instead we find greater focus on Boo Radley, and Tom Robinson's trial is the film's moral centerpiece. As Susan Sage Heinzelman suggests in her essay, the novel represents the social landscape of Maycomb, Alabama, in ways that point to structural and systemic inequalities that are race, class, and gender based. In contrast, the film focuses more on individuals as icons and invites a particularly liberal understanding of race relations, at least thematically. Justice becomes a matter of standing in the shoes of the other, a moral individual's exercise of empathy for those less fortunate; and the film depicts those for whom empathy is impossible—particularly the Ewells—with a level of caricature guaranteed to thwart any spectatorial identification.

And yet aesthetically, the film's noirish chiaroscuro sensibility also complicates the film's moral clarity. In the daylight, reason and affection tend to prevail, but at night, wind and shadows portend the danger always present just under the surface of southern civility. Spectators are invited to identify with the children and their idealized view of Atticus, and the logic of the film's antiracist bent is expressed through and played out in image and sound, heightening and channeling the kinds of affect that underlie the judgments that spectators level—cannot help but level—against the injustices done in Maycomb. And yet, as Ravit Reichman and Colin Dayan in particular highlight in their essays, the film also employs narrative and visual techniques that interrupt and disturb, if only momentarily, the desired trajectory of justice. Atticus Finch, the film's great advocate of nonviolence ("you must not fight," he constantly tells Scout), picks up a gun and proves himself the best shot in the county by shooting an old rabid dog. That he does so in a manner the film represents as reluctant, almost comical, only intensifies the sense that this scene depicts the return of the repressed, exposing the unconscious ways in which even those whose commitment to justice is unassailable can desire and inflict violence on those who are abject. This visually powerful scene, Reichman and Dayan argue, casts a shadow on the legal heroics that come later. It introduces what Peter Goodrich calls the "affect inside legality" made visible in visual representations of law.[14]

The Essays

The kind of textured interpretation we have been describing characterizes our contributors' readings of the film. Two general themes run loosely through the chapters that follow. The first invites us to reconsider Atticus Finch both as an embodiment of principled justice and as a father figure struggling to care for his children. The second moves beyond Atticus to examine the broader community in Maycomb, its fracturings and reconstitutions.

In "Temporal Horizons: On the Possibilities of Law and Fatherhood in *To Kill a Mockingbird*," we argue that the focus on Atticus as both a father and a lawyer fuels the *filmic* appeal and importance of *To Kill a Mockingbird*. As both father and lawyer, Atticus is oriented to the future more than to the present, conjuring what we call "a normative world of becoming more than being." His mode of fathering his children is of a piece with his advocacy on behalf of Tom Robinson: in both he asserts a vision of a future less violent and prejudiced, more just and compassionate, than the present. The film's voice-over underscores that orientation, spoken by a nostalgic daughter who ratifies—indeed idealizes—Atticus as both a father and a lawyer.

Atticus contrasts sharply, we argue, with the film's other father, Bob Ewell. Ewell embodies the honor-based violence of white supremacy and an older version of southern manhood, one that places clan and race above a liberal vision of a just and equal society. Conversely Atticus appears, both as a father and as a lawyer, to be deeply invested in self-control and civilized reciprocal relations with others in the community. And yet, although he acts in principled and decisive ways, his power to control both his children and the legal outcome in Tom Robinson's case is limited. Maycomb's potent social norms have not completely enveloped Scout and Jem; and they have learned from Atticus to question commands, no matter their source, rather than reflexively obeying them. Atticus represents not law as command but rather law that is more contingent and future-oriented, law that works to change the present (however haltingly) by attempting to bring into being a new imagining of community and justice. Atticus's children embody that imagining. They sit with the African American community during the trial, up in the balcony, nearer to heaven, joined in their reverence for Atticus. Insofar as Scout and Jem embody both the vulnerability of a racist present and the promise of a different kind of community, their relation to their lawyer father illuminates the way in which Atticus serves as a bridge to a better future and a redemptive vision of law.

In "I Would Kill for You: Love, Law, and Sacrifice in *To Kill a Mockingbird*," Linda Ross Meyer offers a somewhat different but related reading of Atticus's relations with his children. At the moment he takes Tom Robinson's case he seems, Meyer argues, to choose legal obligation over loyalty to family, and in so choosing he puts his children in real danger. Why won't Atticus defend his family, Meyer wonders? She takes up this provocative question by reading Atticus's actions through the archetypal story of a father sacrificing his son for the law, Abraham and Isaac, as it was interpreted by Søren Kierkegaard in *Fear and Trembling*.

There Kierkegaard suggests two different figural conceits through which we might interpret Abraham's actions: the knight of the infinite, an embodiment of universal principle who makes tragic sacrifices once convinced by reasoned argument that a certain principle is "for the right"; and the knight of faith, who acts not on principle or through deliberation but to obey God's commands in an act of personal loyalty. This is a perilous love, Kierkegaard suggests, an absurd faith, at once terrible and beautiful.

Is Atticus Finch a knight of the infinite? Meyer asks. From one perspective he seems willing to sacrifice his children for the sake of liberal legality. Meyer sees this same conflict between law and loyalty resonating in a number of contemporary circumstances, ranging from cultural responses to 9/11, to the elegiac roles that victims now play in courtrooms, to self-defense doctrines that allow the killing of an innocent aggressor, through "speciecism," a preference for humans over other species. Yet, she argues, Kierkegaard's framework can help resolve this seemingly intractable set of dilemmas. Ultimately, when Atticus concludes that it would be a sin to put Boo Radley on trial for Bob Ewell's death, law loses out to loyalty. In reaching that conclusion, Atticus proves himself a knight of faith. He does not embrace a universalist view of either law or ethics. Rather, in choosing loyalty to Tom over loyalty to his race (having thoroughly denigrated the Ewells), he works to alter the loyalties of his community, to commit to a different future on faith, one that draws its virtues from those already immanent in every member of the community. Focusing on that kind of particularity, the film offers a way out of the tension between law and loyalty that is consonant with the liberalism Atticus seems to embody.

If these two essays both continue the classic line of scholarship that focuses primarily on Atticus Finch as a cultural icon, the essays by Thomas L. Dumm and Imani Perry peel apart his identity and community in ways that complicate his heroic reputation. Noting the film's doublings, cross-connections, and oppositions among various kinds of families, Dumm, in "Motherless Children Have a Hard Time: Man as Mother in *To Kill a Mockingbird*," suggests that the problem of missing mothers signals one of the film's critical subtexts. Even as the film portrays a collection of lonely, isolated selves, Dumm argues, men do much of the mothering—the protective nurturing—of various community members. Atticus himself occupies a complicated place in that dynamic. Dumm asks a question similar to Meyer's: Why do we continue to admire Atticus Finch? Atticus acknowledges that he cannot protect his children from the world's ugliness; yet, Dumm argues, we excuse him because he is a father trying to mother his children and fails because he is in mourning for his lost wife.

Other characters in the film take up the role of mother and wife in various ways. Sheriff Heck Tate acts as both a supportive "wife" to Atticus in the film's curious rabid dog scene and a protector of Boo Radley and Atticus himself in the culminating moment of the drama, when he refuses to arrest Boo. And Boo is defined, in the end, by his protective care of Atticus's children, compensating for Atticus's failure. Ultimately, Dumm argues, the problem of motherless parenting presented in the film anticipates the great dissolution of the American family in the 1960s. It captures a problem both ongoing and unresolvable in American identity—the problem of the lonely self, constituted by the suppression of grief—through the theme of the missing mother. The ways in which various characters negotiate that problem move the film away from the remains of the South's feudal past and toward its liberal future; and in their successes and failures, we are able to glimpse a gentler version of the traditional American family.

In "If That Mockingbird Don't Sing: Scaffolding, Signifying, and Queering a Classic," Imani Perry generalizes Dumm's analysis of the film's gender dynamics both in and beyond the frame of the text. She treats the film as a cultural artifact with pedagogical purposes that exceed the civil rights narrative with which it is typically associated. Drawing on Alain Badiou's concept of "creative repetition" and Henry Louis Gates's analysis of signifying in African American culture, Perry approaches the film intertextually, scaffolding it with other works (including the novel and other texts genealogically related to it) to cast it as an assemblage and thereby offer a fresh interpretation of its politics.

Perry notes a number of details in *To Kill a Mockingbird* that undo the logic of types: the gender inversions in Scout (the tomboy) and Dill (the dandy); the melding of the white children into the black community via Calpurnia, the mother figure; the disability that "acquits" Tom of the crime for which he is convicted; the odd embodiment of Boo, who ultimately is the moral center of the story. If nonnormative characters are a staple of the southern gothic genre, here they constitute the core of the film. Viewed that way, she argues, *To Kill a Mockingbird* is a queer text, one that radically subverts gender and racial types, and in so doing locates an ethos of decency and humanness in an otherwise hierarchical world. By signifying on the southern gothic and on other major texts that surround it, the film can be read as recognizing social stratification and yet destabilizing it, advocating in the end a radical egalitarianism.

In "A Ritual of Redemption: Reimagining Community in *To Kill a Mockingbird*," Naomi Mezey argues that Maycomb, as a community, is both undone and reconstructed through law. Analyzing the film's complex temporality and visual aesthetics, Mezey suggests that the film's viewers understand it as a narrative of racial justice, rather than injustice, precisely because, through Scout, we internalize Atticus Finch's rhetoric and displace the sins of racism onto the past. Noting the ways in which both the Great Depression and the trial of the Scottsboro Boys haunt *To Kill a Mockingbird*, she argues that through a series of displacements—the political is reimagined as religious, the national as personal, the contemporary moment as the 1960s, and the 1960s as the 1930s—the film's audience is distanced from, and even absolved of, its connections with intentional racism.

Mezey focuses on the film's visual strategies and the ways they conjure membership in a community—who is in and who is out. She reads several key scenes as offering evidence of fracture along lines of both race and class: the lynch mob scene as a moment when Scout draws Mr. Cunningham back into the norms of the larger community; and the trial scene, in which the courtroom is a "contact zone" that makes visible the multiple and overlapping alliances among different factions of a community riven along lines of race and class, caught between a variety of modes of judgment (legal, social, moral). The trial, she suggests, functions as an almost religious space that helps spectators think through the recurring problem of racial injustice. Mayella's desperate claim of white privilege contrasts starkly in the film's visual economy with Tom's struggle to tell a story that can save his life, Atticus's stirring indictment of the Ewells' ignorance and immorality, and his appeals to universal values before the jury. Temporally displaced from the immediacy of Tom Robinson's sacrifice by law (a lynch mob by another name), spectators frame their understanding of the events through the camera's vivid unraveling of white solidarity.

Invited to identify not with the Ewells but with the African American community in the balcony, we disown a racist past. Ultimately, Mezey argues, community is reconstituted not through law but by the neighborhood with the subtle substitution of Boo for Tom, such that the ending offers absolution and hope. If our spectatorial perspective on the trial redeems it as an agent of equality, Boo's integration remakes the community of the film anew.

While Mezey reads *To Kill a Mockingbird* as a cultural lens for imagining an inclusive American community, Susan Sage Heinzelman explores the film's place in the British imaginary, particularly in relation to post–World War II racial politics. In "We Don't Have Mockingbirds in Britain, Do We?" Heinzelman frames her analysis with W. E. B. Du Bois's concept of "double consciousness," reimagining the film as a way to describe a kind of post-empire British liberal democracy that accommodates racial difference even as it preserves white supremacy. Britain's cultural and political double consciousness, she argues, mirrors that of America, as part of a "mutually produced, transnational cultural phenomenon." Heinzelman then analyzes that double consciousness in a number of ways. She situates the reception of *To Kill a Mockingbird* first autobiographically, within the context of England's virulent anti-immigrant racism of the postwar period. Reading film reviews of the time, she finds that the film's "high-toned" liberalism sat well with British viewers, who (like their American counterparts, as Mezey proposes) preferred to imagine a national identity untouched by prejudice.

From that contextualization, Heinzelman reads the film as positioning its audience to be educated into Atticus's compromised, morally ambiguous white liberalism: the sense that non-elites should be treated with dignity, but with no critique of race and class hierarchy. The film, she argues, sets aside the complexity of local and historically specific race relations in favor of universalizable moral representations that secure race and class privilege. Boo, the whitest of white men, kills Bob Ewell, the incarnation of low-class whiteness. Moreover, Atticus's shooting of the rabid dog, a metaphor for white privilege, is accomplished with a single shot that avoids suffering. Legitimizing Atticus's violence for that reason suggests not an embrace of fairness and justice so much as a way to avoid confronting the suffering inflicted by an ongoing colonialist ideology. Ultimately, Heinzelman argues, Prime Minister David Cameron's "muscular liberalism," which reinforces a collective sense of Britishness (or the values of the privileged, white, propertied British, anyway), simply reiterates the "double consciousness" so powerfully at work in *To Kill a Mockingbird*, offering yet again a way out of contemporary British conflicts around class and race.

The final two chapters provocatively extend Heinzelman's treatment of the shooting of the rabid dog—the only overt depiction of violence in *To Kill a Mockingbird*. In "Dead Animals," Ravit Reichman understands this scene as one that is ornamental and unnecessary to the film's narrative logic, but also one that is, within the *nomos* of the film, a negative refraction of Atticus's injunction not to kill a mockingbird. For Reichman, the killing of the dog (unnamed in the film but named Tim Johnson in the novel) raises the larger question posed by the text—who or what deserves to die?—and answers it by treating the question itself as unrepresentable, unspeakable, and unassimilable to the larger ethical world of the film. The killing of Tim Johnson does not trouble the moral landscape that the upright Atticus otherwise inhabits; but in accomplishing nothing within the narrative of the film, it suggests that certain significant issues have been bracketed and thus might disrupt the community's ethical core.

Reichman's rendering of the scene emphasizes the ways in which its filmic elements resonate with its larger disruptive effect. Visually, she links it to the genre of the western and likens the conflict between Atticus and the dog to an unequal duel. As Atticus targets his "enemy," who stands uncertain before him, the humans in the scene fall mute. For Reichman that muteness signals an incapacity to assimilate the arbitrary shooting of a living creature to any vision of justice or even to a capacity for self-consciousness. Noting other "pockets of silence" in the film—namely, those delicately pointing to the relation between racism and class status in both the lynch mob scene and Atticus's brutal cross-examination of Mayella Ewell—Reichman points to the ways in which, as she puts it, "there are some things that can't be discussed in Maycomb because they cannot be fully explained."

Reichman explores the symptomatic absence of reflection on and the incapacity to speak about such violence by juxtaposing her reading of this scene with another, from George Orwell's 1936 story "Shooting an Elephant," in which the narrator (a colonial policeman in Burma) painstakingly and agonizingly details his deep ambivalence over shooting a mad elephant. Orwell's story offers the possibility of a counterfactual rendering of violence and power in Maycomb and shows how the film's key conflicts—between Atticus Finch's drive for justice and his expertise in inflicting violence, or between the animality and humanity of man—are left unresolved.

Finally, Colin Dayan's "Humans, Animals, and Boundary Objects in Maycomb" places the shooting of the rabid dog alongside other kinds of epistemic violence done in the film. Dayan focuses on moments that test the boundaries of the human, the management of which subtends who and what are deemed "civilized." When, she asks, can a dog be legally killed? In answering that question, she writes, courts have employed the language of threat and removal. Dayan links the death of Ewell—which, in the film, seems more than justifiable—to this logic of elimination. The shooting of the dog, she argues, prepares us for the knifing of the man. In doing so, the film teaches its viewers whom and what to value.

Analyzing the "dog fable" as a sacred ritual embodying the entwining of white privilege with law, Dayan suggests that the killing is an act of political power consonant with the cruelty of polite society, preserving what is of service to humans and eliminating what is worthless. Indeed Atticus Finch's moral goodness, she argues, depends on rendering certain human and nonhuman animals into "waste products." That dynamic carries over into the courtroom scene. Dayan details the ways in which the film visually represents the Ewells' abjection, describing the trial as a landscape of judicial cruelty leveled particularly against Mayella, a character set apart from Maycomb, already defeated from the very start. Boo Radley, who in his ghostlike body lies somewhere in between human and animal, may be a figure of redemption for the violence that has come before, but he is not, Dayan argues, fully capable of resolving the contradictions that violence produces.

Taken together, the chapters that follow suggest that *To Kill a Mockingbird* is a text that exceeds and subverts the usual platitudes that have enshrined it as an iconic text in the struggle over American race relations. Reimagining Atticus Finch as both heroic and vulnerable, Maycomb as both fractured and regenerated, and humanness itself as a fragile precondition for social inclusion and the doing of justice, they unearth the conditions on which the film's—and therefore our—understanding of justice rests. That the film can invite and sustain such questions once again points to its continuing relevance in an age now far removed from the dusty streets of Maycomb.

NOTES

1. *To Kill a Mockingbird* first appeared as a novel in 1960, winning a Pulitzer Prize; it was made into an Academy Award–winning film two years later. See Harper Lee, *To Kill a Mockingbird* (Philadelphia: J. P. Lippincott, 1960); *To Kill a Mockingbird*, dir. Robert Mulligan (Universal Pictures, 1962).

2. In 2008 the American Bar Association polled a panel of experts to identify and rank the twenty-five greatest law films ever made. While this was not a scientific survey, ranked first was *To Kill a Mockingbird*. See Richard Brust, "The 25 Greatest Legal Movies," www.abajournal.com/magazine/article/the_25_greatest_legal_movies/. Moreover, in the same year, the American Film Institute ranked it number thirty-four in its list of the top one hundred films of the previous one hundred years (www.afi.com/tvevents/100years/movies.aspx), and named Atticus Finch its number-one film hero (www.afi.com/100years/handv.aspx). See also See Mark Holcomb, "To Kill a Mockingbird," *Film Quarterly* 55 (Summer 2002): 34–40. On the postwar "golden age" of law films, see David Ray Papke, "Law, Cinema, and Ideology: Hollywood Legal Films of the 1950s," *UCLA Law Review* 48 (August 2001): 1473–93.

3. Naomi Mezey, "Law's Visual Afterlife: Violence, Popular Culture, and Translation Theory," in *Imagining Legality: Where Law Meets Popular Culture*, ed. Austin Sarat (Tuscaloosa: University of Alabama Press, 2011), 67. On the continuing cultural refractions of race, law, and film in another context, see Marjorie Garber, "Cinema Scopes: Evolution, Media, and the Law," in *Law in the Domains of Culture*, ed. Austin Sarat and Thomas R. Kearns (Ann Arbor: University of Michigan Press, 1998), 121–59.

4. Another way to understand *To Kill a Mockingbird*'s afterlife is to locate it within a history of film, its generic forms, and its mechanisms for producing attachments to particular actors and narrative storylines. As we note in the text, Gregory Peck's signature performance made him the iconic touchstone of the good lawyer; but of course synergistically, part of the film's popularity depended on his star status. On the industry's investment in movie stars and the ways in which they are both produced and consumed, see Richard Dyer, *Stars* (London: BFI, 1998); and Paul McDonald, *The Star System* (London: Wallflower, 2000). The film also invites its spectators into its *nomos* visually by invoking a variety of generic conventions drawn not only from the trial film (the category in legal scholarship with which it is most obviously associated) but also from film noir, the gothic, and the western, as a number of the contributors to this volume suggest. Those generic invocations provide familiar ground that shapes audience responses to the dilemmas the film presents.

5. On the gothic influences in Lee's novel, see Claudia Durst Johnson, *To Kill a Mockingbird: Threatening Boundaries* (New York: Twayne, 1994), 39–70.

6. As the literary scholar Frank Kermode suggests, the film's "weight of meaning" is "thrown forward" onto a future just beyond its immediate present—a future characterized by moral judgment and the promise of justice. See generally Frank Kermode, *The Sense of an Ending: Studies in the Theory of Fiction* (Oxford: Oxford University Press, 1967), chap. 1.

7. Carol Clover, "God Bless Juries!" in *Refiguring American Film Genres: History and Theory*, ed. Nick Browne (Berkeley: University of California Press, 1998), 256–57.

8. See Steven Lubet, "Reconstructing Atticus Finch," *Michigan Law Review* 97 (1999): 1340.

9. "Seeing and telling the truth," Shaffer argues, "was the way Atticus could know who he was and what his community was. It also permitted him to imagine the sort of community he sought to protect for his children and neighbors." Thomas L. Shaffer, "The Moral Theology of Atticus Finch," *University of Pittsburgh Law Review* 42 (1980–81): 189. Shaffer also argues that Finch's truth telling takes on theological (practicing courage as a virtue), political (serving as a source of public morals in Maycomb), and professional (lawyerly) dimensions.

10. Lubet, "Reconstructing Atticus Finch," 1340. This kind of reading accords with more general claims that trial films tend to shore up the legitimacy of legal institutions. See David Ray Papke, "Conventional Wisdom: The Courtroom Trial in American Popular Culture," *Marquette Law Review* 88 (Spring 1999): 487–88: "The symbolic courtroom trial is separate from neither American legal process nor society as a whole. It grows out of American culture in general, and it feeds back into it. It serves in fact as a variety of constitutive social language, that is[,] while drawing from our sentiments, values, and ideologies, the courtroom trial convention reinforces, shapes, and directs. . . . [It] reinforces the ideas that courts work as institutions and that law in general can be trusted both in its articulation and its application."

11. Malcolm Gladwell, "The Courthouse Ring: Atticus Finch and the Limits of Southern Liberalism," *New Yorker,* August 10, 2009, 26–32. There was a notable and heated exchange on this same question of Finch's complicity with or resistance to southern racism in the early 1990s. See Monroe Freedman, "Atticus Finch, Esq., R.I.P.," *Legal Times,* March 9, 1992, 20; David Margolick, "To Attack a Lawyer in 'To Kill a Mockingbird': An Iconoclast Takes Aim at a Hero," *New York Times,* February 28, 1992, www.nytimes.com/1992/02/28/movies/bar-attack-lawyer-kill-mockingbird-iconoclast-takes-aim-he-ro.html; Monroe Freedman, "Finch, the Lawyer, Mythologized," *Legal Times,* May 18, 1992, 25. For other critiques of Finch, see John Jay Osborn, "Atticus Finch—The End of Honor: A Discussion of *To Kill a Mockingbird,*" *University of San Francisco Law Review* 30 (1996): 1139–1142. See also Theresa Godwin Phelps, "Atticus, Thomas, and the Meaning of Justice," *Notre Dame Law Review* 77 (2001–2): 925–36; and Monroe H. Freedman, "Atticus Finch–Right and Wrong," *Alabama Law Review* 45 (1994): 473–82.

12. Gladwell, "The Courthouse Ring," 27.

13. Garber, "Cinema Scopes," 157. On the shifting reception of both the text and Atticus Finch since the novel's publication, see Joseph Crespino, "The Strange Career of Atticus Finch," *Southern Cultures* 6.2 (2000): 9–29. See also Eric Sundquist, "Blues for Atticus Finch," in *The South as an American Problem,* ed. Larry J. Griffin and Don H. Doyle (Athens: University of Georgia Press, 1995), 181–209.

14. Peter Goodrich, "Screening Law," *Cardozo Studies in Law and Literature* 21 (Spring 2009): 1–21.

 CHAPTER ONE

Temporal Horizons
On the Possibilities of Law and Fatherhood in *To Kill a Mockingbird*

AUSTIN SARAT & MARTHA MERRILL UMPHREY

To Kill a Mockingbird, the Oscar-winning 1962 movie based on Harper Lee's novel, is a classic American law film.[1] Its central character, Atticus Finch, an iconic citizen-lawyer in a southern town during the Great Depression, is called on to defend an African American field hand accused of raping a white woman. Indeed some claim that Atticus is popular culture's leading embodiment of lawyerly virtue. "No real-life lawyer has done more for the self-image or public perception of the legal profession than the hero of . . . *To Kill a Mockingbird*," writes Steven Lubet. "For nearly four decades, the name of Atticus Finch has been invoked to defend and inspire lawyers, to rebut lawyer jokes, and to justify (and fine-tune) the adversary system."[2]

Although scholars have criticized Atticus for being too accommodating to the segregated world in which he lives and practices law,[3] many nonetheless acknowledge that he is an antidote to much common criticism of law and the legal profession. As Lubet writes: "Lawyers are greedy. What about Atticus Finch? Lawyers only serve the rich. Not Atticus Finch. Professionalism is a lost ideal. Remember Atticus Finch. . . . Atticus serves as the ultimate lawyer. His potential justifies all of our failings and imperfections. Be not too hard on lawyers, for when we are at our best we can give you an Atticus Finch."[4]

To Kill a Mockingbird is, however, not just, or not primarily, a law story.[5] Scout Finch's portrait of Atticus as a *father* is regarded by many critics as the key to the film's cultural resonance.[6] Told as a daughter's memory of her father, her brother, and the town in which she grew up, the film focuses on Scout's childhood exploits. Without a mother (though partially raised by an African American maid, Calpurnia), Scout, her brother, Jem, and their friend Dill have enormous freedom in the small world of Maycomb, Alabama.

Yet Atticus is a powerful presence in their lives. Scout's memory of him, as she reveals it over the course of the film, is highly idealized, even heroic. As she says of him, "There just didn't seem to be anyone or anything that Atticus couldn't explain."[7] Scout's reflective voice-overs invite viewers to accept her idealized perspective and to take a child's view of the events portrayed in the film.

Scout's dual position as main child protagonist and post hoc narrator also alerts us to the complex temporality of the film, both in its narrative vision and in the social landscape of its reception.[8] That the film, set during the depression, was released in 1962 locates its earliest viewers in the midst of the civil rights struggles of the early 1960s, after *Brown v. Board of Education* but before the 1964 Civil Rights Act. They were, and in a different way we are, situated in the future that the film imagines. In 1962, the conflicts of the 1930s that are represented in the film remained palpable, as did its portrait of the South's hotly contested visions of justice and injustice. Today, some fifty years after its release,[9] viewers know that Atticus's cause will be substantially, if not completely, vindicated, though with much difficulty and long after the period in which the film is set.[10]

In contrast to those who interpret *To Kill a Mockingbird* solely as a lawyer film and those who see it primarily as a fatherhood film, we suggest that it is the *conjunction* of lawyer and father that gives *To Kill a Mockingbird* its appeal and importance. Scout's reflections on her father render the two roles—father and lawyer—inseparable, fusing what she represents as almost magical parenting with Atticus's profound integrity and sense of justice. Many are the moments in the film when Atticus tries to teach Scout how to live a principled life in ways underwritten by his own ideals, which are equivalent to the ideals of liberal legality itself.[11] He lectures Scout, a tomboy who relishes fighting, on the need to restrain herself and avoid violence; he enjoins her to respect everyone, even in the depression-era South's highly stratified society, by imagining living life in another person's shoes; and he offers himself as a role model for those values.[12]

To Kill a Mockingbird shares with many mid- to late-twentieth-century films an interest in exploring the law-fatherhood conjunction, offering viewers a chance to consider what fatherhood can reveal about law and law about fatherhood.[13] Analysis of this canonical film provides an opportunity to explore the role that fathers and fatherhood play in cultural imaginings of law and in exemplifying the various faces of law's power. Atticus Finch is a father/lawyer committed to a particular vision of fatherhood and law, one in which both can transcend, if not transform, the context in which they exist, in which orienting oneself to the future takes precedence over controlling the present, and in which the temporal horizon of law and fatherhood is kept firmly in view. Through Atticus, *To Kill a Mockingbird* suggests that law and fatherhood are powerful and yet limited in their power, that both exist in the present but are oriented toward an as yet unrealized future. In this essay we examine the temporal dynamics that mark the law/fatherhood dyad as they are played out in *To Kill a Mockingbird*.

The film's invitation to imagine law as a father—and a very particular kind of father—resonates with, and yet departs from, a cultural tradition in Judeo-Christian history that, historically, has aroused desire and anxiety. The Abraham and Isaac story is, of course, a paradigmatic exemplification of the claims and powers of law, of the presentation of law as the Father but also the father as law.[14] It is also a story of fatherly failure before the law, of the abandonment of a child, of a father's failure to protect an innocent in the face of an arbitrary and unjust threat.[15] As Jacques Derrida notes, "Abraham is . . . at the same time the most moral and the most immoral, the most responsible and the most irresponsible of men, absolutely irresponsible because he is absolutely responsible, absolutely irresponsible in the face of men and his family, and in the face of the ethical, because he responds absolutely to absolute duty."[16] The law we encounter in Genesis, rather than rescuing us from danger, is the source of danger; rather than preventing loss, it threatens to impose it; rather than allying itself with fatherhood, it exposes the weakness and vulnerability of all fathers; and rather than providing a structure within which to order and reorder the world, it is itself a profoundly disordering force.[17]

In a different vein, legal scholars, following Freud,[18] regularly have called attention to the complex psychological associations of paternity and legality.[19] They have portrayed law as the focal point for a deep-seated longing for paternal authority. Jerome Frank, in *Law and the Modern Mind*, suggests that law, like religion, is a projection of a widely shared human need for certainty and security in a world of danger, and invites us to think of law as the father or, more precisely, as the father substitute.[20] "To the child," Frank argues, "the father is the Infallible Judge, the Maker of definite rules of conduct. He knows precisely what is right and what is wrong and . . . sits in judgment and punishes misdeeds. The Law . . . inevitably becomes a partial substitute for the Father-as-Infallible-Judge."[21] Exploring similar themes, Peter Goodrich notes that "Freud and those who follow him depict a law that is modeled upon the power of the father. They elaborate a symbolic order that is patriarchal in its norms and methods. To some extent that account of the legal order reflects an institution embedded in a history of homosocial power and continuing male privilege."[22]

To Kill a Mockingbird offers, we argue, a view of law and fatherhood quite different from the model of father/law as command or father/law as infallible judge. In the film, fatherhood and law conjure a normative world of becoming more than being, one concerned with legitimate authority rather than raw power. Like Moses leading the Jews out of Egypt, Atticus believes in a "promised land" which he himself may never enter or attain, and he acts, in his role as father/lawyer, as a bridge between the past and the future.[23] The entailments of a racist past are legacies against which Atticus sets himself.[24] He resists the norms and customs of racism and race privilege and of violence that were so deeply intertwined in the mid-twentieth-century American South. In attempting to undo those legacies, Atticus offers his children an example, a different way of being in the world, a model of adult values and sensibilities that foreshadow and also constitute the ideals of liberal legality.

To Kill a Mockingbird dramatizes the aspirations of mid-twentieth-century manhood—its benign paternalism and willed repression of violence—as well as what Kaja Silverman calls "the vulnerability of conventional masculinity,"[25] in Atticus's incapacity to impose his will on the world around him. Yet the film suggests that sacrificing the present for a better future is one key constituent element of a father's duty to his children and of law's commitment to justice. The film's temporal flux—the nostalgia of its narrative voice intertwined with its imagined trajectory toward a new world of racial equality—exposes a complex structure of desire and anxiety that attaches law to fatherhood.²⁶ In *To Kill a Mockingbird*, Scout and Jem embody the hope that through the relation between a lawyer/father and his children, law will reach forward toward justice rather than remain mired in a restrictive and unjust past. At the same time, we see the vulnerability of those figures of hope as well as the incapacity of the father fully to protect them from the dangers of the present.

"What Kind of Man Are You?"

To Kill a Mockingbird is in fact a film about two fathers, Atticus Finch and Robert E. Lee (Bob) Ewell. Both are single parents. Ewell's daughter Mayella is the victim of the alleged rape whose supposed perpetrator, Tom Robinson, Atticus defends. And if Atticus is a fairytale father, Ewell is a fatherly nightmare, crude and abusive with a demonic look.²⁷ In bold and subtle ways the film marks and highlights contrasts between them: while Atticus is soft-spoken, polite, and generally unflappable, Ewell is loud, profane, and threatening; while Atticus is always dressed impeccably in a suit and hat (which he removes indoors as southern custom and good manners dictate), Ewell wears overalls and is generally disheveled; while Atticus eschews violent confrontation, Ewell seems to crave it.²⁸ In cultural terms, Ewell represents the Old South—honor, violence, racism— and Atticus the emerging order of the New South of respect, restraint, and racial equality.

Two scenes in particular highlight the contrast between these two fathers. The first occurs early in the film after a preliminary hearing in Tom Robinson's case when Ewell, exiting the courtroom, confronts Atticus. This confrontation, staged within the space of law, is about racial solidarity in the segregated South and about what fatherhood means in that context. Ewell leaves the courtroom with his hat on his head, defying the demands of propriety, while Atticus, holding his hat in his hand, talks to another man. As Atticus turns to go, Ewell blocks his way and immediately displays his violent disposition: "Cap'n, I'm real sorry they picked you to defend that nigger who raped my Mayella. I don't know why I didn't kill him myself instead of going to the sheriff. It would have saved you and the sheriff and the taxpayers a lot of trouble."

While he spits these words out with venom, "I don't know why I didn't kill him myself" is a question not just for Ewell but also for the film's

Bob Ewell and Atticus Finch at the courthouse

viewers. Perhaps, the question suggests, in spite of his constant aggressiveness and threatening demeanor, Ewell is capable of actual violence only
against children and the weak. While he is the kind of man who can poke
an index finger into Atticus's chest with his thumb pointing upward, as if
to mimic holding a gun during their conversation, he may not be one who
could pull an actual trigger.[29]

Ewell's menacing but flaccid and cowardly display of violence is a
metaphor for the structure of violence underpinning the era's white supremacist values. Those values depend on a kind of racial solidarity that
evacuates the promises of liberalism—on racial loyalty over factual truth,
on caste status over individual merit, and on violent aggression over reason. In their courthouse exchange, even as he notes Atticus's superior
status ("Hey, Cap'n"), Ewell calls Atticus to account in response to an
accusation of racial betrayal, casting his question as an issue of alliance:
"Hey, Cap'n, someone told me just now that they thought you believed
Tom Robinson's story agin our'n. You know what I said? I said, 'You are
wrong, man, you are dead wrong. Mr. Finch ain't takin his story agin
our'n.' Well they was wrong, wasn't they?" Atticus avoids answering the
question about whether he believes Tom, taking on the mantle of liberal
legality rather than that of racial solidarity. "I've been appointed to defend Tom Robinson," he says. "Now that he has been charged, that's what
I intend to do."

As Atticus departs, walking down the stairs and out of the frame, the camera closes in on Ewell, his teeth clenched, calling after Atticus: "What kind of man are you? You've got children of your own." Ewell's question might be read as asking, "What kind of (white) man are you?"—meaning "Are you one who will protect his white daughter from the dangers of racial intermixing? One who will enforce the race line at all cost?" Read this way, Ewell's accusation of betrayal raises questions about the proper role of law in relation to racial hierarchy and racial privilege. His is a call to serve the present, to acknowledge and protect white supremacy. Atticus's flat, matter-of-fact response points to a future in which African American men accused of raping white women will routinely be afforded the full protection of the law.[30]

Of course, that future remains over the horizon. Thus, in spite of overwhelming evidence to the contrary, Tom Robinson is found guilty by an all-white, all-male jury. Sometime later, Tom is shot trying to escape as he is being transported to jail in a neighboring town. The law of the present, it seems, is allied with the entailments of the past. Yet Atticus's cross-examination of Bob and Mayella Ewell during the trial leaves a cloud of suspicion that Ewell had beaten his daughter for her willing dalliance with an African American man and fabricated the rape allegation to cover up her transgression.

The cloud of that dishonorable imputation provokes Ewell to menace Atticus and his children, and that menace lays bare the promise as well as the limitations of Atticus's redefinition of fatherhood and law. In emphasizing the fact that Atticus is also a father, Ewell suggests that lawyerly niceties ought to matter less than remembering what it means to have children. For Ewell, having children is an occasion for and a call to violence, and it is precisely this call that Atticus refuses to heed, for better or worse.

Ewell's spiteful challenge to Atticus's manhood marks one way in which Atticus is vulnerable to violence in the present: through his children, whether it be verbal harassment in the schoolyard or Ewell's final attack on them in the woods. Although the critic Stella Bruzzi observes that Atticus is there "to protect Jem and Scout from the brutalizing adult world Mayella's father embodies,"[31] early in the film Atticus articulates a more tragic understanding of fatherhood. "There's a lot of ugly things in this world, son," he tells Jem. "I wish I could keep 'em all away from you.

That's never possible."[32] Knowing that, Atticus embraces a model of fatherhood and law that aims to build a new and different future rather than remaining tethered to entailments of the past and present. "You're gonna hear some ugly talk about this [his legal representation of Tom Robinson] in school," Atticus tells Scout after her fight with young Walter Cunningham. "But I want you to promise me one thing: that you won't get into fights over it, no matter what they say to you."

This move away from reflexive violence is paradigm shifting in the depression-era South for men (insult demands response in honor-based cultures) as well as for law (contrast, for example, the lynch law demanded by townsmen with Tom Robinson's actual trial).[33] Once again Atticus embodies that shift. Late in the film, after hearing of Tom's death, Atticus and Jem go to Tom's home to convey the tragic news to his wife and family. As Jem sits in the car, Ewell appears out of the shadows and orders one of Tom's relatives to fetch Atticus from the house. ("Boy, go inside and tell Atticus Finch I said to come out here. Go on, boy," he says to a grown man, in true racist fashion.) While they wait for Atticus to appear, the camera brings Ewell and Jem into the same frame. They glance at each other, visually connecting, registering yet again Ewell's awareness of Atticus's vulnerability as a father. In this moment, viewers are invited to take on Jem's perspective as the conflict between Atticus and Ewell plays out.

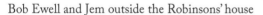

Bob Ewell and Jem outside the Robinsons' house

As Atticus exits the Robinsons' house and slowly walks toward Ewell, the ensuing confrontation occurs wordlessly. As Atticus nears Ewell, Ewell suddenly spits on him. Startled by the violent act, seemingly about to lose control at its deep insult, Atticus takes one step forward, anger registering on his face for the first and only time in the film, as if he were going to defend his honor. Shifting quickly, the camera registers Jem's frightened reaction to the impending violent confrontation. We catch a glimpse of Ewell and, over his shoulder, of Jem, anxiously waiting to see what Atticus will do in response to this gross provocation. Instead of resorting to violence, however, Atticus stops, reaches into his pocket, takes out his handkerchief, wipes the spit off his face with disgust, and steps around Ewell. As he drives away, the car's lights illuminate Ewell's scowling face.

Yet again Ewell has been frustrated. Again he is unable to draw Atticus into his world—now not in the racialized alliance contemplated in their earlier interaction but instead in a confrontation between white men over insults to their honor. Atticus models for his son (and for the film's viewers) the answer to Ewell's question "What kind of man are you?" His version of manliness shows restraint in the face of a crude attack and evokes in that restraint a choice between the world that Ewell inhabits and the one that Atticus seeks to create, a world in which manliness resides in self-control and moral rectitude, not violence or physical confrontation.

Noncompliant Jurors and Disobedient Children

Although the film portrays Atticus Finch as an idealized figure, the fact remains that whether during Tom Robinson's trial or in daily dealings with his children, Atticus is often unable to work his will in the present. Drawing a parallel between the noncompliant jury in Tom's case and Atticus's disobedient children, the film suggests that if the present is the touchstone of his efficacy as a father and a lawyer, Atticus is oddly impotent. The viewer's embrace of him and his vision of fatherhood and law depends, then, on the affection and ratification the narrator's post hoc voice-over provides. Seeing Atticus as his children see him, knowing that the disobedience in the present becomes the embrace of the future, we are able to take the long view of his immediate failings as a lawyer and a father even as we understand their costs.

With respect to the legal present, Atticus's careful, reasoned parsing of evidence, so convincing to contemporary viewers, is of no avail before the film's white male jury. He cannot persuade them to embrace and ratify his civics book belief in equal justice for all.[34] "Now, gentlemen," he tells the jury, as if anticipating *Brown v. Board of Education* and the Warren Court, "in this country the courts are the great levelers. In our courts all men are created equal." Atticus is uncharacteristically animated in his plea to the jury to review the evidence dispassionately and restore Tom Robinson to his family. "In the name of God," he says, his voice raised, "do your duty. In the name of God, believe Tom Robinson."[35]

As he utters these lines, the camera closes in on Jem intently surveying the scene from the "colored" balcony. With the scene's focus on Jem, who has begun to identify powerfully with his father, the film transforms the legal argument before the jury into an instruction from father to son and into an intergenerational family legacy.[36] What Atticus cannot bring to fruition in Tom Robinson's case is left to his children's generation to complete. As he explains to Tom, who is being led from the courtroom after the guilty verdict: "I'll go to see Helen [Tom's wife] first thing tomorrow morning. I told her not to be disappointed, that we'd probably lose this one." Losing "this one" refers to the trial, but also to the legal present. Atticus knows the obstacles he confronts in the Alabama courts, and losing "this one" is Atticus's acknowledgment that the law of the here and now cannot overcome the racism of its cultural surroundings.[37]

Later, after learning of Tom's death, Atticus despairingly tells his children, their friend Dill, and a neighbor: "The last thing I told him was not to lose heart, that we'd ask for an appeal. We had such a good chance. We had more than a good chance." To whom would Atticus have made his appeal? What gave him such confidence in its success? There is a suggestion that Atticus's appeal would be addressed not only to the courts but also to an indeterminate future in which the promise of justice could, and would, be redeemed, a future in which courts could and would indeed be the great levelers.

Just as he is unable to get the jury to do its "duty" and believe Tom Robinson, Atticus frequently is unable to make his children obey him. Indeed, we first meet Jem six minutes into the film in a moment of stubborn defiance, sitting in a tree house and refusing to come down until Atticus agrees to play on a church football team. Atticus calmly walks over to the tree, looks up as if offering a prayer, and asks, "Son, why don't you come down out of there now and have your breakfast?" Jem responds: "No, sir, not until you agree to play football for the Methodists. . . . I ain't coming down." Atticus's response highlights what Jem sees as his father's limitations: "Oh, son, I can't do that. I'm too old to get out there." Yet, as in his confrontations with Bob Ewell, when Jem continues his protest, Atticus turns and walks away, offering a calm rejoinder: "Suit yourself." And so Jem stays in the tree.

Moreover, despite his best efforts, Atticus has great difficulty stopping Scout from fighting with other children at school. "Scout I don't want you fighting," he tells her. "I don't care what the reasons are, I forbid you to fight." In a voice-over Scout acknowledges his point: "Atticus had promised me he would wear me out if he ever heard of me fighting anymore. . . . I was far too old and too big for such childish things and the sooner I learned to hold it in, the better off everybody would be." But, as she puts it, "I soon forgot."

If Scout's and Jem's childishness proves frustratingly resistant to Atticus's incessantly reasonable injunctions, it offers an opening onto a world in which social norms have not completely colonized the children's every thought and action. In their relative innocence, they relate to those around them in ways that, though mildly defiant, unravel the tight fabric of racism bit by bit. In so doing, they provide a vision of a more just social order that is, in the world of the film, incipient and ready for cultivation.

The film conjures that alternative most powerfully in a scene midway through the narrative in which Atticus and his children turn away a lynch mob on the jailhouse steps. Atticus is called to the jail by the sheriff the evening before Robinson's trial is to begin, and he posts himself on the front steps with a chair, a lamp, and a law book—ready to confront impending violence with reason and enlightenment. After Atticus leaves his house, the children and their friend Dill sneak out and follow him. Hiding in the bushes across from the jail, Jem tells Scout: "I just wanted to see where he was and what he was up to. He's all right," as if he were responsible for protecting Atticus. "Let's go back home."

Just as they are about to leave, a group of armed men from Old Sarum, a nearby area in which poor whites live, arrive at the jail and demand that Atticus turn Tom over to them. At this point the children run to

Atticus, making their way through the crowd of men. "Jem, go home and take Scout and Dill home with you," Atticus says when they appear. Jem, slowly surveying the crowd of men, refuses to leave. "Son, I said, go home," Atticus insists, to which Jem replies, "No, sir." Someone in the crowd tells Atticus that he'd better get the children out of there. "Jem, I want you to please leave," Atticus says. "No, sir," Jem repeats. "Jem," Atticus intones, anxiously raising his voice. "I tell you I ain't going," Jem insistently replies.

In this dangerous moment, Atticus once again fails to control his children. Yet Jem's defiance paradoxically is rooted in a deep identification with Atticus. It is almost as if Jem were projecting himself into the future and acting as he imagines Atticus himself would act—indeed, is acting: on principle.

It is Scout, however, who pierces the tension of the moment. She spots Walter Cunningham Sr., a leader of the mob, and, too young to understand his purpose, calls out to him in a friendly way. "Hey, Mr. Cunningham," she says. "How's your entailment going?" She has met him once before, in the film's first scene, when he drops by her house to pay Atticus for legal work in hickory nuts "as part of his entailment," and she knows his son Walter Jr. "Tell him 'hey' for me, won't you?" she says to him. She

Scout and the lynch mob

then strays innocently into a topic with much deeper resonance across the film. "You know something, Mr. Cunningham?" she says. "Entailments are bad."

Cunningham, who has so far been avoiding her gaze shamefaced, begins to look at her quizzically. "It takes a long time, sometimes," Scout continues. (To play entailments out? To get rid of them? Or, perhaps, to lift the burden of the entailments that structure a social inheritance of inequality and injustice?) Then, worried that she has offended him with her forwardness, she quietly retreats. "What's the matter? I sure meant no harm, Mr. Cunningham," she says worriedly. Finally he looks at her and replies: "No harm taken, young lady. I'll tell Walter you said 'hey.'" Turning to the mob he says, "Let's clear out of here; let's go, boys."

Scout, more credulous than defiant, breaks the frame of meaning that has structured the conflict between Atticus and the mob. She reaches across lines of class and racial antagonism and, as her father has always enjoined her to do, tries to stand in the shoes of someone else, attempting to understand the weight of the entailments Mr. Cunningham feels as a poor man—but in the wider world of the film, perhaps as he also stands ready to help lynch a black man.

In this scene Jem and Scout disobey Atticus in the service of some value or principle that Atticus himself might have espoused. By teaching his children about the proper way to live and act, Atticus has given them grounds for disobeying his more immediate paternal commands. The children bring his values to bear, however prematurely, in ways that suggest they have already learned lessons about the kinds of adults Atticus wants them to become. Here again *To Kill a Mockingbird* plays out the temporal horizon of the lawyer/father. Like law itself, Jem and Scout exist both in the here and now and in an incomplete vision of what they can and should be.[38]

The Colored Balcony

This orientation to the future is also captured visually in the positioning of Atticus's children as spectators in Tom Robinson's trial.[39] The courtroom, like the town in which it is located, is rigidly segregated, with whites seated on the first floor and African Americans in the balcony. That Dill, Jem, and Scout cannot find a seat on the first floor among Maycomb's whites but can comfortably join the balcony crowd seems to foretell something about the world into which they will grow up. They find their place as spectators hovering over a classic southern race trial, looked after by an African American minister, Reverend Sykes.

The camera places viewers alongside them, merging our gaze with theirs as we watch the trial proceed. But we also often look up from below to see three white children surrounded, indeed enveloped, by the African American community in a vision of racial integration imaginable within the confines of the law long before it is imaginable in the world outside the courtroom.[40] It is to that imagining that Atticus as lawyer/father orients himself, offering to the law and his children a vision of formal legal equality, embraced in spite of social difference. When Bob Ewell later tries to kill Jem and Scout, he is avenging his own humiliation at Atticus's hands during the trial but also acting to short-circuit the future that Atticus's children embody.[41]

The spectators in the colored balcony are an audience for the jury's verdict in Tom Robinson's case and another kind of jury for Atticus's arguments, for his vision of equal justice under law. Viewers focus on their reaction to the verdict as it occurs: the camera shifts to the African Americans in the balcony and then returns to the jury below. When Robinson is found guilty, we are returned to the balcony, where Jem sits, head down and crying, and Scout stares out glumly, as if imprisoned between the slats of the balcony's railing.

After the rest of the courtroom empties, spectators in the balcony remain to watch Atticus pack his briefcase. As he begins to leave, the camera moves behind him to show the African Americans in the balcony standing in silent tribute.[42] Jem immediately joins them in standing, but the still-untutored Scout remains seated until Reverend Sykes tells her, "Miss Jean Louise, stand up." Scout complies without protest as the minister puts his hand on her and explains, "Your father is passing."

The word "passing" in this deeply affecting scene suggests not just physical movement out of the courtroom but the passing on of a legacy. The lawyer's appeal and the work of the father in passing on his values are joined. The African Americans in the balcony rise for Atticus the way the spectators at a trial stand when the judge enters and exits the courtroom. For Maycomb's African American community, and for his children who stand with them, Atticus is the true embodiment of a law whose gaze is

The black balcony

oriented beyond this courtroom to a time when equality before the law may be achieved, segregation will be ended, and African Americans and whites will sit side by side.

In its temporal orientation, *To Kill a Mockingbird* captures a constituent element of both law and fatherhood. As Drucilla Cornell reminds us, "legal interpretation demands that we remember the future."[43] In that phrase Cornell suggests that law fixes its gaze temporally, not just on the possibilities (or impossibilities) of the present, but on a future promise of justice. For justice, she argues, "is precisely what eludes our full knowledge." We cannot "grasp the Good but only follow it. The Good . . . is a star which beckons us to follow."[44] While justice, what Cornell calls the Good, is, on her account, always present *to* law, it is never completely realized *in* law.[45] The law, writes Judith Butler, "posits an ideality . . . that it can never realize, and . . . this failure is constitutive of existing law."[46] Law exists in time, in the "as yet" failure to attain the Good, and in the commitment to its future realization. Cornell reminds us that there are in fact two audiences for every legal act, the audience of the present and the audience of the future, which stands as a figure of law's redeeming promise of justice. Both audiences seem to be very much a part of the legal and paternal world of Atticus Finch.

Perhaps no one had a deeper and more penetrating understanding of the centrality of the temporal duality that Cornell highlights than Robert

Cover.[47] He compellingly called our attention to law's "jurisgenerative" as well as what he named its "jurispathic" qualities.[48] Law, Cover argued,

> may be viewed as a system of tension or a bridge linking a concept of reality to an imagined alternative. . . . Thus, one constitutive element of a *nomos* is the phenomenon George Steiner has labeled "alterity": the "other than the case," the counterfactual propositions, images, shapes of will and evasions with which we charge our mental being and by means of which we build the changing, largely fictive milieu for our somatic and our social existence. But the concept of a *nomos* is not exhausted by its alterity; it is neither utopia nor pure vision. A *nomos*, as a world of law, entails the application of human will to an extant state of affairs as well as toward our visions of alternative futures.[49]

The *nomos* that law helps to create, Cover believed, always contains within it visions of possibility not yet realized, images of a better world not yet built. But, he reminds us, law is not simply, or even primarily, a gentle, hermeneutic apparatus; it always exists in a state of tension between a world of meaning in which justice is pursued and a world of violence in which "legal interpretation takes place on a field of pain and death."[50] In this sense, law provides "a bridge to alterity."[51]

Taking Cornell's and Cover's perspective, one might say that Atticus Finch's effort to save an African American man accused of raping a white woman in *To Kill a Mockingbird*, while it has little chance of immediate success, provides such a bridge and participates in the logic of what Cover calls "redemptive constitutionalism."[52] Atticus refuses to recognize the injustice of the time and place in which he lives as the defining totality of law and thus acts as the carrier of the vision of a future in which justice might prevail. For people like Atticus, Cover argues, "redemption takes place within an eschatological schema that postulates: (1) the unredeemed character of reality as we know it, (2) the fundamentally different reality that should take its place, and (3) the replacement of one with the other."[53]

Cover uses the example of antislavery activism in the mid-nineteenth century to suggest that the work of "redemptive constitutionalism" reveals "a creative pulse that proliferates principle and precept, commentary and justification, even in the face of a state legal order less likely to hold slavery unconstitutional than to declare the imminent kingship of Jesus Christ on Earth."[54] In this view, lawyers like Atticus Finch speak in a prophetic voice even as they supply the argumentative and interpretive resources to bridge the gap between the present and the beckoning possibility of justice.[55]

To Kill a Mockingbird suggests that fathers also are called on to remember the future and to imagine for their children a time different from, and perhaps better than, the present.[56] As a father and a figure of law, Atticus attends to the demands of the present but keeps the future firmly in view. He cultivates a way of being with his children that recognizes who they are while never forgetting who he hopes they can and will become in the future.[57] Fifty years after its screen debut, many of this film's viewers join Scout—as daughter/narrator—in memorializing and idealizing Atticus precisely because he held firm to his hope for the law he served and the children he raised.[58]

NOTES

The authors are grateful for the skilled research assistance of Matthew Brewster.

1. *To Kill a Mockingbird*, dir. Robert Mulligan (Universal Pictures, 1962). Quotations from the film are personal transcriptions.

2. Steven Lubet, "Reconstructing Atticus Finch," *Michigan Law Review* 97 (1999): 1340. As Pierre Schlag puts it, "Normative legal thought allows us to pretend that we are preparing our students to become Atticus Finch while we are in fact training people who will enter the meta-insurance adjustment business." Pierre Schlag, "Normative and Nowhere to Go," *Stanford Law Review* 43 (1990): 189.

3. See John Jay Osborn, "Atticus Finch—The End of Honor: A Discussion of *To Kill a Mockingbird*," *University of San Francisco Law Review* 30 (1996): 1139–42. As Osborn argues: "Atticus cannot see beyond his law books. Indeed he seems almost scared to do so, as if it would unleash the real demons in the town. He plays along with the system" (1141). See also Theresa Godwin Phelps, "Atticus, Thomas, and the Meaning of Justice," *Notre Dame Law Review* 77 (2001–2): 925; Holcomb, "To Kill a Mockingbird," 36; and Monroe H. Freedman, "Atticus Finch—Right and Wrong," *Alabama Law Review* 45 (1994): 473–82.

4. Lubet, "Reconstructing Atticus Finch," 1340.

5. See, for example, Michael Asimow, "When Lawyers Were Heroes," *University of San Francisco Law Review* 30 (1995–96): 1136.

6. See Stella Bruzzi, *Bringing Up Daddy: Fatherhood and Masculinity in Postwar Hollywood* (London: BFI, 2005), 85–86. Bruzzi argues from a psychoanalytic perspective that "Atticus Finch . . . is the perfect fairytale father. . . . The single father of fairytales feeds a tremendous need not to devalue or forget the symbolic father—and implies a residual fear at his imminent loss. . . . Atticus is a benevolent version of Lacan's fearsome father."

7. Bruzzi argues that it is the film's clear intention to "glorify" Atticus (ibid., 86).

8. For an instructive discussion of the temporality of film spectatorship, see Marjorie Garber, "Cinema Scopes: Evolution, Media, and the Law," in *Law in the Domains of Culture*, ed. Austin Sarat and Thomas R. Kearns (Ann Arbor: University of Michigan

Press, 1998), 121–59. As Garber puts it, "Entering a movie theater[,] . . . . an audience brings its own world to match with the screen's fictions" (143).

9. *To Kill a Mockingbird* first emerged in novel form two years before the film's release. See Harper Lee, *To Kill a Mockingbird* (Philadelphia: J. P. Lippincott, 1960).

10. Today the quest for equal justice under law that Atticus pursued has still other and more complicated resonances. See, for example, Alan David Freeman, "Legitimizing Racial Discrimination through Antidiscrimination Doctrine: A Critical Review of Supreme Court Doctrine," *Minnesota Law Review* 62 (1978): 1049–1119.

11. In one instance, as he tries to explain to Scout that she cannot stop going to school, he says, "Scout, do you know what a compromise is?" to which Scout responds, "Bending the law?" Atticus corrects her, as if delivering a lesson from a first-year contracts course: "No, Scout, it is an agreement reached by mutual consent. Now, here's the way it works. You concede the necessity of going to school, and we'll keep right on reading every night just as we always have. Is that a bargain?"

12. This fusion of father and lawyer is perhaps most explicitly made after Scout has been caught fighting with children who accused her father of being a "nigger lover." Atticus "sits her down on the front steps and teaches her white liberal ideology: how she should substitute 'Negro' for 'nigger' and how he 'couldn't hold my head up in this town. *I couldn't even tell you and Jem not to do something again*' if he did not defend Robinson." Bruzzi, *Bringing Up Daddy*, 88; emphasis added. See also David Ray Papke, "Law, Cinema, and Ideology: Hollywood Legal Films of the 1950s," *UCLA Law Review* 48 (August 2001): 1473–93; and Holcomb, "To Kill a Mockingbird," 36.

13. For a fuller exploration of the law-fatherhood conjunction in contemporary films about law, see Austin Sarat, "Imagining the Law of the Father: Loss, Dread, and Mourning in *The Sweet Hereafter*," *Law and Society Review* 34 (2000): 3–46.

14. "The drama of the Akedah," the binding of Isaac, "takes place in the narrowest arena, between father and son, father and father, solitary and God. The call that starts it all remains a haunting fact: and where obedience seems to be purest it is also most questionable. A voice out of nowhere commands a murder it calls a sacrifice." Geoffrey Hartman, "The Blind Side of the Akedah," *Raritan* 16 (1996): 35.

15. Lippman Bodoff, "The Real Test of the Akedah: Blind Obedience versus Moral Choice," *Judaism* 42.1 (Winter 1993): 71–92.

16. Jacques Derrida, *The Gift of Death*, trans. David Wills (Chicago: University of Chicago Press, 1995), 72.

17. By becoming law to Isaac, Abraham may be said to become a father. Yet Abraham is, in one sense, not present to Isaac at all. He appears before Isaac as a servant of a law that is not his own. He is present only to God. His fatherhood fails before a law that models itself the Father. "To meet the God of whom it was said not once but several times that 'He is gracious and merciful, slow to anger, and of great kindness . . . ,' commanding His favorite to offer up as sacrifice that one's beloved son, is sure to produce . . . fear and trembling." Judah Goldin, introduction to Shalom Spiegel, *The Last Trial: On the Legends and Lore of the Command to Abraham to Offer Isaac as a Sacrifice; The Akedah* (New York: Schocken, 1969), x.

18. Sigmund Freud, *Totem and Taboo*, trans. James Strachey (New York: Norton, 1950).

19. As Louis Althusser puts it: "Any reduction of childhood traumas to a balance of 'biological frustrations' alone is in principle erroneous, since the Law that covers them,

as a Law, abstracts from all contents . . . and the infant submits to this rule and receives it from his first breath. This is the beginning, and has always been the beginning, even when there is no living Father (who is Law), of the Order of the human signifier, i.e. of the Law of Culture." Louis Althusser, "Freud and Lacan," in *Lenin and Philosophy and Other Essays*, trans. Ben Brewster (London: Monthly Review Press, 1971), 212.

20. Jerome Frank, *Courts on Trial: Myth and Reality in American Justice* (Princeton: Princeton University Press, 1949), 196–97.

21. Ibid., 18. "Despite advancing years," Frank argues, "most men are at times, the victims of the childish desire for complete serenity and the childish fear of irreducible chance. They then will to believe that they live in a world in which chance is only appearance, not reality." (19). He later observes: "Driven by fear of the vagueness, the chanciness of life," man "has need of rest. Finding life distracting, unsettling, fatiguing he tries to run away from unknown hazards." (196).

22. Peter Goodrich, "Maladies of the Legal Soul: Psychoanalysis and Interpretation in Law," *Washington and Lee Law Review* 54 (1997): 1047.

23. For this view of Moses, see Michael Walzer, *Exodus and Revolution* (New York: Basic Books, 1986).

24. An entailment at common law is "an interference with and curtailment of the ordinary rules pertaining to devolution by inheritance; a limitation and direction by which property is to descend different from the course which it would take if the creator of the entailment, grantor, or testator, had been content that the estate should devolve in regular and general succession to heirs at law in the statutory order of preference and sequence." *Black's Law Dictionary*, 4th ed., rev. (St. Paul: West Publishing, 1968), s.v. "entailment."

25. Kaja Silverman, *Male Subjectivity at the Margins* (New York: Routledge, 1992), 38.

26. "The psychoanalytic foundational fiction of the origin of the law and civilization is tormented by the dilemma of positing simultaneously that its myth 'really happened' and that its 'memory' is instituted by an unconscious explanation of unnatural restraints on individual will." Jonathan Buyarin, "Another Abraham: Jewishness and the Law of the Father," *Yale Journal of Law and the Humanities* 9 (1997): 350.

27. See Bruzzi, *Bringing Up Daddy*, 86.

28. On this contrast, see Osborn, "Atticus Finch—The End of Honor," 1140.

29. Atticus, by contrast, seldom shows anger and never aggressiveness; but when he's called on by the sheriff to shoot a rabid dog, we (and his children) discover that he is the best shot in the county.

30. However unsuccessfully, Atticus enacts that future as one answer to Ewell's question. After the trial is over and the verdict rendered, when Atticus exits the courtroom, moving down the same center aisle that Ewell had used earlier, the camera shows people looking down on Atticus from the segregated, coloreds-only balcony, where the African American community has risen to pay homage to him. If Ewell's question called forth the logic of racial solidarity under Jim Crow, the action of the African Americans is their tribute to a vision of the future in which law will live up to its promise of equal treatment.

31. Bruzzi, *Bringing Up Daddy*, 88.

32. It is worth noting that Jem and Scout are saved from Ewell's attack by their neighbor, the reclusive Boo Radley, rather than their father, Atticus. Perhaps Boo is able to

take on the mantle of protector because he has lived fully apart from the norms of the community and so remains outside the controversies of the Robinson case, is at least reputedly capable of violence whereas Atticus is reluctant, and has observed—and in his own way befriended—Jem and Scout as they have grown, though he has never actually met them. He sees them in ways Atticus, otherwise preoccupied with the future, does not. He understands how dangerous their world is, even as Atticus refuses to take that danger seriously.

33. See William Ian Miller, *Humiliation and Other Essays on Honor, Social Discomfort, and Violence* (Ithaca: Cornell University Press, 1993); and Richard Maxwell Brown, *Strain of Violence: Historical Studies of American Violence and Vigilantism* (New York: Oxford University Press, 1975).

34. "The reality was that Atticus' defense was doomed from the start." Asimow, "When Lawyers Were Heroes," 1136.

35. As one critic of Atticus Finch puts it: "Finch wants his all white, all male jurors to do the right thing. But as a good Jim Crow liberal he dare not challenge the foundation of their privilege. Instead, Finch does what lawyers for black men did in those days. He encourages them to swap one of their prejudices [about race] for another [about class and respectability]." Malcolm Gladwell, "The Courthouse Ring: Atticus Finch and the Limits of Southern Liberalism," *New Yorker,* August 10, 2009, 32.

36. See Holcomb, "To Kill a Mockingbird," 40. Holcomb calls attention to what he labels "Jem's nascent activism."

37. See Eric J. Sundquist, "Blues for Atticus Finch," in *The South as an American Problem,* ed. Larry Griffin and Don Doyle (Athens: University of Georgia Press, 1995), 181–209.

38. Thomas Shaffer, in "Growing Up Good in Maycomb," *Alabama Law Review* 45 (1994): 553, argues that "the Finch children grow up, subordinate to the direction and witness indicated by faith."

39. That they attend the trial at all marks another instance of their defiance of Atticus. As they sit on the side of the road watching a parade of neighbors heading down to the courthouse, Jem suddenly gets up and begins to join that parade. He says: "I can't stand it any longer. I'm going down to the courthouse and watch." Scout replies: "You better not. You know what Atticus said." Jem answers: "I don't care if he did. I'm not going to miss the most exciting thing that ever happened in this town."

40. Holcomb, in contrast, suggests that the film actually has little to say about race, that it displays "an implicit desire for race and class to simply not matter." Holcomb, "To Kill a Mockingbird," 39.

41. As Shaffer explains: "Robert Ewell . . . was humiliated and saw his daughter humiliated by Atticus in the trial. . . . Robert Ewell became obsessed with his humiliation and with the idea that Atticus was the source of his humiliation. He stalked the Finch children, attacked them, and nearly killed them." Thomas Shaffer, "The Moral Theology of Atticus Finch," *University of Pittsburgh Law Review* 42 (1980–81): 191.

42. The African Americans rise, Bruzzi suggests, to honor Atticus as "the great protector who stands up for the weak and the good." Bruzzi, *Bringing Up Daddy,* 87.

43. Drucilla Cornell, "From the Lighthouse: The Promise of Redemption and the Possibility of Legal Interpretation," *Cardozo Law Review* 11 (1990): 1697. Jules Lobel argues that "even when prophetic litigation loses in court, it often functions . . . as

an appeal to future generations." Jules Lobel, "Losers, Fools, and Prophets: Justice as Struggle," *Cornell Law Review* 80 (1995): 1347.

44. Cornell, "From the Lighthouse," 1697.

45. Drucilla Cornell, "Post-Structuralism, the Ethical Relation, and the Law," *Cardozo Law Review* 9 (1988): 1587.

46. Judith Butler, "Deconstruction and the Possibility of Justice: Comments on Bernasconi, Cornell, Miller, Weber," *Cardozo Law Review* 11 (1990): 1716. Butler argues that "this horizon of temporality is always to be projected and never fully achieved; this constitutes the double gesture as a persistent promise and withdrawal. . . . Cornell argues that it is necessary to repeat this gesture endlessly and thereby to constitute the posture of vigilance that establishes the openness of a future in which the thought of radical alterity is never completed."

47. For a collection of his work, see Martha Minow, Michael Ryan, and Austin Sarat, eds., *Narrative Violence and the Law: The Essays of Robert Cover* (Ann Arbor: University of Michigan Press, 1993).

48. Robert Cover, "The Supreme Court, 1982 Term—Foreword: *Nomos* and Narrative," *Harvard Law Review* 97 (1983): 4–68.

49. Ibid., 9.

50. Robert Cover, "Violence and the Word," *Yale Law Journal* 95 (1986): 1601.

51. Cover, "The Supreme Court, 1982 Term," 9.

52. Ibid., 34.

53. Ibid.

54. Ibid., 39.

55. Lobel, in "Losers, Fools, and Prophets," 1337, explores the utility of the idea of prophecy to the work of lawyers who serve losing causes. Phelps, in "Atticus, Thomas, and the Meaning of Justice," 932, argues that Atticus's vision of justice is too "closely aligned to due process" and suggests that, like Captain Vere in Melville's *Billy Budd,* he is "complicitous in an unjust status quo."

56. See David Dollahite and Alan Hawkins, "A Conceptual Ethic of Generative Fathering," *Journal of Men's Studies* 7.1 (1998): 109–32.

57. On the theme of hope in *To Kill a Mockingbird,* see Shaffer, "The Moral Theology of Atticus Finch," 221.

58. As Bruzzi puts it in *Bringing Up Daddy,* 87–88, "*Mockingbird* . . . wants its audience to believe in the peculiar brand of patriarchy and paternity Atticus represents—benevolent, just, and innately traditional."

 CHAPTER TWO

I Would Kill for You
Love, Law, and Sacrifice in
To Kill a Mockingbird

Linda Ross Meyer

I believe in justice, but I will defend my mother before justice.
Albert Camus, Stockholm interview, December 14, 1957

To Kill a Mockingbird, the film, is now over fifty years old.[1] When I first saw it, around its twentieth anniversary, it seemed quaint, a black-and-white slice of history we had moved well beyond. Atticus Finch's famous "in our courts, all men are created equal" closing argument registered not as progressive but even as itself regressive, addressed as it was to the white "gentlemen" of the jury, and failing as it did to acknowledge the racism and sexism that mere legal equality simply papered over.[2] Sure, the movie was brave for its time, portraying the stark injustice in a trumped-up cross-racial rape case against Tom Robinson, an innocent black man, years before the last miscegenation statute was declared unconstitutional. But, we thought, we were far smarter about racism in 1982. We had moved beyond the ideal of mere "legal equality" to an understanding that something more, such as affirmative action, was required to undo the generations of de facto inequality and subconscious racism that made any playing field racially uneven—especially that of the court system. And by 1982 we could see the racism inherent in the 1962 film's portrayal of Calpurnia, the Finches' black housekeeper, and Tom, and we were embarrassed even by Atticus's white noblesse oblige.

But still, in 1982 our endgame was the same; one way or another, we and Atticus were on the same road toward giving our children a world in which "there's just one kind of folks. Folks."[3] And Atticus's faith that "it's not ok to hate anybody,"[4] because "most people are [nice], . . . when you finally see them,"[5] was still our faith. The clannish Ewells and Cunninghams were bad only because they were ignorant, and eventually that ignorance could be overcome through education and reason. Eventually class, race, and all tribal divisions would be overcome in favor of the principled moral universalism and equality that Atticus exemplified, and the new global community we anticipated as a result. Law still provided the framework for this universalism, with its demand for universally applicable principles and other-embracing neutrality. And many of us, including me, marched off to law school with Atticus as our icon.

But some three decades later I see the film's conflicts touch closer to home. *To Kill a Mockingbird* no longer seems quaint. The film is above all about the conflict between our particular loyalties (to family, class, country, race, religion, species) and the possibility (and desirability) of a vision of a universal order of law or ethics applicable to all. The film also asks what price we will or won't pay for our loyalties—both to specific communities and to our vision of universalized law itself. What moral compromises will we make to keep our families safe? What risks to our families are we willing to accept in order to vindicate our vision of "liberty and justice for all"? In our post-9/11 era of deep religious conflict, fear of worldwide terrorism, and factional war, the film's themes of fear and mistrust, tribal loyalty, and the failure of a universalized vision of justice are more salient and contested than they have been perhaps since it first came out.

Horton Foote's screenplay of *To Kill a Mockingbird,* while generally quite faithful to Harper Lee's novel, changes the book's framing and its perspective to pose more dramatically this question of loyalty: Is there a place for loyalty and love that allows me to die for you, and even to kill for you? The movie explicitly understands that Maycomb is prepared to sacrifice Tom, not out of justice, but out of love and fear: to demonstrate its loyalty to Mayella Ewell, to her tribe, and to the white racial hierarchy of the town's heritage and history. White Maycomb is willing to kill (and torture) innocents—Tom, Atticus, and maybe even Atticus's children, Scout and Jem—for its own survival. It seeks to kill the innocent aggressor in defense of its own, for Tom, though innocent, has compromised Mayella's honor.

Director Robert Mulligan and screenwriter Horton Foote emphasize this conflict between law and loyalty in several ways: they sustain a camera focus on Jem (who feels this particular conflict most intensely) rather than Scout; they bookend scenes on the Finches' front porch (one of them not in the novel), both of which force Atticus to choose between law and loyalty; and they add several other scenes and dialogue involving Bob and Mayella Ewell that are not in the novel but that also pose the conflict explicitly.

Both the filming and the sequencing of scenes focus not on Scout (the first-person narrator in the novel) but rather on Jem. Although he is relegated in the book to a less central role, the film takes Jem to the center. In fact Jem is so thoroughly the central character through whom we see the story—leading the action, understanding and reacting to events, taking most of the close-ups—that Scout's voice-over often seems jarring, a shift of perspective that we do not expect and that often does not fit the film's attentive focus on Jem's point of view. The movie begins and ends with Jem. Although Scout's naïve encounter with Walter Cunningham informs us of the social hierarchies at play in Maycomb, the first conflict in the film is with Jem—and it is a departure from the novel. Jem refuses to come down from his tree house to eat breakfast because Atticus has declined to play football for the Methodist church team. Atticus explains: "I'm too old to get out there. After all, I'm the only father you have. You wouldn't want me to go out there and get my head knocked off, would you?"[6]

But Jem understands only that his father is "too old for anything," adding: "He won't let me have a gun. And he'll only play touch football with me, never tackle." Atticus is a disappointment as a man and as a father. He won't use violence or dominance, even in play, and Jem is left both without a role model for leaping the gap between childhood and manhood and without a staunch protector against the evil he is beginning to see in the world. From Jem's perspective, Atticus lacks courage and won't "man up" to the demands of loyalty—not for the Methodists and not even for his own children. Atticus never seems to choose loyalty over law. And that leaves Jem, throughout the movie, feeling both exposed to danger and pushed into taking on himself the role of defender and protector that Atticus refuses.

Foote thus places this conflict between loyalty and law not just in the courtroom but also on the front porch of Atticus Finch's house. He does this by inventing an early scene on the porch that is the parallel to the powerful ending, in order to frame the film even more explicitly in terms of Atticus's personal conflict between his role as a lawyer and his role as a father. Atticus "denies" demands of loyalty to his children twice (explicitly) within the course of the film in these parallel scenes on the front porch, when he is faced with a choice between them and the demands of universal law and duty. The first choice comes at the beginning of the film, when Atticus agrees to take the Robinson case, the second at the end, when Atticus is prepared to put Jem himself on trial for the death of Bob Ewell.

The first time we see Atticus choose legal obligation over personal loyalty, he has just put the children to bed and is sitting on the porch. He overhears as Scout asks Jem about their mother:

"How old was I when Mama died?"
"Two . . ."
"Was Mama pretty?"
"Um-hm."
"Was Mama nice?"
"Um-hm."
"Did you love her?"
"Yes."
"Did I love her?"
"Yes."
"Do you miss her?"
[silence]

We feel the mother's absence in Jem's silence as Atticus swings alone on his porch. Yet immediately after this exchange Judge Taylor stops by, introduces the topic of Tom Robinson, and says tentatively: "I've been, ah, thinking about appointing you to take his case. Now, I realize you're very busy these days with your practice. And your children need a great deal of your time . . ." Judge Taylor breaks off, waiting for Atticus to respond, giving him an out.

"Yessuh," says Atticus. He looks down, thinking it over, and the camera pans back to Judge Taylor, who is waiting in silence. It is clear that Atticus could refuse this case—a case he knows will bring his family trouble. The judge will not force the issue.

But finally Atticus looks up. "I'll take the case," he says after a moment.

"I'll send a boy around," the judge replies, reminding us that even the judge who wants to see Tom defended is still part of Maycomb's complex social and racial hierarchy. And then, as the judge steps off the porch, he says, "Thank you."

"Yes, sir," replies Atticus in a tone that suggests that it was no small matter.

This invented scene explicitly gives Atticus the choice to make,[7] underlining the conflict between loyalty and justice not only in Tom's trial but also in Atticus's own willingness to put his small, motherless family at risk for the sake of law—the same man who wouldn't risk a football injury for the sake of the Methodists.

The seriousness of this choice between justice and love is reemphasized shortly afterwards, when Atticus faces Bob Ewell at the arraignment—another scene not present in the novel. Atticus is dressed in an impeccable light linen suit; Ewell is grubby, in overalls, with his stained, mangled hat still on his head in defiance of courthouse etiquette. Atticus's distaste is patent.

"Well, hey, Cap," Ewell greets Atticus with folksy jocularity.

"Mr. Ewell," Atticus counters with stiff formality, emphasizing with his own "Mr." Ewell's lack of courtesy and the social distance between them.

"Cap, I'm real sorry they picked you to defend that nigger that raped Mayella. I don' know why I didn't kill him myself instead of going to the sheriff. Woulda saved you and the sheriff and the taxpayers a lot of trouble."

"Excuse me, Mr. Ewell, I . . ." Atticus tries to move past Ewell, but Ewell steps in.

"Hey, Cap, somebody told me just now that they thought that you believed Tom Robinson's story agin our'n. You know what I said?" Ewell grins and laughs. "I said you wrong, man, you dead wrong. Mr. Finch ain't takin' his story agin our'n." He looks for Atticus to react, but Atticus is stony. "Well, they was wrong, wadn't they?" Ewell's good-old-boy familiarity takes on an edge of menace.

Atticus draws himself up. "I've been appointed to defend Tom Robinson, and now that he's been charged, that's what I intend to do," Atticus replies, and begins to push forward past Ewell.

Ewell tries to block him. "You're takin' his—" But Atticus interrupts.

"You'll excuse me." Atticus brushes past Ewell and descends the stairs toward the courthouse door.

The camera moves in on Ewell, "a short, bantam cock of a man."[8] He looks incredulous. He leans over the banister to deliver his parting shot, his tone biting and nasal, drawing out the diphthongs, his hat shading his face: "What kin'a man are you? You got childun of ya own!" While James Anderson's delivery carries this line as a half threat, foreshadowing the attack on Jem and Scout, Foote's stage direction is that the line is to be uttered in astonishment, not in attack.[9] Ewell simply cannot believe that Atticus would trade off the interests of a white daughter for a black stranger.

The film has a subversive edge. Ewell's question recalls the frightened faces of the children on the steps of the schoolhouse after the *Brown v. Board of Education* decision. Ewell asks the questions that families both black and white in Topeka must have been asking in 1954: Even for your children, won't you do a little injustice? Won't you fight? Won't you kill?

The question reechoes as Atticus turns down opportunities to fight Ewell, even when a drunk Ewell menaces Jem and Scout in the car at Helen Robinson's house. He tells Jem, who is clearly frightened: "No need to be afraid of him, son, he's all bluff." But Jem is not so sure. He looks back through the car window as Ewell raises a hand in threat.

Later, back on the front porch, the film's potent symbol of the threshold between safety and danger, public and private, home and the larger world, youth and maturity, Atticus tells Jem: "There's a lot of ugly things in this world, son. I wish I could keep them all away from you. That's never possible."

But from Jem's perspective, it is not so much that Atticus can't protect them but that he won't protect them. Atticus is the best shot in the county, but he refuses Jem a gun. He won't fight Ewell, and the only categorical rule he gives his children in the entire film is: "I don't care what the reasons are. I forbid you to fight." Why won't Atticus defend his family? What kind of father is he?

How can we understand Atticus's choice to endanger his motherless children in a hopeless cause? Why is Atticus such a figure of admiration? If, on the one hand, we side with Atticus, does that make us lunatic idealists, suicide bombers who would sacrifice our own families to an abstraction? On the other hand, if we side with the Ewells, does that make us narrow-minded tribalists, doomed to torture and kill in order to save "our'n"?

The classic story of a father sacrificing his own child is, of course, the biblical story of Abraham and Isaac, and commentary on that story sheds some light on Atticus Finch's character. Although many authors have discussed the story,[10] one author in particular, Søren Kierkegaard, asks us to linger on the aspect of it that is most troubling: Abraham's immediate and firm commitment to kill his only, beloved son, for no good reason. Other authors, for example, Emmanuel Levinas, skip quickly to the happy ending, emphasizing God's grace or Abraham's openness to the angelic voice that forbids the final act of sacrifice.[11] But these authors seem to make the story too easy. Abraham took *days* to journey to Mount Moriah and came to the very brink of murdering his son before divine intervention stopped him. How could a father do such a thing? How can Abraham be admirable? Do we admire Abraham because he was following law at all costs, sacrificing his son to a universal good? And is that also why Atticus is admirable? But what is admirable about a pointless sacrifice, doomed to failure?

First, I describe Kierkegaard's understanding of the Abraham story. Next I suggest four aspects of this conflict between law and loyalty that I see in contemporary legal life. I then return to the film to explore how it resolves the conflict.

The Knight of the Infinite and the Knight of Faith

The grounding idea of liberal legalism is the premise that reasoned debate can unfold principles applicable to all "like cases." All persons are equal before the law; reasons valid in one instance are also valid for all other instances of the same sort. One person cannot be given preference over another; my child cannot be preferred over someone else's. Logically, at least, the perfect agent of universal law must be prepared to sacrifice himself and all he loves to the "universal law."

Søren Kierkegaard, in *Fear and Trembling*, offers us the embodiment of universal principle in his character of the tragic hero, or "knight of the infinite," a dutiful Kantian who is willing to sacrifice everything dearest to himself if necessary to do his duty and to uphold the universal law.[12] The knight of the infinite may suffer for his adherence to principle, but his suffering is articulable and understandable, and all reasonable beings must honor him for it. The knight of the infinite has a duty to deliberate with other reasonable beings, but once convinced by rational argument, the knight of the infinite is the firefighter who must ascend the stairs of the burning tower though it cost him his own life, the man who must hold to his marriage contract even when his affections have turned elsewhere, the judge who must condemn even his own errant child according to the law. These sacrifices are tragic, but they are undeniably "for the right"; we admire and applaud them and take comfort in the security that such knights abide by their principles no matter what. We can rely on those principles, predict them, state their premises and their conclusions in a common tongue amenable to logic. We need only talk together reasonably to reach the right answer.

Kierkegaard points out, however, that religion requires a knight of faith, not a knight of the infinite. Abraham is commanded by God to sacrifice Isaac. There is no reason given for this commandment. It is not demanded by ethical principle, and is even forbidden by ethics, for ethics considers it an unjustified murder of the most heinous sort, as well as a breach of a prior contract between Abraham and God. Abraham does not doubt or complain about this command; he consults no one; he deliberates with no one; he knows that rational debate is of no use. God has commanded it, and it must be done. Abraham's love for God and absolute obedience to him must come before the law, before reason, before sanity, before comprehension. The act of offering Isaac is an act of personal loyalty, demonstrating that Abraham will sacrifice everything—human love, sanity, cosmos, sense, and even reason—to God. The only gain to be attained is that Abraham "becomes God's intimate acquaintance, the Lord's friend . . . whereas even the tragic hero only addresses Him in the third person."[13]

Hardest of all, Abraham has no guarantee that the request is divine rather than demonic; he must recognize the command in and of itself. He must do without Kant, who asserts that we recognize God only because he is good.[14] Yet if Abraham had not carried through, or if he had asked to be spared the trial, "then he would have borne witness neither to his faith nor to God's grace, but would have testified only how dreadful it is to march out to Mount Moriah."[15]

C. S. Lewis sees the same conflict in the more human experience of eros. The divinity of sexual love rests in its self-abnegation—its willingness to do anything for the beloved.[16] Eros affirms the infinite value of *this* person, *this* child, *this* lover. Who in love wants to be equal to all others? One wants to be above all others, unique, essential, irreplaceable. As Lewis points out, the divine potential is also the demonic potential, for the lover is willing even to sacrifice his own nobility, honor, and principles to the beloved. As tragedy attests, the lover drowns her children, kills her husband, betrays her family, prostitutes herself—anything for love. The irony, of course, is that in debasing herself for love, she becomes unlovable and even demonic—a Medea. As Lewis points out, though eros prefigures the passion of Kierkegaard's knight of faith, such love and loyalty to another human being is idolatry. Absolute love beyond ethics, says Lewis, belongs only to God.

Even such devotion to God is perilous, Kierkegaard reminds us. What if Abraham is mistaken? He has nothing but his own faith to reassure him that it is God and not some demon that instructs him. If he is mistaken, "what can save him? He suffers all the pain of the tragic hero, he brings to naught his joy in the world, he renounces everything ... and perhaps at the same instant debars himself from the sublime joy which to him was so precious that he would purchase it at any price. Him the beholder cannot understand nor let his eye rest confidently upon him."[17] Yet the marvel for Kierkegaard is not that Abraham proceeds to follow the command but that he believes firmly that in doing so, all will be well—not in some other life but in this life. This faith in miracle, in the impossible, in the absurd is what Kierkegaard admires in Abraham but cannot achieve himself. "At the moment when the knight made the act of resignation, he was convinced, humanly speaking, of the impossibility. This was the result reached by the understanding, and he had sufficient energy to think it.... This is quite as clear to the knight of faith, so the only thing that can save him is the absurd, and this he grasps by faith. So he recognizes the impossibility, and that very instant he believes the absurd."[18]

An old doctrine of criminal law acknowledges the dilemma of Abraham. Generally, a person who understands the law and knows what he is doing is criminally responsible for his acts.[19] In other words, one who is capable of the Kantian ethical deduction must follow the universal principle and is criminally responsible if he, for weakness of will, does not do so. Some old cases, however, recognized an exception where the defendant believes that God has commanded the criminal act.[20] In that case, the defendant is excused by reason of insanity even though he knew that the act was against the law. The law makes Kierkegaard's point: we excuse, and we may even admire, the knight of faith, but we cannot make sense of his actions. The law recognizes the "higher obligation," but only as a species of insanity, and as an "excuse," not a justification. The law cannot take the step of faith—cannot affirm an impossibility or acclaim a miracle.

Nonetheless, Kierkegaard says that he admires Abraham's faith, especially his confidence that all would be well—a confidence that is absurd in the face of the horror of what God had commanded him to do. Because of Abraham's confidence, God's grace was affirmed and Abraham became God's *friend*, not merely a dutiful agent of universal law.

Kierkegaard urges on us both the terror and the beauty of the knight of faith. Loyalty and love treasure the person infinitely in her peculiarity, not as an "equal" member of a class of reasonable beings, the same as all others.[21] The nature of the bond cannot be articulated, parsed, or reduced to a list of qualities, but is always whole and incommensurable. Yet its very incommensurability is also its unreason and unlawfulness. In the name of love, every ethical abomination is possible—and every miracle. Only an unreasonable, "absurd" faith in the goodness of God rescues the knight of faith from despair.

Law and Loyalty

Kierkegaard's knight of the infinite and knight of faith embody and explicate the deep conflict between law and loyalty that is so central to *To Kill a Mockingbird*. In this section I briefly outline four aspects of this conflict in contemporary legal life before returning to the complex story presented by the film and the ways in which that conflict is itself interrogated and interpreted through the character of Atticus Finch.

Americans versus Terrorists: Torture and the Ticking Time Bomb

To Kill a Mockingbird was released into a world of riot, violence, and fear not unlike our own post-9/11 times, and its conflicts between loyalty and law parallel our own. In 1962 racial conflict in Alabama was felt and framed like our "ticking time bomb," threatening the destruction of "the homeland" and its way of life. "It's the race agitators that causes the trouble," declared Attorney General Albert Patterson as he ran for governor of the state in 1958. "We cannot afford to take a chance anymore. We have got to have someone in the governor's office who will stand up and fight for the rights of the people on this segregation question."[22] Patterson's refusal to protect the Freedom Riders gave permission and even authorization to the mobs that beat, burned, cursed, humiliated, and killed peaceful civil rights protesters. The protesters, or "agitators," were innocent of violence, but from the perspective of the segregationists, the threat they posed to the white South struck at the very definition of southern community and the fragile sense of security of the white minority in power.

Now, at an increasing distance from 2001, we have seen the horrors of our own loyalty- and fear-driven responses to terrorism. We have gone to war, with all its inevitable collateral damage. We have tortured and killed innocent people, hoping for information, but sometimes just for humiliation and revenge. In Abu Ghraib, Bagram, Fallujah, and elsewhere, our own soldiers, incited by patriotism, hate, and revenge, have committed murder, rape, desecrations of the dead, and other acts of brutality and abuse. Like Governor Patterson, some of our leaders have turned their eyes away and given at least tacit approval.[23]

Paul Kahn, speaking of our own violent responses to terrorism in his book *Sacred Violence: Torture, Terror, and Sovereignty,* puts it like this: "The real conflict is between an ethos of love for a particular community and a moral universalism. Our attachments to the state are not justified in the language of morality. Rather, attachment to a community has a history and a destiny to which the individual finds himself bound."[24]

Kahn argues that our violent responses to terrorism also resound in tribalisms like those of the Ewells and the Cunninghams: we love our country so much that we are willing to die for it, to kill for it, and to torture for it. If we succeed in torturing our enemies until they abjure their own fidelities, then we win: we undermine their commitments and truths, and we reinforce our own. Kahn makes clear that in the language of sacrifice and love, true love (which is the only truth for love) is only as true as the intensity of the pain we will endure to validate it. And that blood sacrifice in turn ties us even closer to "our" country as we honor, grieve for, and remember the dead, and pledge more blood so that their blood won't have been shed "in vain." To be truly committed to the continued existence of one's country, one's family, or one's way of life, one must be willing to die, and to kill—even innocents. Kahn also calls up the story of

Abraham and Isaac: in order to prove his commitment to God, Abraham had to be willing to sacrifice his innocent son. Likewise, Kahn says, we prove our commitment to and love of country by killing and torturing even innocent "enemies." This is the sacred violence that witnesses and seals the bonds of community. It is part and parcel of why we account "noble" the sacrifice of those willing to die for their country.

Funerals in the Criminal Courtroom

A second resonance of the movie's conflicts in our current domestic legal system comes in the courtroom, as victims and victims' families become key players in the criminal process. Since the advent of the victims' rights movement, victims are far more visible in the criminal justice system than ever before. They are present at pretrial hearings and sentencings, not just at trials; they have input in the exercise of the prosecutor's charging and bargaining decisions; they return post-trial to dispute parole or probation decisions.

Victims' families often demand "justice" for their lost loved ones not to achieve a universal equality but as a kind of personal, sacrificial memorial. Hence their presence in the legal system often confuses the norms and scripts of the funeral with the norms and scripts of the criminal trial. Victims bring large gilt-framed pictures or slideshows of their deceased loved ones, with devotional captions in flowing script. Victims report that they want the prosecutor, the judge, the jury not just to convict but to sympathize and grieve with them. We find it difficult to resist the power of victims' demands for loyalty. Who can quibble with an elegy? Sentences become gravestones, the more expensive, the greater the sacrifice, and the more honorable the victim. A short sentence is like a cheap casket; it seems to demonstrate disrespect or lack of love for the victim. Conversely, we are mystified when victims' families do not fight for long sentences or the death penalty, because it too seems to signal disrespect or a failure to honor the victims. One flummoxed prosecutor even asked a bereaved mother who refused to support the death penalty whether she "really loved" her murdered daughter.[25]

The confusion of elegy with justice reaches the legislature as well as the courtroom. For example, a bill to abolish the death penalty in Connecticut was derailed by the personal plea of victims' family members.[26] While legislators largely agreed that the death penalty was not sensible policy for a host of reasons, they felt the awkwardness of "quibbling with the elegy" when they tried to explain their position to passionate victims who demanded that we act out of love for their lost family members— and who demand that we kill in order to prove that love. As state senator Edith Prague put it, explaining why she switched her vote from for to against repeal after meeting with the victims' family members: "Whatever he [the father and husband of the victims] would have asked me to do, I would have done, because that family doesn't deserve any more stress or aggravation. . . . So, I'm going to honor their request. I want to do a little something for them."[27]

Though articulated as a demand for justice, the victim's voice resists the forum of reason and insists on particularity. It is the loss of *this* child, *this* lover that the victim wants us to feel, not an abstraction of desert or a principle of equal justice. As Antjie Krog, reporting on the South African Truth and Reconciliation Commission, writes, "The victims ask the hardest of all the questions: How is it possible that the person I loved so much lit no spark of humanity in you?"[28] As with the fight for the "homeland," we are caught between the urgent demands of loyalty—that we courageously fight or kill the enemy to prove our love—and the demands of a disembodied legal principle that leaves us cold.

Self-Defense

Woven deeply into the fabric of the criminal law is the conflict between loyalty and law, which we usually fail to notice. The law of self-defense allows one to kill when necessary to prevent imminent death or serious bodily harm, but only when the one threatening death is an "aggressor." Self-defense, after all, is a justification, not an excuse. The claim must be that one has killed rightly, stopped a greater evil from occurring. Correlatively, the traditional law of duress does not provide an excuse to one who kills an innocent person, even when one's life is forfeit if one does not. These doctrines together raise the problem of the "innocent aggressor"—the baby with the handgun who is about to pull the trigger without realizing what will happen. Even if we assume that killing the baby is the only way to stop him, it is hard to argue that killing this baby is "right" or that self-defense should apply here (though scholars do try). Why should I be able to prefer my life to the baby's life? Or if the baby is aiming at someone else, why should I prefer that person's life to the baby's life? (The question of abortion to save the mother's life also encounters this difficulty.) Yet, scholars tend to assume that I do have the "right" to defend my life over another's in such a situation, just because it's "mine." Loyalty and love allow, in these circumstances, the killing of an innocent being in order to prefer oneself (or one's friend) to someone else. But "principled neutrality" cannot justify it.

Writ large, self-defense against the innocent aggressor is the justification for killing the conscripted enemy soldier and the justification for "collateral damage" necessary to war. It is the rationally dubious ground that allows preferring one's own countryman to another's, the instinct of the tribe.

Speciesism

Finally, we see the conflict enacted in the context of our relation with animals. Peter Singer accuses us of "speciesism"—the unjustified preference for humans over other species. He and others explicitly compare our treatment of animals to the treatment of racial minorities: we kill animals for the benefit of humans without a thought, just as whites killed blacks or loyalists kill adversaries. But according to Singer, pain is pain, whether it is suffered by human or nonhuman animals, friends or enemies. A truly universalist ethical perspective, he argues, would not treat nonhuman animals differently from humans but would weigh all pain and suffering equally in the utilitarian world scale of pleasure and pain.[29] Singer's opponents, he says, make the same kind of argument that the Ewells do: Why shouldn't I prefer my own children, my own countrymen, my own race, my own species? Wouldn't you save your child from a burning house before you saved the dog? Wouldn't you kill a dog who, without criminal intent, was attacking a child? Isn't there a place for loyalty and love that allows me to kill for you, just because you are one of "mine"?

Atticus Finch and the Choice of Law or Loyalty

One way to characterize the conflict in *To Kill a Mockingbird* is to think of Atticus as a "knight of the infinite," who will sacrifice even his family for his commitment to reason and to law's resolution of conflict through reasoned debate. He tells Scout that he must defend Tom Robinson to the best of his ability. Failing that, "I couldn't hold my head up in town," he

tells her. "And I couldn't even tell you or Jem not to do something again."
Later, in his closing argument to the jury, he urges: "I'm no idealist to believe firmly in the integrity of our courts and our legal system. That is no
ideal to me; it is a living, working reality."

In these moments Atticus seems to work out the conflict between loyalty and universal law much as George Fletcher tries to in his 1993 book
Loyalty: An Essay on the Morality of Relationships. There Fletcher spells out
the importance of loyalty as "an expression of the historical self."[30] Rituals
of attachment and devotion secure the bonds of a real, living, historical community, bonds that sustain the public trust of daily life and make
possible the rich, fully imagined understanding of individual selves who
receive their identity from their loyalties and attachments. But Fletcher
cautions:

> The challenge for our time is uniting the particularist leaning of loyalties with
> the demands, in some contexts, of impartial justice and the commitment, in all
> contexts, to rational discourse. As much as I make this plea for loyalty, I make
> a stronger plea for the qualities of mutual respect and reasoned discourse that
> make this or any argument worthwhile. There is no point to an argument that
> would be accepted or rejected on the basis of personal loyalties. The text stands
> as an argument that, if worth making, has no ties to my time, my place, or my
> community. It is an appeal to discourse across time, across space, and across
> culture. We learn we have roots by transcending them.[31]

In other words, yes, be loyal. But your highest loyalty must be to reasoned
argument itself, so that your other loyalties may be subject to dissent and
contestation—and therefore growth and change. In the courtroom, that
forum of rational debate, the "great leveler," all of us count the same.

The movie, more explicitly than the book, asks if Atticus is willing to
make such a sacrifice for his commitment to a universalized law—to sacrifice Mayella, and even to sacrifice his own children. One reading of the
film is that Atticus puts his children at risk in order to follow his principles of liberal lawfulness. He will risk his children to uphold his principles
because, as Martha Umphrey and Austin Sarat suggest in the preceding
essay, that is the best legacy he can give them, for although he cannot
protect their lives, he can give them a reason to live, a pride and honor in
"holding their heads up."

But the film does not leave us with liberal lawfulness triumphant—
neither in result nor in process, nor even (I would argue) as a foreseeable
future. The camera cuts to Jem during Atticus's closing argument, and we

can see that Jem wants to believe in the force of reason too. He wants to believe in the triumph of politeness, civility, good manners, forbearance, and reasoned debate. Jem has tried to follow Atticus's lead; he has kept Scout from fighting. He comes to a tentative willingness to believe in Atticus's world of law, reason, civilized disagreement, nonviolence. He sees it as a "good sign" when the jury has been out for two hours. But Jem's fleeting belief in Atticus's optimistic future is short-lived. The guilty verdict surprises and crushes Jem. Although Atticus is ever optimistic, his mind moving immediately to the "good chance" in an appeal, Jem is defeated. When neighbor Maudie tries to comfort him, telling him that his father is one of those "who are born to do our unpleasant jobs for us," he rudely tells her to "go away."

Throughout the film Jem seems less optimistic than Atticus, and in some ways seems the wiser, or more "realistic," character of the two. Jem anticipates dangers that Atticus does not: he follows his father to the courthouse to guard Tom, and he refuses to leave when the mob surrounds them. He doesn't trust that this conflict will be worked out "reasonably." He doesn't trust that loyalties can be articulated in universal terms and that the mob can be "talked out of" their objective. Jem also does not believe that Ewell is "all bluff." He fears Ewell, and, left alone to stay with Scout at night, he is unnerved by his fears, and he panics and runs through the dark and windy streets. Nor is Jem shocked by the news of Tom's death, though Atticus is.

Jem tests his courage against the darkness of these fears—represented by his obsession with the dark secrets of the Radley household, his willingness to cross the boundaries of safety, and then his clandestine correspondence with Boo Radley. And of course it is Jem who ultimately has to find the courage to fight Ewell and to try to protect his sister—by force, not argument. He ends up unconscious, his right eye as black as Mayella's, his left arm as useless as Tom's. Jem pays the price for Atticus's defense of law in Maycomb. As the book has it, "Jem was a born hero." He and Boo, his alter ego, are the ones who keep justice alive in Maycomb the old-fashioned way, by engaging in bloody battle, in silence, without reasons, by night, not by day. They kill the bad guy; they do not try to reason with him.

At the movie's end, it is not universal principle or reason that prevails. When Atticus learns from Heck Tate that Ewell has been stabbed to death, he is appalled. For the first time in the film, we see Atticus not in command of himself or the situation or even the law. He fumbles. "I guess the thing to do is, uh, good Lord, I must be losing my memory. I can't remember whether Jem is twelve or thirteen. Anyway, it'll have to come before the county court. 'Course it's a clear case of self-defense, but, well, I'll run down to the office . . ."

Atticus is ready, again, to sacrifice Jem to the law, to have him tried for the murder of Ewell. His optimism is still intact but shaken, anxious. We can hear the unspoken questions running through Atticus's mind: Is Jem twelve or thirteen? Will he be tried and sentenced as an adult? Will he be treated as legally responsible for his actions—accountable as a "reasonable man?" Will the jury believe a boy? Will they believe Boo Radley, the neighborhood "monster" who has a violent past and is not quite sane? The jury did not believe the "boy" Tom. In this speechless moment on the porch, law and its rational discourse seem to unravel, and Atticus falters, vulnerable. He recedes into the background, no longer the commanding figure he has been throughout the film.

Atticus is rescued and upstaged at this point by Heck Tate, his good-old-boy social inferior. Tate takes the Ewell position of loyalty, not reason. "Mr. Finch, do you think Jem killed Bob Ewell, is that what you think? Your boy never stabbed anyone." Tate looks meaningfully at Boo Radley, quietly swinging in the porch swing with Scout. Then he resumes: "Bob Ewell fell on his knife. He killed himself." He pauses, looking at Atticus, but Atticus says nothing. For the first time, he has no defense of law to give. Tate continues:

> There's a black man dead for no reason. Now the man responsible for it is dead. Let the dead bury the dead this time, Mr. Finch. I don't know of any law that makes it a crime for a citizen to do his utmost to keep a crime from being committed, which is exactly what he did. But maybe you'll tell me that it's my duty to tell the town all about it, not to hush it up. But you know what'll happen then. All the ladies in Maycomb, starting with my wife, will be knocking on his door, bringing angel food cakes. To my way of thinking, to take a man who has done you this great service, to take him and drag him into the limelight with his shy ways, to me that's a sin. It's a sin and I'm not about to have it on my head. I may not be much, Mr. Finch, but I'm still sheriff of Maycomb County and Bob Ewell fell on his knife. Good night, sir.

This speech is thematically parallel to Ewell's speech on the stairs of the courthouse. Ewell says he should have killed Tom himself to save the town, taxpayers, and Finch the trouble. And Atticus should have stood by his people, believed "our'n" against the race of the other. Closed ranks. After all, what kind of man are you, Atticus? You have children of your own. But of course this time, when Heck Tate presents the very same argument, Atticus goes along with it. Boo Radley and Jem will be spared the "trouble" of a trial because "Bob Ewell fell on his knife."

Tate's speech suggests that law, legal process, trial may not be the glorious workings of equality and reason that replace violence but something that themselves amount to, as Scout sees it, "killing a mockingbird." Perhaps a second reading of the film is that Atticus's "law" loses out to Jem's and Tate's (and Ewell's) "loyalty" after all. The last voice-over of the movie tells us that Atticus spent the night at Jem's bedside and was there when he woke up in the morning. In the film's final scene, subversively, Atticus seems to choose loyalty, not universal law.

The Catholic Legion of Decency, which provided ratings for the film, was so troubled by this ending that it initially rated the film as suitable only for adults, because adolescents should not be taught that the "official rules by which we live may be set aside when special circumstances demand." Only after the scene was recut to make Atticus less complicit in the "saving lie," and after a personal plea by Gregory Peck that Atticus's "stunned emotional state" was a "morally acceptable explanation of why the father . . . did not resist the Sheriff's deception," was the rating changed to recommend the film for both adults and adolescents.[32] Even so, *New Yorker* reviewer Brendan Gill complained that the scene suggested that "while ignorant rednecks mustn't take the law into their own hands, it's all right for *nice* people to do so."[33]

But I would suggest that there is something about Atticus that we have not yet fully understood. There may be another way to understand Atticus's character—not as a knight of the infinite but as a knight of faith. His faith, however, is not in God's goodness but in Maycomb's.

Atticus's defense of Tom is laudable and courageous. His speeches inspire us. But Atticus's treatment of the Ewells is openly contemptuous. Even in his court of law, the great leveler, Atticus Finch, employs every weapon of class ridicule against them, and as Paul Kahn reminds us, "ridicule stands with torture as a form of degradation."[34] His defense of Tom is not a neutral one. Atticus does not play fair. In his argument there is force and cruelty, and words are a sharp weapon.

The prosecutor's sneering sexual insinuations during his cross-examination of Tom are nearly matched by Atticus's condescending treatment of Bob and Mayella Ewell. Atticus first pricks Ewell's pride by asking if he can read or write. Ewell, with hesitancy and great embarrassment, agrees to demonstrate, writing his name on Atticus's tablet so everyone can "see" that he is not unlettered. But the test is a trick. Atticus does not give Ewell the satisfaction of proving to the courtroom that he can write. He does not show the writing tablet to the jury but pointedly tosses it carelessly aside. He smirks. He has scored off Bob Ewell. He preyed on Ewell's class insecurity to divert his attention from the real point of the exercise: to demonstrate that Ewell is left-handed.

Ewell is furious at how Atticus's ploy has revealed his self-consciousness, tricked him, and underscored the difference in social rank between them, all at once. Later Ewell tries to settle the score by provoking Atticus into a fistfight. Ewell spits in Atticus's face, a custom that for Ewell would require a trial by battle to settle this debt of honor. And though Ewell does succeed for a split second in making Atticus lose control, again Atticus triumphs over him. Loftily Atticus pulls out his gentlemanly handkerchief and wipes his face, then drives off in his fancy car. Atticus's gesture is condescending, not peacemaking. His refusal to fight is an insult, a refusal to meet Ewell as an equal. It is war by other means, war by humiliation, and Ewell has no weapons for it.

Atticus's treatment of Mayella at trial is of a piece with his treatment of Ewell. He condescendingly says he pities Mayella for her ignorance and flusters her with social forms and rules that she does not know how to respond to—insulting her with every gentility. Mayella's accusatory response, resounding through the courtroom, cuts to the heart of the conflict. The choice as she understands it is not between universal law and tribalism but rather between different tribal loyalties—between the "elite" and "regular white folks." Dignity must be paid for in blood, not words. Mayella is powerful in this moment. Her face fills the screen; her voice rings out: "I got something to say. And then I ain't gonna say no more. He took advantage of me. And if you fine, fancy gentlemen ain't gonna do nothing about it, then you're all a bunch of lousy yella stinkin' cowards. The whole bunch of you. And your fancy airs don't come to nothin'. Your ma'aming, and your Miss Mayella'in—it don't come to nothin', Mr. Finch!"

The courtroom reverberates in the silence after her passionate out-burst, men shift in their seats, and Ewell almost, but not quite, offers Mayella a gesture of protection as she folds herself out of view again in her courtroom seat. Mayella has named the elephant in the room. She has put her finger on what is at trial, and she has uncovered the bias in the supposedly unbiased trappings of the law. Instead of truth she demands manhood, the courage to stand by her, protect her reputation, protect her dignity. The trial is not between true and false. The trial is between "his'n" and "our'n."

After Mayella's speech the camera cuts to Jem's face. His brow is fur-rowed; he feels the strength of her accusation too. Atticus has crossed the boundaries of politeness, the boundaries of race, has abandoned Mayella to scorn and worse in even suggesting that she was attracted to Tom. And he has a daughter of his own.

While it is hard now to understand how Mayella could ask the jury to sacrifice Tom's life for her "honor," Mayella's "honor" in depression-era Alabama is not merely a question of whether or not she is invited to join the Junior League. Admitting to an attraction for a black man in the Maycomb of this era could be fatal for a woman like Mayella. Within memory, at least, white women in the South who crossed racial boundar-ies were beaten, raped, tortured, and murdered by Klansmen. According to Martha Hode:

> Like black women, white women who defied the rules of patriarchy could not count on ideology about female purity to absolve them of alleged illicit sexual activity. Poorer white women whom Klansmen and their sympathizers judged to be lacking in virtue were subject to abuse that ranged from insulting language to rape. After Georgia Klansmen shot a black man "living in adultery with a white woman," they "strapped the woman across a log, and whipped her so severely that she could not sit up yesterday." Klansmen also sexually mutilated white women who lived outside the boundaries of sexual propriety. In the Georgia case of cohabitation in which the black man was castrated with a butcher knife, a witness recounted (perhaps exaggerating, perhaps not) that Klansmen "took the woman, laid her down on the ground, then cut a slit on each side of her orifice, put a large padlock in it, locked it up, and threw away the key, and then turned her loose." In North Carolina, a white girl with a bad reputation was assaulted by the Klan; one witness testified that "they took her clothes off, whipped her very severely, and then lit a match and burned her hair off, and made her cut off herself the part that they did not burn off with the match."[35]

If vigilante enforcement of racial apartheid remains strong in depression-era Maycomb, Bob Ewell's appeal to Atticus as a father is not rhetorical. Ewell is likely a Klan member himself, and in putting out the story of Mayella's rape, he may be protecting his daughter from Klan retribution. Mayella's plea for loyalty from the jury is a genuine plea for protection, and they grant it, albeit reluctantly (given how long the jury takes to reach its verdict). Either Tom or Mayella will suffer for the sin of crossing racial boundaries. The white fathers on the jury decide it will be Tom, not Mayella.

Atticus cannot be neutral in this conflict. He must and does take sides. And he takes "his'n." His compassion and friendship for Tom moves beyond the chilly defense of reason; Atticus likes Tom, he admires Tom, and he cares about Tom. Atticus does not "merely" defend Tom in court. He counsels him, visits his house, meets his family. When Tom is threatened by a lynch mob, Atticus sets up his "theater of reason" in front of the jail the night before the trial, arming himself with his reading lamp and his law book, those symbols of the power of truth and law over violence. But in the film there is also a long, thin, rifle-like shadow across Atticus's lap. Although he has left his gun at home, the violence of law itself is present, and the bargaining with the crowd takes place in the shadow of the law's violence. Atticus is willing to die—and perhaps kill—to keep Tom out of the hands of the mob. He does not leave, even when Jem and Scout show up and the mob begins to turn ugly. And Atticus himself crosses racial boundaries when he chooses to go himself to Tom's house to inform Tom's wife, Helen, of Tom's death. When she faints, Atticus is the one who catches her and carries her inside. And so the movie portrays Atticus's commitment to Tom as itself a loyalty. Atticus recognizes that mere equality is not enough: he tells Jem that "cheating a Negro is ten times worse than cheating a white man."

At the same time, and against all odds, Atticus really does believe that Tom will be vindicated. Atticus is not jettisoning his loyalties to his community but hoping for the amendment of them—against all the evidence. Harper Lee's novel makes clear in prose what the filmmakers make clear by Atticus's clothing, style, and manner of address. He is a white southerner of the upper classes, steeped in the privilege of southern hierarchy and apartheid. He is a Finch of Finch's Landing, a man with a Name and an Old Family, a man to be addressed not as "boy" or as "Atticus" but as "Mr. Finch." The only man Atticus "sirs" and addresses by title (outside the formal context of the courtroom) is Judge Taylor; others—Heck Tate, Walter Cunningham—he addresses by their first names, though they address him as "Mr. Finch." Atticus does not seek to put away this history, his community, or his social standing. In the book, Lee gives us this snatch of dialogue from Atticus to Scout: "This time we aren't fighting the Yankees, we're fighting our friends. But remember this, no matter how bitter things get, they're still our friends and this is still our home."[36] Atticus will not see even the Ewells as his enemies. He believes in the compassion and humanity of his fellow Alabamians against the evidence, and he is willing to test that faith with the safety of his own children. Atticus hopes he can bring out the best in his friends; he believes that their basic goodness will come through, as Walter Cunningham's does in the lynch mob scene. And Atticus asks the jury members not just to "do your duty" but also to have faith in their own neighbors, black as well as white. Tellingly, Atticus's final words to the jury are "In the name of God, *believe* Tom Robinson"—a line that is not in the novel.

So a second interpretation of the film is not that Atticus embodies the "knight of the infinite," committed to an equal, universalizable law. Instead the "law" Atticus champions is a way of life that commits to a particular vision of a future—not a future dictated by reason alone, not a mere "ideal," but a "living, working reality"—in which revenge and honor killing are forsworn, hatred is countered by kindness, politeness, and dignity (whether addressed to a lynch mob, a Negro, or a crabby old white lady), and compassion and friendship both grow out of and outgrow the boundaries of race and tradition. In the novel Scout asks about the trial, "Atticus, are we going to win it?" And Atticus replies: "No, honey. . . . [But] simply because we were licked a hundred years before we started is no reason for us not to try to win." Then Scout says, "You sound like Cousin Ike Finch," who, Lee tells us, is Maycomb County's sole surviving Confederate veteran.[37] Lee wants us to see that Atticus looks for a New South to take root right in the midst of the worst of the Old South—and Atticus will fight this new losing battle with the same stubborn tenacity with which the South fought the North. Horton Foote put it this way in a note to the filmmakers in which he defended the tone of the original draft of Atticus's closing argument:

I think it should perhaps be kept in mind that particularly at this period a Southerner like Atticus is not an unprejudiced man speaking to a group of prejudiced ones. He is surely a man that has had to fight the prejudice in himself, so in a measure one might say he is addressing the speech to a part of himself as well as to the jurors. In other words, he is not a "noble man" explaining the obvious facts to a group of ignorant, unenlightened dirt farmers, but a man who has shared their prejudices, struggled with them, and who is determined to be free of them at all costs. And, too, he knows the depths of the complexity of the prejudices that he is trying to get them to renounce in themselves.[38]

Despite Atticus's absurd faith in his neighbors, Tom is convicted, and he is shot while trying to run "like a crazy man."[39] There is no miracle, no change of hearts and minds in Maycomb. But Atticus's response is not to blame the court system or the jury or even the times. Instead Atticus says that "the last thing" he told Tom was that he should not "lose heart." He should not have fled. Tom lacked faith; he succumbed to despair. Despite the objective evidence of deeply rooted hatred and prejudice in Maycomb, Atticus believes it is Tom's lack of faith, not the injustice of the verdict, that is responsible for his death. And though there is no miraculous exoneration of Tom, the film ends with a miracle of another sort. Atticus, like Abraham, is saved from the necessity of his sacrificial offering: Boo Radley rescues Scout and Jem from the murderous knife of Bob Ewell.

But it is a very close thing. What if Scout or Jem had been raped or murdered? The film's uncomfortable final scene on the front porch leads us to question Atticus's trust in the law and in his neighbors, as Atticus himself stumbles over Jem's age. Faith in the humanity of "others"—enemies, outcasts, criminals, and misfits—exacts a heavy price for our loyalty. Do we think terrorists should get "the same" legal protections as citizens? Do we endanger and dishonor the victim when we trust the offender with a second chance? Do we put our "own" species, country, family, clan at risk from "others"? Do we refuse to defend ourselves against innocents who threaten "our" way of life? Do we draw up our wills and board the Greyhound bus for New Orleans and pray that our enemies' humanity will finally prevail over their hatred? Do we send our innocent black children over the threshold into the angry all-white school? The time bomb, after all, is ticking.

And yet, if we do not put all at risk for our faith in the absurd impossibility of growing through our old loyalties into new ones, we will not be able to hold our heads up and stand as witnesses to that actuality, to call the other "friend." Atticus is a towering figure not so much because he stands for equality, universal principle, and cool reason against tribal loyalty, but because that very tribal loyalty has taught him to have faith, perhaps even an absurd faith, in the possibility that his fellow southerners will come around.

Atticus's tenacity and power arise from the same roots as the Ewells' tribal hatred, but he looks more closely at the particular. What Atticus sees that Ewell does not is that the very virtues of the honor culture that Ewell professes are present not in white men by virtue of their pedigreed white maleness but in outcasts, Negroes, old women, children, and poor farmers. Throughout the story Atticus finds virtues in unlikely places: gentlemanly restraint and compassion in Tom's kindness to Mayella, courage in Mrs. Dubose's fight against addiction, friendship in the reclusive Boo Radley, pride and gentility in poor Mr. Cunningham. The cultural definitions of the tribal boundaries between "us" and "them," "white" and "black," are themselves abstractions that break down in the face of concrete gestures of courage, compassion, gentility, and perseverance.

This is not to say that we can replace "universal law" talk with "universal virtue" talk. Being able to see these virtues as virtuous requires personal and concrete experience. The film tells us that you have to know the Cunninghams to understand why stubbornly refusing a teacher's quarter is a sign of nobility, or why Mr. Cunningham would prefer not to be thanked for his offerings of food. You have to know Boo Radley to understand why he isn't dangerous and why telling people of his heroic act would be like killing a mockingbird. Atticus teaches Jem and Scout to know right from wrong when they see it, just as Abraham "just knew" it was God who commanded the trip to Mount Moriah. There is no logical protection provided by universal principle or law that can keep us from forming mistaken loyalties. There is only the close attention to the particular persons around us, to what they do and how they affect others, in the light of what we know from our embedded tradition and our own historical past about good and evil deeds. If we keep our loyalties personal and do not abstract them, then we are less liable to frame conflicts as generalized wars of "us" against "them." And if we remain open to experiencing "others" as persons, irreducibly unique and full of contradiction, then it becomes much more difficult to fear and to hate them. Atticus's ethic is the ethic of novel and film: both arts bid us to take the time to bide, to inhabit the character of an other.[40]

And just as virtue has to be seen in the particular encounter with another person, the promotion and advocacy of virtue cannot be abstract either. Atticus can keep faith with his neighbors only by risking his children. It has to be personal. If Atticus had been some northern lawyer who came down on the train from New York to defend Tom, then all the universal principle or virtue talk in the world wouldn't matter. Atticus succeeds in changing (some) hearts and minds in Maycomb, like those of Heck Tate and the Cunninghams, not because his legal principles are right or universal, but because his neighbors know him—because he is the best shot in Maycomb County, because he accepts produce in lieu of payment, because he can, with a straight face, tell Mrs. Dubose she "looks like a picture," because his children go to school with everyone else's, and because *Atticus,* their neighbor and friend, believes in Tom. And even though, from the perspective of universal law and reason, this personal faith, this loyalty, is absurd, miracles do happen. Just as Scout and Jem arrive on Halloween at Maycomb's Mount Moriah, the most dangerous "maniac" of all, the monstrous Boo Radley, the crazed one every sane person in Maycomb fears and no one trusts, "Lord knows what he's doin' or thinkin'," comes to the children's rescue—a deus ex machina, absurd, insane, impossible, and true.

So in our own conflicts between loyalty and law, Atticus offers us only the injunction that we avoid abstraction in both. Never assume you understand a person "until you climb inside of his skin and walk around in it." This is not loyalty to ideas, positions, sides, races, religions, causes, abstracted political groups, or rules, but a way to reach a "compromise" with particular people or situations and to "get along a lot better with all kinds of folk." It requires an absurd, risky faith that we *can* understand one another, we *can* step out of our own skin to walk around in another's, and that we are willing to do so. The film, in other words, offers us a way out of the conflict between law and loyalty, *if* we can believe Tom Robinson.

NOTES

My thanks to Austin Sarat for hosting the symposium that prompted this essay, and to Austin Sarat, Martha Umphrey, Trisha Olson, Max Simmons, Claire Katz, and the other contributors to this volume for excellent criticisms, insights, and suggestions.

1. *To Kill a Mockingbird,* dir. Robert Mulligan (Universal Pictures, 1962).

2. Harper Lee, *To Kill a Mockingbird* (New York: Harper Perennial, 2002), 233.

3. Ibid., 259.

4. Ibid., 282.

5. Ibid., 323.

6. All quotations from the film are my own transcriptions, unless otherwise noted.

7. In the novel Atticus tells his brother, "You know, I'd hoped to get through life without a case of this kind, but John Taylor pointed at me and said, 'You're It.'" *To Kill a Mockingbird,* 100.

8. Horton Foote, *Three Screenplays: The Trip to Bountiful, Tender Mercies, To Kill a Mockingbird* (New York: Grove Press, 1989), 23.

9. Ibid., 23.

10. The story of God commanding Abraham to murder his son is a difficult one to understand and/or accept, and generations of theologians have pondered it. See, e.g., Edward Noort and Eibert Tichelaar, eds., *The Sacrifice of Isaac: The Aqedah (Genesis 22) and Its Interpretations* (Boston: Brill, 2002). Some commentators avoid the difficulty of imagining a God who would order child sacrifice by suggesting that Abraham misunderstood God's instructions, or that God was using this opportunity to teach Israel that child sacrifice (which existed in surrounding cultures) was not acceptable. Other Christian theologians interpret the story as an extended prophetic allusion to the future crucifixion of Jesus. But whether or not those are convincing interpretations of the text, they duck the philosophical problem that I wish to pursue here, a problem that has fascinated philosophers as well as theologians: Is God's command what makes right, or is God bound by a prior morality or "natural law"? See, e.g., Edward Wierenga, "A Defensible Divine Command Theory," *Nous* 17 (1983): 387–401; and John Chandler, who writes in "Divine Command Theories and the Appeal to Love," *American Philosophical Quarterly* 22 (1985): 231, "Probably the two most important traditional objections to the D.C.T. [divine command theory] are, firstly, that the theory entails that actions such as cruelty or rape, which we are certain are wrong, would become right, and indeed obligatory, were God to command them, which is absurd; and secondly, that the theory logically precludes its supporters from describing God as good in any significant sense." The debate is, of course, also closely related to the positive law–natural law question of whether a law is properly law only if it is good, and if not, whether laws that are not good retain any morally obligatory element just by virtue of being laws. See Peter Cane, ed., *The Hart-Fuller Debate in the Twenty-first Century* (Portland, Ore.: Hart, 2010). The problem reechoes in criminal law doctrine as well. See note 20.

11. Emmanuel Levinas, "A Propos of 'Kierkegaard Vivant,'" in *Proper Names,* trans. Michael B. Smith (Stanford: Stanford University Press, 1996), 76–77.

12. Søren Kierkegaard, Fear and Trembling *and* The Sickness unto Death, trans. Walter Lowrie (Princeton: Princeton University Press, 1968).

13. Ibid., 88.

14. Immanuel Kant, *Foundations of the Metaphysics of Morals,* trans. Lewis White Beck (Indianapolis: Bobbs-Merrill, 1959), sec. 2, 25: "Even the Holy One of the Gospel must be compared with our ideal of moral perfection before He is recognized as such."

15. Kierkegaard, *Fear and Trembling,* 37.

16. C. S. Lewis, *The Four Loves* (New York: Harcourt Brace, 1960).

17. Kierkegaard, *Fear and Trembling,* 71.

18. Ibid., 57–58.

19. *M'Naghten's Case,* 8 *Eng. Rep.* 718 (1843).

20. See, e.g., *State v. Cameron,* 100 Wash. 2d 520, 674 P.2d 650 (1983); *State v. Crenshaw,* 98 Wash. 2d 789, 659 P. 2d 488 (1983) ("Although the woman knows that the law and society condemn her act, it would be unrealistic to hold her responsible for the crime, since her free will has been subsumed by her belief in the deific decree").

21. See, e.g., Martha Nussbaum, "Love and the Individual: Romantic Rightness and Platonic Aspiration," in *Love's Knowledge: Essays on Philosophy and Literature* (New York: Oxford University Press, 1990), 314–34; "Symposium: Conference on Law and Love," ed. Linda Ross Meyer and Martha Merrill Umphrey, special issue, *Quinnipiac Law Review* 28.3 (2010).

22. *The Freedom Riders* (2011), PBS documentary, available at http://video.pbs.org/video/1560084046/.

23. Jeremy Brecher, Jill Cutler, and Brendan Smith, eds., *American War Crimes in Iraq and Beyond* (New York: Holt, 2005).

24. Paul W. Kahn, *Sacred Violence: Torture, Terror, and Sovereignty* (Ann Arbor: University of Michigan Press, 2008), 88.

25. Susan Campbell, "Death Penalty vs. Life: An Issue of Closure vs. Peace," *Hartford Courant,* October 6, 2010.

26. The bill passed in the succeeding legislative session, but in a form that was prospective only, so that, on its face at least, it would not undercut the death verdicts in this case. David Ariosto, "Connecticut Becomes 17th State to Abolish Death Penalty," April 25, 2012, CNN, http://articles.cnn.com/2012-04-25/.

27. Susan Haigh, "Connecticut Death Penalty Repeal Appears in Doubt," Associated Press, May 11, 2011, http://abclocal.go.com/wabc/story?section=news/local/northern_suburbs&id=8126266.

28. Antjie Krog, *Country of My Skull: Guilt, Sorrow, and the Limits of Forgiveness in the New South Africa* (New York: Three Rivers Press, 2000), 60.

29. The same argument holds for other animal rights advocates who would use "reason" or "sentience" as the dividing line: we must treat all reasonable creatures, whether dolphins or humans, alike, and presumably all nonreasonable creatures, whether hens or severely mentally disabled humans, alike.

30. George P. Fletcher, *Loyalty: An Essay on the Morality of Relationships* (New York: Oxford University Press, 1993), 77.

31. Ibid., 173.

32. R. Barton Palmer, *Harper Lee's To Kill a Mockingbird: The Relationship between Text and Film* (London: Methuen Drama, 2008), 212–13.

33. Quoted ibid., 212.

34. Kahn, *Sacred Violence,* 166.

35. Martha Hode, *White Women and Black Men: Illicit Sex in the Nineteenth-Century South* (New Haven: Yale University Press, 1999), 161.

36. Lee, *To Kill a Mockingbird*, 87.

37. Ibid.

38. Quoted in Palmer, *Harper Lee's To Kill a Mockingbird*, 228.

39. Barton Palmer (ibid., 232–33) points out that Lee's novel makes Tom's death much more problematic and less believable: he is shot seventeen times. The film glosses over this fact as well as the fact that Atticus takes this explanation at face value instead of suspecting an official lynching, preserving an overly heroic picture of Atticus and underplaying the racism and violence that Atticus's optimism in the novel repeatedly overlooks or over-discounts.

40. See Martha Nussbaum, "'Finely Aware and Richly Responsible': Literature and the Moral Imagination," in *Love's Knowledge*, 148–67. For an application of such insights to international conflicts, see Nir Eisikovits, *Sympathizing with the Enemy: Reconciliation, Transitional Justice, Negotiation* (Amsterdam: Republic of Letters, 2010).

CHAPTER THREE

Motherless Children Have a Hard Time
Man as Mother in *To Kill a Mockingbird*

THOMAS L. DUMM

To Kill a Mockingbird is a film that resists itself. Every temptation toward easy sentimentality and simplistic characterizations of good and evil— even in the representations of the politics of racial segregation and sexuality—is subverted, not just by the carefully rendered dialogue and the narrative, both of which follow closely the main lines of Harper Lee's novel, but by a structural element that introduces a quasi-tragic element to the film. More so than the novel, the film highlights the isolation of each of the major figures in this tale even as it shows, rather than tells, why and how there can be no easy choices for any of the protagonists and antagonists. With its double conclusion—the deaths of Tom Robinson and Bob Ewell—*To Kill a Mockingbird* becomes a parable of the ongoing and unresolvable conflicts at the core of American identity, lonely selves who cannot reach beyond their loneliness and who misidentify each other in the search for resolution of their loneliness.

To Kill a Mockingbird not only has a double conclusion but also presents an entire series of doubles that brings into the open many of the ongoing tensions characteristic of the segregated South, so much so that one is tempted to think of the film as an extended dialectic of paired contradictions, never fully resolved. Especially the Finches and the Ewells as one pair, and the Cunninghams and the Robinsons as another, mirror each other in ways that intensify and deepen the narrative of the film, allowing viewers to imagine these characters more fully than we would otherwise be able to do.

In this essay I focus on one of those oppositions in order to show how *To Kill a Mockingbird* unwittingly prophesies the fate of the modern American family in the decades following the 1960s.[1] The freshness of this film, its contemporary feel, even as it pretends to be about the past, is a consequence of this buried prophetic narrative, which is only further hidden by its being a film that was produced in 1962 concerning events in the American South during the decade of the 1930s. (One need only look at the stylized modern font in the titles to note that this is to be an unusual exploration of the past.) In its sustained reflections on the problem of motherless parenting, the film uncannily anticipates what we might call the great dissolution of the American family later in the twentieth century. That it largely succeeds in this prophetic role is a consequence not so much of the particular genius of Harper Lee and the filmmakers, but instead of the uncanny unfolding of racial, sexual, and class politics in the United States during the era that followed its release.

Missing Mothers

How are we to mother our motherless children? Elsewhere I have suggested that this is one of the hidden problems of modern life, the problem of the missing mother being engendered in the production of the modern individual as subject and object.[2] The autonomy of the modern self has been a product of a particular kind of suppression of grief, a massive misunderstanding of the meaning of individuality, the creation of what could be termed "the lonely self." The struggles we have inherited from the lonely self are intimately connected to the ways we negotiate social circumstance, the meaning we impute to others, how we love (and hate) one another within families, communities, and polities.

The missing mother plays a significant role in the development of the lonely subject, in large part because of its powerfully evocative force. We might trace that force through what literary theorists would call the constitutive power of the metonymic chain the mother has inhabited as a word. If we look to the etymological root of the term *mother* we find that its meaning has shifted from one of its earliest definitions, from the

Greek *huster-ikos,* meaning "of the womb," or *hysteria,* to mother as *matrix,* meaning "womb." A disorder of the womb, in Elizabethan parlance, was described as a rising, suffocation, or swelling upward of the mother, that is to say, hysteria. Moreover, in an associated slang term, also Elizabethan in origin, the female genitalia were called "hell."[3]

The presence of such a demonized mother has always been problematic. She serves the purpose of psychologically reassuring men of their superiority, but simultaneously is frightening to men because of her demonic power. So one way in which Western cultures have attempted to deal with this paradox is to make her disappear. The image of the mother is recuperated by killing her off, figuratively. We can find examples of dead mothers in all sorts of literatures. More parochially, American culture has had many examples of motherless children in literature both high and low, but especially in literature and films that target children as audiences, in an appeal to the fantasy of the child to be without the mother. The disproportionate number of motherless children in fairy tales has carried over to Disney-fied children's films: *Snow White, Cinderella, Pinocchio, Bambi, The Lion King, Aladdin* are but a few examples, each of which features a child or children who are motherless.

But it is also the case that we can find dead mothers literally reflected in murder rates. Although they do not specifically record the killing of mothers by their husbands, the FBI Uniform Crime Reports nonetheless do note the relationship status of women and men known to each other who are killed by each other. There is a clear and obviously disproportionate level of women killed by men as opposed to men killed by women. For instance, in 2010, within families in the United States, 105 husbands were killed by wives versus 603 wives by husbands. Figures for the same year show a similar proportion among unmarried couples: 131 boyfriends killed by girlfriends versus 492 girlfriends killed by boyfriends. This ratio, somewhere between five to one and six to one, remained remarkably stable over the first decade of the twenty-first century.[4]

In a vein not dissimilar to the concept of the missing mother, Martha Fineman has referred to what she terms "the neutered mother," the idea of a mother who, in being given formal equality with men, is rendered neutral in regard to her gender. Fineman notes that in the context of continued cultural and economic biases that work against substantive equality for women, especially for mothers, who continue to be charged with the primary task of child care, this neutrality is pernicious. Neutrality in this context operates as a form of neutering. This neutering then contributes to the further demonization of mothers, especially along class and racial lines, and provides a legal weapon for men in divorce and custody disputes, another way of eliminating or expelling mothers from the nuclear family.[5]

The emergence of the neutered mother is a contemporary masculinist legal solution to an older problem concerning the ongoing predicament of motherhood as the primary target of misogyny. Supposedly empowered through a political right to equality, the mother is socially disadvantaged further by taking on more responsibilities in the public sphere while continuing to maintain an unequal burden of private responsibility in the care and nurturing of children. Furthermore, through the neutralization of her engendered powers, she is made, in a sense, to disappear from that private sphere. That is to say, she is torn apart by the added burden of being equal in the public sphere, with all of its attendant responsibilities, while remaining tied down in the domestic sphere. It is a lose-lose situation. Moreover, while she has achieved equality in legal terms, the de facto situation is such that she must still struggle over the lack of substantive equality at work and in other public venues.

Of course, prior to the development of modern medicine, the death of the mother in childbirth was the most common way in which the problem of the mother was solved. And it provided an added benefit for the father, an ability to sentimentalize the dead wife, and to enjoy the favors of a new wife to whom the old one would be compared. In a sense, the figure of the mother would be best served—more respected, more loved—by dint of her absence.

What is striking about *To Kill a Mockingbird* is both the ubiquitous presence of the problem of the missing mother and the variety of familial relationships that illustrate it. If we consider the primary families that are presented to us—the Finches, the Radleys, the Ewells, the Cunninghams, Dill's family, and the Robinsons—only the Robinson and Radley families are presented explicitly as including living mothers. And of course the tragic death of Tom Robinson makes his wife, Helen, a widow.

There is a pattern of contrasts at work here. Atticus Finch and Bob Ewell are both single fathers. Atticus is at the top of the social hierarchy, and Bob is at the bottom. Atticus's children are being raised to be self-confident, literate, and aware of others. Bob's daughter Mayella is so lacking in a sense of self that when she is addressed with respect during the trial, she assumes she is being mocked, and it is not unreasonable for Atticus to ask Bob if he knows how to write his name. If we compare the Radleys and the Robinsons, we immediately note that the Radleys are recluses, while the Robinsons live in an extended and open family and community. Boo's disability—his pathological shyness—keeps him indoors; Tom's disability—his crippled left hand—does not. If we work on the assumption that the Cunningham family is intact, we can compare them to the Robinsons and note that the primary opposition between those two families is that Walter Cunningham Sr. is part of the mob that wants to lynch Tom, while Tom, of course, is the prisoner on trial. Walter Sr. is in debt to Atticus, but Tom has no debts even though he seems as poor as the Cunninghams. If we assume that Walter Sr. is a widower, we can make a comparison with the Finches. Walter Jr. hunts with his father, whereas Atticus gives Jem an air rifle only after this information is revealed, and with reluctance. Walter is in debt—he has an "entailment" to Atticus—and his son Walter Jr. is in direct conflict with Atticus's daughter, Scout, at school.

The richness of these various cross-connections serves as a background for the entire story. Beneath the overt narratives of the courage of Atticus Finch, the coming of age of Jem, and the trial of Tom Robinson, these families of a depression-era southern town tell us another story, about the persistence of the lonely self in a place where American liberalism would not imagine it to prevail, the Deep South, where modernity is in conflict with the feudal remnants of antebellum America famously limned by Louis Hartz.[6] (If one of Hartz's claims, that the antebellum South was relatively underdeveloped as a consequence of slavery and its legacy, then what we are seeing in *To Kill a Mockingbird* is the fitful stirring of liberalism in the ruins of the Jim Crow South.)

But Hartz doesn't account for the status of women in his work. For a better analysis of the political demonization of women during the cold war era, which is precisely at its midpoint when *To Kill a Mockingbird* appears, we must turn to another theorist of American political culture, Michael Rogin. In his analysis of cold war cinema from 1946 to 1964, Rogin found there to be a persistent theme linking "Momism" with communism. "Momism" is a term developed by a popular writer of the time, Phillip Wylie, to refer to the situation in which the modern mother, no longer having to perform the many housekeeping duties that were central to the activities of mothers in the past, had too much time on her hands and became a shrew. Rogin writes:

> Mom, in Wyie's depiction, was a self-righteous, hypocritical, sexually repressed, middle-aged woman. Having lost the household function of preindustrial women, according to Wylie, mom got men to worship her and spend money on her instead. America, insisted Wylie, was "a matriarchy in fact, if not in declaration," in which "the women of America raped the men." Mom dominated her husband and encouraged the dependence of her son. She elicited his adulation to repress his sex and transferred the desire that ought to go to another woman into sentimentality for herself.[7]

Rogin demonstrates how this demonization of mothers came to be closely interlinked with anticommunism. Communists supposedly gained advantage over Americans by subverting the family, the source of the American way of life. The films of the era, according to Rogin, "subordinate political consciousness to sexual unconsciousness."[8] He suggests that there is both a depoliticizing of communism into a form of sexual desire and a politicizing of the family by its enlistment into the fight against subversion. In commenting on one example in the genre of anticommunist films, Rogin quotes the narrator: "I woke up one morning and found I had a Party card. . . . It was like finding yourself married to a woman you hate."[9]

To Kill a Mockingbird would seem not to fit into the genre of anticommunist movies, but only if we forget the continued accusations made against the leaders of the civil rights movement, that they were part of a communist conspiracy. The FBI was particularly interested in exposing Martin Luther King Jr.[10] Although the setting of the movie is the rural South of the 1930s, the book and film appeared at the peak of both the cold war and the civil rights movement. The makers of the film, it would seem, were perhaps unconsciously trying to remove the thorny and difficult issue of subversion from the picture. By eliminating the presence of mothers and minimizing the roles of women characters who are more prominent in the novel, they succeeded in turning the focus away from the national traumas associated with the emerging civil rights movement and bringing it back to the more universal, and less politically charged, issue of injustice.

How these various families negotiate the problem of the missing mother is a critical subtext of the film. At crucial moments, mother surrogates play key roles in pushing the narrative forward. It is in these moments that we notice the glimmers of a hoped-for liberal future emerging from the feudal past. Put negatively, the bonds of a small-town community are shown being torn asunder in this film. And every surrogate mother plays a role in either easing the pain or inflicting it. Put positively, the characters in this drama are fitfully moving toward a dissolution of the missing mother, one that is enabled by a legal order that is being called into question as inadequate to the demands of motherly care. The creation of surrogate mothers, who attempt to make up for the missing mother in partial and incomplete ways, illustrates this ongoing struggle to address and in a sense overcome the social limitations imposed by masculinist versions of motherhood, providing a transitional moment, so to speak, from the realm of the missing mother to that of the neutered mother.

Yet at the same time, the men in the film are valorized, not feminized, because their roles as protectors of the American way renders them heroic. They do the work that must be done, as Scout is told at film's end. They may be mother surrogates, but their true roles are as surrogates, not as mothers; and as men they successfully put to an end any doubt that they may be advancing the terrible subversions associated with "Momism."

In what follows I provide an extended example of one of the most important mother surrogates in action. I focus on the *male* rather than the *female,* in part because, as I noted, the roles of the women surrogates—Calpurnia, Mrs. Dubose, and Maudie Atkinson—are relatively underwritten in the film. But more important, the men as mothers overcome the suspicion that they may be "moms" in Wylie's sense of the term.

That said, there is a subversion of gender and patriarchy at work in this film more generally that pulls in a different direction from that of the male mothers. Scout's boyishness, Dill's femininity—he is a character based on Harper Lee's friend from boyhood through adulthood, Truman Capote—and the fact that Atticus's children address him by his first name all are signs of an ongoing instability in gender roles. In the end, the men as mothers illuminate a corner of the film, and of its time, that, while not the most explicit theme in *To Kill a Mockingbird,* nonetheless is present, and in its presence signals the emergence of a new form of family in the decades that followed the 1960s. I focus first on Sheriff Heck Tate, and then on Atticus Finch. Their fates are intertwined at several levels, but it is in their attempts to mother that we might see another way in which this film continues to resonate in the twenty-first century.

Sherriff Heck Tate as Successful Mom

Sheriff Heck Tate is an unlikely motherly figure. He is the agent of the state who arrests those who violate the law. His relationship to the man who has been appointed to defend the man he has arrested should be formal, distant, and official. Yet this is not the case. Partly it is the informality of small-town life in the South that is the reason. But beyond that, the intimate relationship of Heck to Atticus Finch is much more personal in character, and in the end goes to the heart of the outcome, not only in the case against Tom Robinson, the killing of Bob Ewell, and the exculpatory decision concerning Boo Radley, but also in the rehabilitation of Atticus as a surrogate mother to his children. That he is the chief law enforcement official of the county underscores the complicated relationship of law to motherhood, even though the substance of that relationship remains unspoken.

Heck appears in motherly guise in two crucial scenes—the shooting of the rabid dog, and his discussion with Atticus concerning what happened to Jem and Scout on their long walk home the night of the Halloween pageant. The earlier scene foreshadows Heck's more full-blown role as a surrogate mother to Atticus, when he gives his rifle to Atticus, almost demurely, telling Atticus that he would feel a lot more comfortable with him shooting at the dog, and saying to the children, "Didn't you know that your father was the best shot in all of Maycomb?"[11] By telling the children of a skill that their father has, a hidden talent that he exercised before they were born, Heck is behaving like a proud wife who would brag about her husband the father when trying to make her children take pride in his role as a respected man. Heck and Atticus, as mother and father, stand united to protect the children from a dangerous world.

So in this scene Heck is mothering not Atticus but Jem and Scout. They respond to Heck's claim concerning their father with wide-eyed amazement. Their prior understanding of Atticus is clear: he is a man not of action but of contemplation, a lawyer whose skill is drawing a water-tight will, as Maudie puts it when defending Atticus's reluctance to play football. Heck's reference to his sharpshooting refigures Atticus in the eyes of his children as a physically brave man.

It is symbolically interesting that Atticus throws his glasses on the ground before shooting the dog. He is casting aside his lawyerly equipment in order to become the killer. Here the film is anticipating the scene in which Atticus exhibits physical courage against a lynch mob. exercising it quietly but clearly. Jem had earlier been deeply impressed by Atticus's behavior in shooting the dog.[12] But now, while guarding Tom Robinson at the jail, Atticus is wearing his glasses again, reading under the floor lamp he has brought from home. That Jem refuses to leave him, sensing that he is needed by his father, is an example of how Heck has taught Jem his lesson. In the scene at the jail, Heck's absence is noted by the lynch mob, and this also suggests that Jem must step in to support his father.

But it is in the second key scene with Atticus that Heck Tate fully becomes the protective mother. I refer to the penultimate scene in the film, after Heck has arrived upon being called by Atticus. The very fact that Atticus calls Heck, though obviously because Heck is the sheriff, is nonetheless of interest. He addresses Heck by his first name, not by his title, and asks him to come because someone has attacked his children. That Atticus is counting on Heck to protect his children suggests that Heck is now the father figure, replacing the impotent father that Atticus has become. But it also suggests that Atticus is counting on Heck to provide him with the comfort and reassurance that is the role of the mother.

After Heck arrives, the two men look in on Jem, introduce Scout to Boo Radley, who has been hiding in the shadow of the doorway to Jem's bedroom, and have Scout take Boo out to the porch so they can discuss matters. Heck then demonstrates the wisdom of someone who has long experience with the community he has served as sheriff. In doing so, he mothers Atticus himself.

Heck first corrects Atticus concerning Jem's supposed commission of the act that resulted in the fatal knife wound suffered by Bob Ewell. "Mr. Finch, do you think Jem killed Bob Ewell? Is that what you think? Your boy never stabbed him." Then, continuing this scene of true instruction, the sheriff explains to Atticus how he will dispose of the case.

Bob Ewell fell on his knife. He killed himself. . . . There's a black man dead for no reason. Now the man responsible for it is dead. Let the dead bury the dead this time, Mr. Finch. . . . I never heard tell it was against the law for a citizen to prevent a crime from being committed, which is exactly what he did. But maybe you'll tell me it's my duty to tell the town all about it, and not to hush it up. Well, you know what'll happen then. All the ladies of Maycomb, including my wife, will be knocking on his door, bringing angel food cakes. To my way of thinking, taking one man who has done you and this town a big service, and dragging him, with his shy ways, into the limelight, to me that's a sin. It's a sin, and I'm not about to have it on my head. I may not be much, Mr. Finch, but I'm still sheriff of Maycomb County, and Bob Ewell fell on his knife. Good night, sir.

Heck presents the problem in terms of a heightened contrast between public right and private good, and comes down firmly on the side of private good. His use of the term "sin" to suggest what it would be like to treat Boo Radley as a hero is indicative of Heck's sophisticated understanding of the distinction he is making. He does not suggest that what would happen to Boo would be a crime. But for Boo to be subjected to the tender care—ironically, the mothering—of the women of Maycomb would be a torture for the poor man. This sphere of civil society at its most basic is what the lonely Boo has been spending his life trying desperately to avoid. Since it is in Heck's power to help Boo evade that fate, he feels compelled to do so.

Indeed, by using his officer's discretion to reach his conclusion, stretching that discretion to the breaking point by claiming that Bob Ewell fell on his knife, he protects not only Boo but Atticus as well. The duty to the public, to the law, that Atticus has been suggesting in a fumbling way— Atticus is so stunned by the accumulated details of what has happened that he has forgotten whether Jem is twelve or thirteen years old—is acknowledged by Heck but at the same time rejected by him. It is as though Heck recognizes that Atticus is trapped by his sense of duty. The morality exhibited by Atticus, however, is akin to that of an adolescent who thinks of justice as being a matter of following the letter of the law or the rules of the game. Atticus notes his duty to the law immediately prior to suggesting that Jem must submit to a hearing in order to clear himself of responsibility for killing Bob. But Heck recognizes a larger duty to justice that Atticus in his shock cannot for the moment comprehend. Heck, balancing the scales between the commission of a crime and the commission of a sin, chooses to commit a crime rather than a sin. He does so because he discerns what Atticus cannot, that sometimes justice is better served by leniency than by strict observance. Heck behaves here like a mother, because it is the mother's designated role to soften the harsh judgment of the father.

Yet Atticus is not behaving as a father here; rather he is groping with an imagined dilemma, and he is unmanned by it, so to speak. In this scene on the porch, we are given other clues as to the mothering role that Heck plays. Atticus's body language conveys his inability to grasp what has just occurred. He holds a handkerchief in his hands, which he continually wrings; his expression is abstracted; he is positioned in the background, while Heck is in the foreground of the frame. The usually eloquent lawyer stumbles over his lines, while the plainspoken sheriff finds the right words. His parting line, "I may not be much, Mr. Finch, but I'm still sheriff of Maycomb County," implicitly suggests that he realizes that his public status may be lower than Atticus's—Atticus refers to Heck by his Christian name, but he is always Mr. Finch to Heck—but in his domain of discretion, turning a public matter back into a private one, he is in control. Heck's decision is designed not to further the ends of law but to provide comfort and protection to those who have suffered a terrible trauma (Scout and Jem), the person who saved them (Boo Radley), and finally to Atticus, the father who has just failed to protect his children and needs now to be mothered.

The impact of Heck's decision has immediate ramifications. First, as soon as the sheriff departs, Scout asserts to her father that Heck is right. Atticus asks her what she could possibly mean, and she reminds Atticus of what he himself had said about its being a sin to kill a mockingbird. Her reminder seems to bring Atticus out of his confused state. Seeming newly aware of the presence of Boo on the porch, he walks over to him and says, "Thank you, Arthur. Thank you for my children." This is a telling line. What does he mean? At the most obvious level, Atticus is thanking Boo for saving his children's lives. But the phrasing is peculiar. As he puts it, Atticus could be thanking Boo for giving his children to him. In this way Boo has in a sense given a new birth to Jem and Scout. Their passage from childhood to adulthood is to be marked by the trauma of this event. Boo's rescue of the children, it is implied in the film (and made more overt in the book), is no coincidence. Boo has been watching over them since the beginning of summer, at least since the evening Jem found his pants neatly folded over the fence in the Radley garden, and probably since the incident when Scout crashed up against the Radley porch in a tire and Jem ran up and touched the front door. In this sense, Boo too is behaving as a mother.

At the Finches' house, after Jem has been treated by the doctor, Scout invites Boo to "pet" Jem, claiming that he can do so only while Jem is asleep, for Jem would resist such a gesture if awake. The gesture is a loving one. And in his protective role, his watching over the children, the little gifts that he has left them through the summer, it would seem that he has embraced that role, and that Atticus is recognizing him for it in his thanks.

It is also relevant that Boo is a recluse. Although Stephanie Crawford, Dill's aunt, repeats the gossip concerning the attack Boo made on his father, supposedly stabbing him in the leg with scissors and then calmly continuing to cut out pictures from a newspaper, this is not how he is depicted by Atticus or Heck. Both men understand that Boo and the Radley family need to be left alone, not because they are dangerous but because they have suffered some unknown unhappiness. Boo is surely a damaged person, but the gothic narrative is undermined by his rescue of the children.

Atticus Finch as Failed Mom

Atticus Finch is a father trying to mother his children. He cares for Jem and Scout by giving them wide latitude to explore their children's world, while gradually introducing them to the traumas of the adult world they are eventually to inhabit. His tender scenes with Scout, including correcting her while she sits on his lap, showing her the watch that he is going to give to Jem, making a compromise concerning his reading to her at bedtime, all indicate his deep involvement in parenting his children, which may not seem unusual to contemporary viewers but would, even in 1962, have struck many as being quite unusual behavior for a father, let alone a father at the height of the Great Depression. He explains to Jem after the conviction of Tom Robinson that he won't always be able to protect him from the harsh realities of the world they inhabit. He is always listening to his children, and is ready to hear what they have to say at breakfast and at the dinner table. The gendered division of labor would excuse him for handing off these responsibilities to the housekeeper, Calpurnia—who shares in disciplining and caring for the children—or Maudie, who has an obvious interest in the widowed lawyer who lives across the street. But he does not pass on these responsibilities.

In protecting his children, he underplays the extent to which other families differ from theirs. When Walter Cunningham Jr. comes to dinner, he is polite and conversational, as though a diet of squirrel and rabbit were ordinary and normal, not a sign of extreme deprivation. When Walter asks for syrup to pour on his food, Atticus simply has Calpurnia get it for him. (Pouring syrup on food to hide the rancid taste is an enduring habit of poor people.) When Scout, early in the film, asks Atticus whether the Cunninghams are poor, he is straightforward and clear, but he also answers her question concerning their own family in the same way. He tries to protect Walter Cunningham Sr. from embarrassment (providing a model for Scout later on, when she attempts to explain to the teacher why Walter Jr. won't accept a handout at school). His injunction to Scout not to fight with other children no matter what they may say about him also goes against the grain of the time. He doesn't tell her that it is unladylike for her to fight. In fact his order extends to Jem as well. Most fathers of the period would likely have taken pride in their children's defending the family honor. But Atticus is not most fathers.

Atticus is especially circumspect in discussing the Ewell family with his children. Bob Ewell, father of a large brood of children, forces Mayella to stay home and watch over the younger ones. Mayella herself has been physically abused by her father, and may be the victim of incest. (In *Fearful Symmetry*, the documentary on the making of *To Kill a Mockingbird*, Collin Wilcox, who portrayed Mayella in the film, overtly suggests that she played the character that way.)[13] Atticus is dismissive of Ewell, understanding him to be a blowhard drunk and not wanting Jem to fear him.

But he also is concerned to protect Jem and Scout from the ugliness of the Ewells of the world. In this task he fails miserably. Scout and Jem roam free through the town at all times, and as a consequence are shot at by Mr. Radley. They are easily able to sneak into the trial of Tom Robinson and to witness the ugly and graphic testimony of Bob and Mayella. They almost witness an angry mob attempting to lynch a black man. Jem is indulged in his wish to accompany Atticus to the Robinsons' home, and is as a result terrorized by a drunken Bob Ewell. The film ends with Atticus sitting up to await his son's return to consciousness after the brutal attack by Ewell, a man whose violent streak Atticus obviously underestimated.

This continual failure on the part of Atticus does not seem to detract from the almost universal admiration the character has received over the decades. Why is that so? The answer lies in the implicit recognition that Atticus is a father trying to mother his children. We indulge the character, make excuses for his failures, for his permissiveness with his children, because we feel sorry for a widower who is so deeply attached to his children that he allows them to mother him as he mothers them. But Atticus, surrounded by a supportive and sympathetic community, still fails in his responsibilities to his children.

Why would that be the case? That is, why would such a conscientious and thoughtful man not realize what he is doing? I would suggest that Atticus Finch is akin to Shakespeare's Lear, in the very limited sense that he misreads signs of love all around him. He is akin to Hamlet, again in a limited sense, in that he broods, and broods, and fails to act. His stoicism is both what is admirable about him and the source of his flaws. He takes on the case of Tom Robinson out of his sense of duty, to be sure, but he does so knowing that such a task is not only thankless but also dangerous. That he does not seem to see the danger is almost comical, or would be if the consequences were not so tragic.

He is terribly distracted throughout the film. The difficulty Atticus seems unable to work through, what is understated in many ways but also so obvious as almost not to bear noting, is that he is doing the work of mourning. He is still a grieving widower, and his mourning has turned into a form of melancholia. Atticus Finch does not know what to do or where to turn for help, except to Heck Tate. That the lawyer needs the sheriff to tell him what is just and unjust is ironic, but that a confused father turns into a helpless child in need of a mother's aid and advice is somehow an inevitable consequence of his circumstance.

So where does this leave us in interpreting *To Kill a Mockingbird?* I began this essay by asserting that we can see the emergence of a form of southern liberalism out of the remnants of a feudal South in this film. The complication of the cold war, and the conflation of the subversive with mothers and minorities, made that task more difficult but not impossible. It required eliminating mothers from the story and rethinking the politics of racial injustice. I suggest that it is the giving over of their masculine identities in the name of nurturing and protecting—that is, in assuming the identity of mother—that the male characters in this film as I have described them push us into the modern age of the American family. Instead of the traditional mother, we have mothering coming at us from all directions, but at sporadic moments and in fragmented pieces. The American family in question has so reached the point of fragmentation that in the United States since 2007 the largest category of heads of households has been single adults.[14] But there is no collective village to help these single parents and nurturers raise their children.

Of course, the mothering of children is only one thematic strand in a very complex film. But the undercurrent of emotion that is carried by these counterintuitive movements toward nurturing (and away from it) helps make *To Kill a Mockingbird* a film that remains contemporary for us. What we see in the dilemmas faced by Atticus Finch, and responded to so thoughtfully by Heck Tate, is a vision for a gentler future for the American family, one that unfortunately has not come to be.

NOTES

1. On the role of prophecy in the political history of the United States, see Sacvan Bercovitch, *The American Jeremiad* (Madison: University of Wisconsin Press, 1978); and George Shulman, *American Prophecy: Race and Redemption in American Political Culture* (Minneapolis: University of Minnesota Press, 2008).

2. See Thomas Dumm, *Loneliness as a Way of Life* (Cambridge: Harvard University Press, 2008), especially the prologue.

3. Ibid., 6–8. The misogynistic rage of Shakespeare's King Lear provides a telling example: "Beneath is all the fiends': There's hell, there's darkness, there's the sulphurous pit,/ Burning, scalding, stench, consumption" (*Lear* 4.6.129–31).

4. These numbers are drawn from the Federal Bureau of Investigation Uniform Crime Reports, www.fbi.gov/about-us/cjis/ucr/ucr.

5. Martha Albertson Fineman, *The Neutered Mother, the Sexual Family, and Other Twentieth Century Tragedies* (New York: Routledge, 1995).

6. See Louis Hartz, *The Liberal Tradition in America* (New York: Harcourt Brace Jovanovich, 1955), especially part 1, "Feudalism and American Experience."

7. See Michael Rogin, *Ronald Reagan, the Movie, and Other Episodes in Political De-monology* (Berkeley: University of California Press, 1987), 242. Rogin is quoting from Philip Wylie, *Generation of Vipers*, 2nd ed. (New York: Rinehart, 1955), 73, 78–79, 122, 127.

8. Rogin, *Ronald Reagan*, 245.

9. Ibid., 250.

10. See Taylor Branch, *Pillar of Fire: America in the King Years, 1963–1965* (New York: Simon and Schuster, 1998), especially 200–205.

11. Quotations from the film are my transcriptions.

12. For another take on this scene, see Colin Dayan's essay in this volume, "Humans, Animals, and Boundary Objects in Maycomb."

13. *Fearful Symmetry*, dir. Charles Kiselyak (Universal Pictures, 1990).

14. See United States Census, 2010, "Heads of Households," http://2010.census. gov/2010census/.

 CHAPTER FOUR

If That Mockingbird Don't Sing
Scaffolding, Signifying, and Queering a Classic

IMANI PERRY

Hush little baby, don't say a word,
Papa's gonna buy you a mocking bird
If that mockingbird don't sing,
Papa's gonna buy you a diamond ring.
Traditional African American lullaby

In the classic African American lullaby "Hush Little Baby" the restless child is promised all kinds of wonderful things if she will simply settle down. The promise of a mockingbird is one among a number of proposed offers. It is a good one. The mockingbird is a beautiful aural fixture of the American landscape. It is the bird with countless songs. It mimics other birds, thereby producing a living sonic collage. Because this repetition is "natural" rather than technologically made, it can be excellent but not identical to the original. Between the cardinal's whistle and the mockingbird's copying response there is a subtle difference even if our ears aren't sophisticated enough to hear it.

This film, whose title reminds us of the preciousness of mockingbirds, is on repeat in our culture. It is on numerous lists of greatest films, just as the novel that it is derived from has a place on many lists of greatest novels. We revisit it constantly, and that is part of what marks it as a classic film. It becomes a "common text" by adolescence. Junior high and high school students across the nation read the book in school and see the film as well, even now, more than fifty years after it was first released.

In this essay I am inviting the reader to understand the film as a cultural artifact that has important pedagogical purposes. The commonplace understanding of the pedagogical lesson, beyond the fact that it is a captivating story, is the moral dictum of human decency and a belief in racial equality. It is an important post–*Brown v. Board of Education* film that reimagines (or perhaps a better word is awakens) the conscience of white southerners, perhaps even white Americans in general, through the fair-minded heroic figure of Atticus Finch and the protagonist, his daughter, Scout. Today, in the post–civil rights context, struggles for civil rights have been integrated into the American narrative of a constant striving toward a more perfect union framed by principles of equality and liberty. The canonization of *To Kill a Mockingbird* suits this nation-crafting and narrating practice perfectly. But although this conception of the film serves a particular culturally based ideological function, if we limit our reading of the film to these terms, we sell it short. It teaches us far more.

I am arguing instead that we read *To Kill a Mockingbird* as a work with a much greater capacity, one that is of especial use to twenty-first-century viewers. The language I use to gird together my readings is that of the philosopher Alain Badiou. He speaks of acts of "creative repetition."[1] With this term Badiou is describing how a philosophical gesture or idea has a particular "form," which has variations that come and go in accordance with events, conflicts, social pressures, and transformations. But the Idea, Badiou argues, ideally has some core resilience through the variations. Indeed, the trials the Idea faces in the battleground of thought actually modify and improve the quality of the Idea even though in essence it remains the same.

I hope it is not too materialist to translate this insight to a consideration of the artifact of the film itself as a gesture or an Idea, a "thing" vested with meaning, which in the creative repetition of repeated watchings by thousands of eyes and minds is being re-created. With this analogy I am engaging in a reading of the film that examines the nature of its creative repetitions at multiple levels, both internal and external to the film.

Internally, I am arguing, the repetitions are disruptive of the common impression that Atticus occupies the role of the masculine ideal. In the midst of this disruption is a deeper argument about human value and difference. The repetitions have artistic and cultural forms, heavily relying on what the literary critic Henry Louis Gates Jr. has described (borrowing from the vernacular use) as signifying,[2] as well as the tradition of the southern gothic. The way signifying and the southern gothic are at play (and I use that word consciously) allows for the simultaneous recognition of the social stratification that existed in 1930s Alabama and its destabilization as a legitimate social ordering or ideology.

The film prunes some elements that illustrate these points quite dramatically in the novel, however; but taking a cue from Badiou and Gates, I am arguing that we scaffold the film with readings of Harper Lee's novel, as well as other literary works and films that influenced or were contemporaneous with *To Kill a Mockingbird*. These other works can be understood as commentary, supplement, even competing events that shape how the film exists. I understand that this kind of project challenges the integrity of the form, the boundaries of the film, which subtends with its temporal and sensory frames, but it also challenges the integrity of the form of this essay as it dances in and out of readings of film and text. Or to state it another way, although genre subtends, signifying upon it subvents and often subverts.

Ultimately this kind of reading serves the goal of rethinking what it is that *To Kill a Mockingbird* can and should do for us as students of this artifact. This is an intertextual reading but also something more specific: a claim that the philosophical gesture, the "Idea" at the heart of this artifact, is an egalitarianism that is far more radical than what we have taken it to present.

In other words, I am interested in allowing the mockingbird to sing by pulling it into harmony and sometimes polyphony with other "artifacts" that we can read alongside it, historically and culturally. In the 1955 recording of the eponymously titled "Bo Diddley," the bluesman played with the words of "Hush Little Baby," giving them a rock-blues pacing and mixing them with the "hambone," a traditional African American knee-slapping rhyme-song. He brought the new form "rock" and his weird square guitar to the old forms of the African juba beat and the hambone. In the multiple recordings of the song they each take a different form, some with the mockingbird reference, some without. I mention Bo Diddley here not just because he sang about the mockingbird but as an artistic corollary to the kind of contemporary intellectual work that this essay finds itself a part of: just as Ivy Wilson reads affect theory back into nineteenth-century contestations over race and citizenship,[3] and Alexander Weheliye reads

the late-twentieth-century musical form of the re-mix into a theorization of the bricolage of early-twentieth-century modernity,[4] I read *To Kill
a Mockingbird* as a "queer text" in the sense that it performs what queer
theory has described as "radical subversions" of gender and its normative
ideals. In this queering we find an ethos of decency and humanness. Bo
Diddley brought the new to the old to the new again. I hope to do some
of the same.

In the language of Hollywood, the characters of the film are archetypes:
Scout is a tomboy. Dill is simply an orphan. Boo is a haunting figure.
Tom Robinson is an abused Negro. Alone, the film can be "read" as cutting them down to those simply understood "roles." But attention to the
film alongside the novel challenges any archetypal readings. True, Atticus
Finch is a widower. He's an aristocratic lawyer who is decent to a fault,
perhaps. Read singularly, he is an ideal man. He even prefigures the common "white savior" role of civil rights memorialization in late-twentieth-
century Hollywood films.[5] This film, just six years post-*Brown*, offered a
vision of a "way to be" in light of the upheaval wrought by the burgeoning
civil rights movement and answered the cold war anxieties about American apartheid with a dashing movie star. But Atticus, even in the form of
Gregory Peck, is not a normative male, not really, despite the cut of his
suit and the sharp jaw line. He is heroic without fitting social norms. In
fact, as Martha Umphrey noted in response to an earlier version of this
essay, there are virtually no "normative" family units in the film. This can
be an entry point to thinking about the film as a sort of "queering" in the
theoretical sense. Queer theory subverts the pejorative for same-gender
romantic love, "queer," to challenge conceptualizations of gender and nor-
malcy that function to delimit, exclude, shame, and degrade.

In making these claims I am also borrowing from Thadious Davis's idea
of a "compensatory reading," which she performs with one of Faulkner's
character from *Go Down Moses,* the escaped slave Tomey's Turl.[6] Davis
takes Tomey's Turl from the margins to the center of the text by reading
his gestures as manipulations of the law of property, despite his status
as a chattel slave, and she does so with detailed attention to the law of
property in Mississippi history. In a structural parallel to Davis, I am reading other imaginative works alongside *To Kill a Mockingbird,* in historical
context, as both jewels and ropes wrapped about the neck of this cultural

artifact, with the ultimate purpose of creating an assemblage that enables a fresh or refreshed interpretation.

There are of course two intersecting primary stories in the film. The children's saga is largely about getting Boo Radley to come out of the mysterious house in which he hides (or is held captive), and the other is about the false accusation made against Tom Robinson for the attempted rape of Mayella Ewell. In the case of Boo Radley, the film mutes valenced readings of "queerness" that are readily apparent in the text. Visually, we see the oddness and disability of Boo, as well as his heroic actions, but it is only textually that we can recognize all of what draws the children to him. The film read alone can allow us to interpret their attraction as standard child haunted house fare. The novel suggests they are seeking something more. Their wanting him to come out is an insistence on an exposure to a specter of humanity generally obscured within the category of heroic acts. But Boo, odd and disabled, is both nurturer and protector. With the novel, we might interpret the yearning for Boo as connected to a complicated longing, as the children mark their play with all kinds of transgressions. Scout's best friend, Dill, prompts their efforts to get Arthur "Boo" Radley to come out of seclusion. Harper Lee based Dill on her childhood friend Truman Capote. Dill bounces from home to home, neglected and displaced, carrying his vivid imagination along with him. Like Scout and her older brother, Jem, he is "incomplete" domestically according to the ideals of the day; they are motherless, he is fatherless, and sometimes motherless as well, while at other times he has temporary father figures.

Understanding the multiple valances of getting Boo to "come out" is aided by Eve Sedgwick's attention to "queer nuances," such that we don't have to read this as a literal metaphor (although I think a good argument can be made for a reading that raises questions about sexual identity); but undoubtedly the child "others" living inside Maycomb are seeking out an adult counterpart. Indeed David Halperin's description of queerness as that which "is at odds with the normal, the legitimate, the dominant . . . an identity without an essence,"[7] or Eve Sedgwick's discussion of how queerness ventures beyond sexuality, in which she describes "one of the things that 'queer' can refer to: the open mesh of possibilities, gaps, overlaps, dissonances and resonances, lapses and excesses of meaning when the constituent elements of anyone's gender, of anyone's sexuality aren't made (or can't be made) to signify monolithically,"[8] facilitates a reading of queerness that encompasses all three children, each of whom tips along the boundaries of race and gender in one way or another. In the text, the spelling of Jim is feminized to Jem. At the same time, the name invokes Twain's Nigger Jim. In retaliation for his efforts to get Boo to come out, Boo's father, Mr. Radley, shoots at Jem, referring to him as a "nigger." Scout, a little girl with a gender-neutral name, is often reminded not to be a girl but rather to "be a gentleman." Dill moves between their beds when he stays overnight, promising Scout marriage but swimming naked with Jem. At various points Dill is told that he is not a boy, Scout that she is not a girl or, worse, sometimes too much of a girl. She and Jem are mothered by their black housekeeper, Calpurnia, and all three of them sit with the Negroes at Tom Robinson's trial. In seeking to pull out the most "queer" adult in their small world, they might be seen as searching for a role model, and not simply exhibiting the gothic curiosity that so characterizes southern literature and language. Although the film doesn't offer this level of detail, it signals what the novel signifies: Scout is an awkward tomboy with a bowl cut and too short overalls, while Dill is a knock-kneed dandy dressed in linen.

The children's connection with Boo is remote yet tender. He gives them carved toys and sticks of gum. He stealthily covers Scout's shoulders when she shivers as they watch a fire burn down a neighbor's home. Most important, he rescues Jem from the murderous rage of Bob Ewell. With Atticus as a counterpoint, we might simply read Boo as the lesser man to Atticus. He is a shut-in, removed from society because of his family's shame. But perhaps we should read him as the greater man. Certainly the risk and courage he demonstrates over the course of the film—coming out of the house, protecting Jem is as great as if not greater than the courage Atticus displays in defending Tom Robinson. Robert Duvall plays Boo with a tender nervousness, light hair, dark brows, and a face that retreats from the body. Boo Radley is presumed to be dangerously mentally ill, and Duvall, as classically handsome as Peck, performs that difference in his deliberately "queer" or odd embodiment. In Boo's queerness, which provides an intensive if remote connection with the children, we find a moral center of the text.

Because of the history of race, and the brutal exploitation of both labor and sexuality that characterized slavery in the South, the body figures prominently in southern literature, and distinctions between mind, body, and soul are often elided, troubled, and blurred. In his depiction on film, Boo Radley manifests his nonnormative "mind" with a ghastly appearance. As the disability theorist Rosemarie Thompson argues, the encoding of certain bodies as deviant and deficient is a social construction that supports hierarchies of humanity.[9] Harper Lee anticipates such critique by authoring a binding intimacy among the transgressive and liminal figures in the white population which overtakes the community in our vision such that the oddity subverts the normative. Distinctiveness is rule rather than variation. And the most marginal of the distinctive are among the best of them.

To Kill a Mockingbird is not unique in its fixation on the nonnormative. Indeed the southern gothic literary tradition depends on it. The mentally unstable, broken spaces and spirits, haunted people and places, odd accents (linguistic and social) and episodes are signature features of the southern literary tradition as it has been consumed by the American public, which seems to have a voyeuristic desire for those features of southern culture. What is distinctive about *To Kill a Mockingbird* is the clearing away of ethical ambiguity in this oddity. The odd are sources of good. Their bodies are not representative proxies for sin or danger. Additionally, while the incapacitated in southern gothic are sometimes used to represent innocence, and are morally redemptive because they are untouched by the world, it is rarely if ever because of their own analytic capacity. But here they act with clarity and capability. We are unconflicted about the decency of the queered subjects, just as we are unconflicted about the indecency of the one clearly self-proclaimed patriarch and white supremacist, Bob Ewell. The work pushes forth a humane ethics, in the stead of the illegitimacy of the moral code of white supremacy and the procedural failures of the legal system when Tom Robinson is convicted. We know what is wrong and right by the emotional work of the text better than by the rule of law, or the logic of Atticus. And significantly it is Boo, not Atticus, who beats back Ewell's evil. It is Dill, among the white people, who cries at the cruelty exhibited to Tom Robinson at trial. It is Jem who rages. They are not compliant with the rules of their race and gender. And yet they witness the cost of becoming a man like their friend Boo, and it is far greater than the social cost to Atticus of defending Tom Robinson.

In light of this, Atticus as THE model of courage is at the very least challenged, and his subscription to a reasonable man standard in an unreasonable society is as ridiculous as it is noble. Atticus is a man at the crossroads between the ordered injustice, the legal fiction of an abstract code of "justice," and the decency found in the family of nonnormative humanity. In the novel, we see how he wavers under the influence of his sister-in-law, chafing under the gender and class order of the South, and yet also tries his best to subscribe to it and sustain his own decency even as it isn't consistent with his own ways of being. Atticus tries to play both sides against the middle. This proves nearly impossible. At the same time, the fact that Atticus is depicted without this vulnerability in the film (his sister-in-law doesn't appear in the movie, for example) perhaps facilitates our frequent mischaracterization of him as an idealized hero, a man who Stephan Metcalf describes "as a cartoonlike vessel of stoical wisdom. . . . He is the Sermon on the Mount, the Kantian moral law, and the Golden Rule, all rolled into one parched apothegm."[10] But I have grown some disagreement with this depiction through conversation with my co-authors in this volume. Textually he is vulnerable, and self-doubting, albeit devoted to procedure and rule of law. His family is very "odd." Not only is he a single parent, but also he fails to offer "proper" gender education to his children or to restore the heteronormative domestic ideal by remarrying. And then he nearly falters when he thinks that Jem is the one who has killed Bob Ewell. He gestures toward an intent to turn his child in to the authorities until Sheriff Heck Tate counsels him otherwise, explaining that it was a defensive gesture, a paternal gesture ostensibly, on the part of Boo that led to Ewell's fate. Here, Atticus's Abrahamic devotion to law is not a test of loyalty but a revelation of error, both technical and moral.

Henry Louis Gates Jr. brought an African American oral culture to literary theory with his theorization of the folk term "signifying," at the same time making an ambiguous reference to semiotic theory and the uncertain and contingent relationship between word or symbol and referent. Gates employs signifying to describe an African American literary tradition of dialogic subversion through the use of wit and play, a repetition of features of earlier texts, with different strategic goals, structurally consistent with the actions of trickster figures in diasporic folk cultures. Although Gregory Peck as Atticus Finch is a dashing hero, we might read the displacement of Peck with the nervously acted Boo character as the protector of Jem as a signifying moment. Perhaps Atticus isn't the guide for us all. Perhaps Atticus is simply less afflicted than most, but not the beacon of justice we take him to be. The stones thrown away in this world, Boo and the band of children, are in fact cornerstones to an improved moral code in this text. They are not innocents, they are decents.

Critics have often read Tom Robinson's character as a relatively hapless black victim, noble but impaired. He is by turns paralyzed and desperate. But the layers of signification at work in Tom Robinson are more complex than this characterization allows, and also are aided by a consideration of the scaffolding texts. In the novel Tom is paralleled to Atticus's son, Jem. Recall that the novel begins with a mention of Jem's nonnormative body, "His left arm was somewhat shorter than his right,"[11] a detail that is repeated exactly in Tom Robinson's form, his left arm twelve inches shorter than his right. They are both disabled, yet physically competent, Jem to play football, Tom to bust up chiffarobes and do plantation work. In the parallel descriptions of the bodies of Jem and Tom, Tom is a "role model" for Jem, a figuration of an adult Jem, but one whose fate is determined by the rules of race.

Tom Robinson is falsely accused of raping Mayella Ewell, the adult daughter of a widely disparaged poor white family. The denouement of the trial occurs when it is discovered that because of his disability, in contrast to Mayella's girth, strength, and lies, it impossible to believe that he committed the crime. Tom's disability provides the evidence of his innocence. But it also queers his masculinity. He is not weak, but he is incapable of physically dominating Mayella.

The story feature of Tom's disability echoes Mark Twain's novel *Pudd'nhead Wilson,* in which the mark of the body (in the latter case the fingerprint) is the exculpatory evidence. Evidence of truth emerges from the deficiency or deviation (in the former case Tom Robinson's short arm, in Twain's novel the actions of the "pudd'nhead" lawyer who has been bizarrely recording fingerprints, which had operated as evidence that he was a pudd'nhead).

Whereas Mark Twain's fiction frequently allows ambiguity as to his take on the idea of racial equality (his character Tom in *Pudd'nhead Wilson* is a slave switched at birth who unwittingly passes for a white master, and in that role is cruel and immoral), there is no question that Harper Lee's Tom is a decent human being. Twain's Tom is morally deficient, and it is unclear whether that deficiency is a product of nature or nurture. This Tom, however, dark-skinned and unquestionably black, is unequivocally righteous.

The great offense that Tom Robinson performs is not rape; rather it is in expressing how he felt sorry for Mayella as his motivation for assisting her. He ought to have felt compelled by racial hierarchy according to the order of the day, not by common humanity. There is laughter from the jury in response to his sensitivity, and Tom looks stricken. He recognizes the transgression and glances, regretfully, toward Atticus, who slides back in his seat. The case quietly hinges on this moment, much more so than the revelation of Tom's disability. The empathy Tom feels belies a simple sense of race as a blunt stratification, and that is the law that has been broken. Intimate association existed within white supremacy, and through Tom we see that articulated in a distinctive way, not in terms of sexual intimacy between white men and black women as most accounts describe or imagine, but in emotional resonance between a white woman and a black man. His emotionalism itself gives him an interior sensitivity generally denied in depictions of men of both races.

Despite his obvious innocence, Tom loses at trial. Waiting in prison for his appeal, he climbs the prison gate in plain view and is shot down. This occurs off camera so viewers are left to imagine it (and perhaps even question the veracity of it). A common reading of this moment is as an act of desperation, born of the reality of Jim Crow justice. He knows he will be hanged and therefore tries to escape. But if we contrast this work to a best-selling novel published in 1940, Richard Wright's *Native Son* (the first African American–authored title to be selected for the Book of the Month Club, which was also made into a limited-run Broadway play in 1941), we might read Tom's action as something beyond desperation. Bigger Thomas, Wright's antihero, is chauffeur to a blind white woman, Mary. He brings Mary upstairs to her room after a drunken night with her and her communist boyfriend, Jan, who has frightened Bigger by espousing radical racial politics. Hearing the approach of Mary's mother, Bigger is terrified of being found in her bedroom and accused of sexual impropriety. So in a panic he suffocates Mary. White supremacy, with its terrorizing effects, has destroyed his capacity for humanity in that moment. In contrast, Tom Robinson's humanity is intact unto his death, even as his body is less than whole. In the end he pays the ultimate price, like Bigger, but the logic of the novel and the film is not predicated on a socially deterministic reading of his condition the way Wright's novel is. Tom, in expressing thought and emotion contradicting the logic of the social order, is individuated. He is a free man held captive. *To Kill a Mockingbird* is a humanist work of art, in contrast to the more social-scientific one that Wright offers. But in signifying upon Wright, Lee is also providing Wright with something he requested of his readership. When Wright explains of his writing, "I would hurl words into this darkness and wait for an echo, and if an echo sounded, no matter how faintly, I would send other words to tell, to march, to fight, to create a sense of hunger for life that gnaws in us all,"[12] he registers a desire not simply for an emotional reaction to his work but for resonance. He seeks a repetition, which he describes as an echo, a return depicted metaphorically as sound. Lee provides such a repetition, although she articulates the gesture of the black male subject quite differently. What matters for these purposes, however, is that the repetition does occur, and it is not simply a repetition of circumstance but a repetition of an argument against said circumstance. Both are forms of "protest novels" against American racism.

Of course, we might choose to make more of the distinctions between the characters—the fact that Tom Robinson is still in the rural South, while Bigger has suffered the devastating reality of the extension of the politics of white supremacy into the promised land that Chicago represented, a dream that "exploded" into the ghetto reality that is Bigger. In the open pages of the novel, Bigger is symbolically represented as a rat in a rat trap, which Chicago slum kitchenette apartments often in fact were. This representation reflects the repetition over generations of the core anxiety of chattel slavery and the core conceit of eugenics: the idea that black people exist at the very margins of the species, perhaps even venturing over into the category of other types of sentient beings. Toni Morrison makes this horror plain in her novel *Beloved* with the description of the slave woman Sethe's horror of being recorded in writing with some characteristics written on "the animal side of the paper" and others on the human. For Tom Robinson, his animal parallel is the dog, Tim Johnson. But this is not how he chooses to define himself. It is the social order that Lee always reminds us of, even as she challenges it with the characters' words and deeds. In Tom's autonomous actions he parallels himself not to an animal but to Atticus, to the thinking man. He becomes an agent rather than a product of his society. In attempting to escape, he insists on a stark performance of southern justice, which is a bloody summary justice for black citizens under Jim Crow. Tom's staging of southern law is more accurate than that of Atticus, albeit effectively suicidal. This allows for the narrative of the film to close in a way that is both poignant and powerful, particularly in 1962. The first viewers watched it in the midst of massive resistance to integration. The Supreme Court had proven incapable of enforcing the Constitution. The substance of law was right, but the process was hampered. Tom's performance instantiates what Robin West so aptly describes as the logic in *Pudd'nhead Wilson:* "Niggers are guilty."[13] And though the work looks back to the 1930s, it has a lesson for its present and our present.

Tom falls according to the rules of the society. As Tom signifies upon the social order, however, the novel and the film signify upon it as well. And this repetition of signifying captures one of the most salient of the parallels between law and literature: they share the required labor of taking a bunch of messy details and interpreting some Idea or ideal or rule or form out of all this stuff. There is a contingency about whether this is going to be done correctly, effectively, or with fidelity to the Idea. But each iteration (a given work of art or a case) itself is instructive, albeit fraught with difficulty and the threat of tragic failure. Likewise, we might read Lee's signifying upon Wright as a matter of Gates's notion of signifying, a repetition that entails a subversive strategy consistent with James Baldwin's critique of *Native Son:* "The failure of the protest novel lies in its rejection of life, the human being, the denial of his beauty, dread, power, in its insistence that it is his categorization alone which is real and which cannot be transcended."[14] At the same time, we might read it as a signifying that operates as a subvention on *Native Son,* a form of supplementation or assistance to an understanding of black subjectivity under the force of white supremacy better suited to a postwar context in which socially deterministic left politics held less sway. In either case, *To Kill a Mockingbird* finds a place within a tradition of argumentative literature that is both literarily compelling and political at its core.

Early in the novel, Calpurnia tells Scout and Jem that her son learned to read by digesting Blackstone's commentaries. This absurd detail should prompt the reader to think about the subjectivity of African Americans in law, as thinkers and therefore authors and judges of morals, ethics, and law, even as they are excluded as citizens. Let's imagine Tom Robinson as the center of this text, empathetic, generous, a person who is not simply acted upon but who acts. His indictment of the society is incisive, and yet his emotional sensitivity is moving. He traverses the boundaries of gender as well as race.

In the film, the second-generation American Brock Peters plays Tom. Peters plays him with the exaggeration of enunciated dialect that characterized classically trained black actors in the early to mid-twentieth century. And though he mouths southern speech, and his acting is emotionally affecting, in his voice we hear his African, Caribbean, and New York roots, not unlike in the performances of his contemporaries Sidney Poitier and Harry Belafonte. Brock Peters provides an interesting counterpoint to Gregory Peck and Robert Duvall. Their black counterparts of that era would have been the dashing leading men Poitier and Belafonte. But Brock Peters was a character actor, and his distinct elocution and stage-like acting in this particular role read as a signification upon the text of the film itself. We are reminded, through his performance, of the constraints of the film era for black actors. That is not simply in the limited number of roles for them but in the nature and quality of those roles. Peters's performance, which (though emotionally effective) veers into the melodramatic and has a Brechtian self-awareness about it, reminds us that as an actor he is painfully confined by the theatrical world to a narrow range of types, automatically cast out of the spotlight even among black actors, with his dark skin, full lips, large eyes, and flared nostrils. And yet we also see that he exists beyond the categorical limits of this world. In his voice he signifies something further afield. Contrast Peters as Tom Robinson to Gregory Peck's performance of Atticus, in which Peck adds a natural quality to a character who is, relatively speaking, quite archetypal in the unflinching moral uprightness of all of the words he is given. Rather than seeing the chiasmus between melodramatic and natural, between real and archetypal, as merely differences between the film and the text, I would argue that with them the film extends the signifying play that the novel engages in. Indeed the invitation in the layers to interpret the characters in different ways offers the opportunity for what can be called compensatory readings.

Brock Peters as Tom Robinson is one of many mid-century instances in which filmic representations of black Americans anticipate the current scholarly interest in the global South. For this second-generation immigrant, his personal South stretches farther than the southern tip of the United States. But then again, so does Atticus Finch's. Early in the novel we learn that the family history of the Finches includes England, Philadelphia, Jamaica, and Mobile, Alabama. These are people produced by ports and their trade in goods and chattel. Scout tells us that Atticus was related by blood or marriage to nearly every other family in town and makes no caveat for race. Later, Scout and Jem have a conversation in which she asks how Jem knows that they aren't Negroes. And Jem explains that their uncle has told him they really don't know, although as far back as they can trace, they're white. Scout replies that if it's as far back as Bible times, it's too long ago to matter. But then Jem reminds her of the one-drop rule.

Intimated here is the manner in which the South itself, decried for brutality and consumed for its local color, is part of a queer geography—the gothic horror, the other within, and the gateway to the global South, situated literally at the borders of abjectness and alterity as represented by "colored" nations of the Caribbean. The jabs thrown about what is niggerish and who is a nigger lover, the spontaneous violence over insults about legitimacy and decency pepper the text and depict a collective sense of indeterminacy and anxiety, but also a truth about ambiguity, admixture, and therefore common humanity.

In this case the point being made is not the indeterminacy and absurdity of race. So many other novels that might fit into what one could call a critical racial realism tradition are centrally concerned with that point. Although that is an expression of this text, the point here is that the soul of the novel, yea of the nation, lies in those who cross the color line in moments of human affection and decency, who embrace our contingencies and fellow feeling that cannot subscribe to simple categories. This is not simply technically crossing the color line; it is crossing the line of feeling.

Throughout the text and film the ambiguous and absurd humor of southern speech adds "color" to the prose, but perhaps nowhere as provocatively as in the sentence about Tom Robinson as he appears before the court: "If he had been whole, he would have been a fine specimen of a man."[15] In the African American critical tradition there is a preoccupation with the anxiety of (white) influence. There is an exceptional ever-present challenge to identifying an African American literary tradition, simply because of the pervasive intertextuality with authors such as Twain, Poe, Melville, and Faulkner that one finds in African American literary production. Far less attention has been paid to influence working the other way—at least textual influence. The music and language of African Americans have been acknowledged influences on white American literary production, but literary craft, too, has been influential. In *To Kill a Mockingbird* we see the influence of the best-selling texts *Native Son* and *Invisible Man,* but one also finds echoes of Zora Neale Hurston's *Their Eyes Were Watching God* (1937). These complex genealogies, in which one sees cross-generation, cross–color line repetitions, also rupture a sense of wholeness to identity, and specifically whiteness. The brokenness or incompleteness that these genealogies threaten also provide an opening. Hence in the language of the second epigraph to this chapter, in which we recognize the falsity of that which subtends, we are better able to subvent our understandings of humanity and ultimately subvert that which ails us.

In both *To Kill a Mockingbird* and *Their Eyes Were Watching God,* the killing of a mad dog is an important symbolic moment. In the midst of a storm, Hurston's dog threatens the heroine, Janie, and her lover, Tea Cake, battles the dog to its death:

> The dog stood up and growled like a lion, stiff-standing hackles, stiff muscles, teeth uncovered as he lashed up his fury for the charge. Tea Cake split the water like an otter, opening his knife as he dived. The dog raced down the backbone of the cow to the attack and Janie screamed and slipped far back on the tail of the cow, just out of reach of the dog's angry jaws. He wanted to plunge in after her but dreaded the water, somehow. Tea Cake rose out of the water at the cow's rump and seized the dog by the neck. But he was a powerful dog and Tea Cake was over-tired. So he didn't kill the dog with one stroke as he had intended. But the dog couldn't free himself either. They fought and somehow he managed to bite Tea Cake high up on his cheek-bone once. Then Tea Cake finished him and sent him to the bottom to stay there.[16]

Tea Cake's reason is ravaged by the disease he has caught from being bitten by the dog. The course of events that follows is tragic. Tea Cake tries to shoot Janie, and she kills him in self-defense. The scene in *To Kill a Mockingbird* is different. Although in shooting the dog, Atticus is said to be acting in defense of his family, Colin Dayan's chapter in this volume significantly calls into question whether this preemptive assault can be assumed to be a defensive act. The dog is clearly mad, but will he actually hurt anyone? Atticus reluctantly takes aim and shoots the dog. The dog crumples into a heap. Atticus is detached from it, his act a necessary evil. We ought to wonder again about the legitimacy of Atticus's simple procedural fidelity here. If, as stated before, he is a crossroads figure, one of the queer and one of the respectable at once, isn't this an instance in which we might wonder whether his respectability has gone awry?

The dog in *To Kill a Mockingbird* is a "liver-colored dog" and the dog in *Their Eyes Were Watching God* is a "yellow dog," although given the popular expression "lily-livered," they both seem to connote fear and anxiety in their coloring. And of course there is a meditation on that aforementioned anxiety about race and the borderlands of species which the figures of the dogs portend.

For Hurston, Tea Cake has become the dog. And there are incisive feminist readings that can be made about how the consequence of the gendered act of violent protection of the woman is that Tea Cake takes on the role of violent aggressor and cannot escape it. Race and gender symbolism work in tandem. In *To Kill a Mockingbird,* the dog bears a name similar to that of the black male character Tom Robinson: Tim Johnson. The anxiety, however, is less about who Tom is becoming by virtue of this association than how he is seen or treated. Maybe this is because the concern with the destructive impact of racism on the souls of black folk is less potent for Lee than the impact on that of white folks. Her concerns are more principally with white characters, though not at the cost of recognizing the humanity of black characters. It may be that as a daughter of the South, Lee also was sensitive to the costs of any moral ambiguity in black characters in the white southern imagination. It would have been too easy for the image to slide into confirmation of stereotypes if Tom Robinson were to "act out" in ways consistent with the way he had been treated.

When Lee plays upon Ralph Ellison's National Book Award–winning novel *Invisible Man* (1953) by broaching the subject of incest, she changes the race of the parties from black to white. In Ellison's novel, the Invisible Man comes to the home of a rural southern black man named Trueblood as he is driving one of the wealthy white benefactors of Tuskegee University, a Mr. Norton. The Invisible Man, a young college student, tells Mr.

Norton that the two women in the household are mother and daughter, and both are pregnant by Trueblood. We read Trueblood's story, repeated by our narrator, the Invisible Man. Trueblood was in bed with both his wife and daughter because of the cold and awoke to find himself having sex with his daughter. His wife strikes him with an ax. He flees. Later he returns and cares for his wife and children. It is clear, the narrator notes, that Trueblood has recounted the story many times. And when Mr. Norton hands Trueblood a hundred-dollar bill for telling him the story, it becomes apparent why. A prurient interest in this horrific story has proven gainful for Trueblood.

In *To Kill a Mockingbird,* the storyteller is not the man who commits incest, Bob Ewell, but his daughter Mayella. She scrimps for coins, granted no assistance by the respectable people who have consigned her to a space beyond the margins of the community. Her recounting of sexual transgression is not prideful but filled with shame. She cannot bear to admit her lie about Tom, either, because it is the only leverage she has. But perhaps there is another signification. Trueblood, a sickening abuser in the logic of race and sex, goes without punishment (as would Bob Ewell were it not for his attempt upon Jem's life), but the fellow feeling between a black man and a white woman leads to Tom Robinson's death. The film removes any reference to incest, and makes Mayella smaller and more conventionally femme than she is presented in the text. It thereby reduces the discomfort of the trial and all that emerges in the facts surrounding it. But the ultimate truth is apparent anyway: that the kind of intimacy that is punished in this society is simply wrongheaded, and that which is horrific is granted silent assent.

The film and its texts are rife with repetition. *To Kill a Mockingbird* signifies on these African American texts, an action that dismantles a form of white literary subjectivity, fracturing the supposed wholeness in white normativity, and then challenges the legitimacy of "whole men" as the source of wisdom, knowledge, and full humanity. Lee does so without engaging in an archetypical heroic underdog story; in fact she retains the social order as it is understood to be, but pursues truth through characters and their relationships. This itself is a queering of American courtroom fiction, and a worthy one at that. If Tom and Boo are too fragmented to be fine specimens of men, they are better specimens of humanity. The paradigm shift that the term "queer" signals, then, is a shift to a model in which identities are more self-consciously historicized, seen as contingent products of particular genealogies rather than enduring or essential natural kinds. As stated earlier, in literary history it is rare for the influence of African American authors on white authors to be considered, although the other way around is generally accepted. This subversion is both, it seems to me, a self-conscious act, a claim to the kind of complex southern genealogy that Lee describes in the Finch family tree, and also a de-essentializing of craft that serves the larger point about a more radical conception of who matters, who is worthy, and who is righteous. Reading the concept of "queer," which is of recent theoretical vintage, back into this work is truly revelatory.

But it is in putting the film in the context of other films that the most challenging double readings emerge. Because while the text itself is doing some queering that challenges us to rethink ideals, norms, and stratification, the reading of the film in the context of other films helps us see that the very stratification it is part of undoing is at play in the celluloid world.

The British film *The L-Shaped Room*, directed by Bryan Forbes, came out in 1962 as well. In the film Leslie Caron plays a young single Parisian named Jane, living in a bug-infested boardinghouse in Notting Hill in London. Her character is pregnant and caught between the affections of two men. One of her boardinghouse-mates is played by Brock Peters, in a dramatically different role from the one he plays in *To Kill a Mockingbird*. He is a gay Jamaican jazz trumpeter named John, who struggles mightily with revealing his sexuality. Although he is a secondary character, John's interior life is lingered upon in the film. He and Jane have late-night conversations, each lying in his or her own bed, sharing confidences and emotions. John is in love with Jane's boyfriend, Toby. And though he loses in this love triangle, this loss doesn't entail exclusion or alienation from the intimate circle of friends. This is not a representation of a fearful black male sexuality, but neither is it a tentative portrayal of emotional intimacy between a black man and a white woman. It is hard to imagine that a gay black male character, with a desire for a white man and intimacy with a white woman, would have been greenlighted by an American studio mid-century. The contrast between the two films, combined with an understanding of what has been muted in the film version of *To Kill a Mock-*

ingbird, indicates the limitations of time and context, but also show why we should be open to broader readings, given how the society has changed and is changing.

Interestingly, in contrast to the politics of editing in the U.S. context, the film version of *The L-Shaped Room* prunes the repulsion Jane feels for John in the novel on which it is based, with only the affection remaining. Additionally, the film adds an older, sympathetic lesbian character who doesn't appear in the book. It is an important film in the history of queer cinema, and it is extremely progressive in content, albeit not explicitly didactic when it comes to sexual politics. Notably, the *New York Times,* in reviewing the movie, makes no mention of the two gay characters, instead offering this opaque description:

> Around his principal players Mr. Forbes has placed an appropriate mobile frieze of colorful rooming-house characters to reflect the pulsations of their hearts. He casts Brock Peters as a gentle Negro jazz musician who occupies an adjoining room and finds his feelings of friendship toward the two [Jane and Toby] rather shockingly torn. Avis Bunnage is the sleazy landlady with a heart of lead, and Cicely Courtneidge is a faded vaudeville actress who lives with her cat on the ground floor. And Mr. Forbes has Emlyn Williams as an unctuous illegal practitioner, Patricia Phoenix as a rooming-house harlot and Bernard Lee as her customer.[17]

That prostitution is referenced while two gay characters are not suggests the particular bent of American sexual conservatism, which has more often been to police the form of sexual behavior rather than its substance. The outer limit has rarely been that which is explicit, but is more often that which falls outside ideas of the norm. Race, of course, has always been deeply embedded in this policing, and the rules about manhood and womanhood, desire and decency, and who belongs to which group are repetitions that work to ensure social stratifications. *To Kill a Mockingbird* challenges these rules, not by simple transgression but through the ethical force of Lee's queered characters. And yet the film, and the way it was cut for a mass market, is subject to the force of these very rules Lee challenges. It mutes rather than transforms. And the question is whether we can read in ways to turn the volume back up.

A comparison to another work of art allows us to tease out this question further. In 1959 Lorraine Hansberry's play *A Raisin in the Sun* opened on Broadway. It was the first work by an African American woman to earn that honor. In 1961 a film version of the play was made. Like *To Kill a Mockingbird*, *A Raisin in the Sun* is a fixture in American schools. And as with *To Kill a Mockingbird*, this status appears to have short-changed its critical consideration. Hansberry's play about the efforts of a black Chicago family, the Youngers, to move out of their kitchenette apartment and into a house with the insurance money left after their patriarch's death was almost immediately misunderstood as a simple American Dream aspirational tale. In fact, Hansberry was depicting the crushing inequality of the urban North and its deleterious effects on the hopes and dreams of second-generation migrants. In the tiny kitchenette space she captures the complexities of gender and race in the realm of the imagined self and its failures.

Hansberry fought back against the mischaracterization of her project. She decried those who referred to it as a "universal" and therefore not just a Negro play by calling it a Negro and specifically a Chicago Negro play. And she rejected the American Dream reading as well. Her response to one critic who said that the play had a happy ending, with the family moving into a lovely house, but in a hostile white neighborhood, was "If he thinks that's a happy ending I invite him to live in one of the communities where the Youngers are going."[18] Perhaps the New York audience, so distracted by the actions of southern massive resistance, had forgotten the bloody history of northern mob resistance to black integration.

When Hansberry wrote the screenplay for the 1961 film, she tried to recover some of the politics of the play. She wrote in the kind of racism black people faced day in and day out with scenes between Lena Younger and her employer, Lena's going to the grocery store and seeing the poor quality of the produce, her traveling out to white neighborhoods to shop and being mistreated there. She also included a scene in which three characters listen to a street corner black nationalist. Additionally, she wanted the film to begin with a view of the South Side of Chicago in all its ghetto realism. Virtually all of her political revisions ended up on the cutting room floor.

Hansberry was also subject to scathing criticism from the black left for what was termed a "middle-class play" devoid of political content. As time passed, however, this tide would turn. In 1987 Amiri Baraka wrote an article titled "A Critical Reevaluation: *A Raisin in the Sun*'s Enduring Passion" after seeing a production of the play that included several scenes omitted from the first Broadway production. In it he argues that he and others who had criticized the play's values were incorrect:

> We thought Hansberry's play was part of the passive resistance phase of the movement. We thought her play was middle class in that its focus seemed to be on moving into white folks' neighborhoods. . . . We missed the essence of the work—that Hansberry had created a family on the cutting edge of the same class and ideological struggles as existed in the movement itself and among the people. What is most telling about our ignorance is that Hansberry's play still remains overwhelmingly popular and evocative of black and white reality, and the masses of black people dug it true. . . . It is Lorraine Hansberry's play which, though it seems conservative in form and content to the radical petty bourgeoisie . . . is the accurate telling and stunning vision of the real struggle.[19]

The revival Baraka saw developed into the PBS *American Playhouse* version in 1989, directed by Bill Duke and starring Esther Rolle and Danny Glover. Critically acclaimed, it speaks to the cultural moment of the late 1980s in its own way. In the aftermath of the Reagan era dismantling of civil rights remedial efforts, in the midst of the crack epidemic, and at the beginning of the culture wars which continue to threaten the U.S. government's support of the arts, the play appeared as an undeniable expression of black poverty quite distinct from images of welfare queens and Willie Hortons. It is a redemptive image of the black and poor. Rather than being described as lower middle class in reviews, the Youngers were referred to as working class or poor. Unfortunately the production's cultural impact was limited to the world of PBS and had nothing close to the scope of the 1961 project.

More recently we have witnessed the Broadway revival and the 2007 film version, which aired on ABC. In that version the politics of the play are almost completely expunged. In the case of *A Raisin in the Sun*, the different versions in performance and the author's revisions quite explicitly reveal the creative repetition of which Badiou speaks. *To Kill a Mockingbird* has not been re-filmed, and the fact that Harper Lee at this writing remains a recluse who has given only the rare interview and has not written another novel makes the workings of the creative repetitions more opaque. Moreover, the modest critical treatment of the novel and film abet this difficulty.

This volume, however, which brings together twenty-first-century viewers, readers, and critics to comment on a mid-century text depicting the Great Depression, becomes an instantiation of creative repetitions, eliciting useful reconsiderations of the "ideas" and gestures that animate this film. For me, the Idea that emerges most strongly as the one that animates the work is this: in this cast of queerly beautiful subjects with complex humanities we find the basis for arguing against the stratifications in American life. *To Kill a Mockingbird* is filled with a passel of "no's" to normativity, rich with a great big "yes" to a transgressive humanity, and an overarching admiration for decency above all else. That is the song the mockingbird keeps singing.

NOTES

1. Alain Badiou, "Philosophy as Creative Repetition," *The Symptom* 8 (Winter 2007), www.lacan.com/badrepeat.html.

2. Henry Louis Gates Jr., *The Signifying Monkey: A Theory of African American Literary Criticism* (Oxford: Oxford University Press, 1988).

3. Ivy Wilson, *Specters of Democracy: Blackness and the Aesthetics of Politics in the Antebellum U.S.* (Oxford: Oxford University Press, 2011).

4. Alexander Weheliye, *Phonographies: Grooves in Sonic Afro-Modernity* (Durham: Duke University Press, 2005).

5. See *Mississippi Burning* (1988), *The Long Walk Home* (1990), *Ghosts of Mississippi* (1996), *The Help* (2011).

6. Thadious Davis, *Games of Property: Law, Race, Gender, and Faulkner's* Go Down Moses (Durham: Duke University Press, 2003).

7. David Halperin, *Saint Foucault: Toward a Gay Hagiography* (Oxford: Oxford University Press, 1997), 62.

8. Eve Sedgwick, *Tendencies* (Durham: Duke University Press, 1993), 8.

9. Rosemarie Thompson, *Extraordinary Bodies: Figuring Physical Disability in American Culture and Literature* (New York: Columbia University Press, 1996).

10. Stephan Metcalf, "On First Looking into *To Kill a Mockingbird*," *Slate*, June 9, 2006.

11. Harper Lee, *To Kill a Mockingbird*, 40th Anniversary Edition (New York: HarperCollins, 1999), 2.

12. Richard Wright, *American Hunger* (New York: Harper & Row, 1975), 77.

13. Robin West, *Narrative Authority and Law* (Ann Arbor: University of Michigan Press, 1993), 110.

14. James Baldwin, "Everybody's Protest Novel," *Notes of a Native Son* (Boston: Beacon Press, 1955), 23.

15. Lee, *To Kill a Mockingbird*, 212.

16. Zora Neale Hurston, *Their Eyes Were Watching God* (New York: Harper Perennial, 2000), 205.

17. Bosley Crowtherm, review of *The L Shaped Room* (1962), *New York Times*, May 28, 1963.

18. Robert Nemiroff, introduction to Lorraine Hansberry, *A Raisin in the Sun* (New York: Vintage Book Edition, 1994), viii.

19. Amiri Baraka, "A Critical Reevaluation: *A Raisin in the Sun*'s Enduring Passion," in A Raisin in the Sun *and* The Sign in Sidney Brustein's Window, ed. Robert Nemiroff (New York: New American Library, 1987), 10.

CHAPTER FIVE

A Ritual of Redemption
Reimagining Community in
To Kill a Mockingbird

NAOMI MEZEY

This essay explores how different depictions of local community are figured and reconfigured in the film version of *To Kill a Mockingbird* in such a way as to provide a redemptive ritual for reimagining a national community committed to racial equality. In the film, communities of color, class, neighborhood, and family are unraveled and reconstructed through the law; national and historical conflicts overlap, collapse, and are reimagined in a personal narrative and the imaginary space of law. Most notably, the film depicts how the rape trial of Tom Robinson occasions the unraveling of a white solidarity by exposing the cleavages of class and realigning elite whites with blacks in the legal imaginary.

Paradoxically, however, the film's aspirational vision of a racially integrated community is experienced emotionally through the local integration of Boo Radley, the neighborhood's white recluse and outcast, rather than by the failed legal defense of Tom Robinson and the national struggle over civil rights. The political is reimagined as religious, the national as personal, and the audience is absolved of the sins of racism by temporal displacement. The community is always imagined and juxtaposed against the outcast and the stranger. The children's imaginary relationship with Boo Radley is expressed visually throughout the film, haunting the neighborhood, until he literally emerges from the shadows and is made a neighbor.

.   .   .

To Kill a Mockingbird has rightly been called "an inescapable fact of America's civic religion."[1] The novel won the Pulitzer Prize, is an established part of the literary and educational canon, and is always cited as among the most influential books in the United States.[2] In the UK, it has edged out the Bible as the most inspirational book of all time.[3] This comparison tells us something not just about the popularity and influence of the story, but about the sort of influence it has had and the sort of reverence readers and viewers have for it. The film, which was nominated for eight Academy Awards and won three, brought the story to even wider audiences. In Monroeville, Alabama, the town on which Maycomb is based, the book wasn't a sensation when it was first published. According to a local reporter, "folks didn't take much notice until the movie came out."[4] Now Monroeville has embraced its role in this civic religion, its residents quote the book like scripture[5] and imitate the art that imitated and reimagined its municipal life. The Old Courthouse has become a museum, and a play based on the book is performed there each spring by a group of local actors.[6] Outside the courthouse is a statue erected by the Alabama Bar Association in 1997 of the fictional lawyer Atticus Finch,[7] who was chosen by the American Film Institute as the single greatest movie hero of all time.[8] Thus the town is home to local monuments to the book and movie, works that are themselves national monuments to a local vision of racial inclusion.

By focusing in particular on the story in the film, I consider how this narrative is told and why it has become part of our civic religion, asking what purposes it served in the early 1960s to imagine the 1930s through a personal history of race and community, and what purposes it continues to serve, more than half a century later, to worship at the altar of this rendition of justice and community. If religion provides anything, it provides a set of rituals for dealing with recurring problems. *To Kill a Mockingbird* has become a legal and cultural ritual for helping us—its audience, understood within the film as white—think about the recurring problem of racial injustice, how we narrate our national sins, and the possibility of community over time. This ritual functions through temporal and narrative displacement, converting the anxieties of the present into the resolved problems of the past, and the politics of history into personal memory, to convey and reimagine the problems of community as local rather than national, as neighborly rather than political. Within the fraught complexities of local community, *To Kill a Mockingbird* unravels the solidarities of race and class inside the spaces of the law, only to remake the community anew at the end of the film, not through the legal inclusion of Maycomb's poor blacks, but through the neighborly inclusion of the white symbolic outcast, the reclusive Boo Radley.

The film is quite a different text from the novel, conveyed in a different medium, told in a different set of languages. By focusing attention on the film rather than the book, I seek to read the story visually as well as thematically. In some ways the novel's problems are better suited to a movie; its unsteady narrative voice that moves between child and adult and its "episodic tendencies"[9] work well as discrete scenes in a memoir that is told both through the lines of the child's character and the voice-over of the adult. The voice-over and the cinematography together elevate nostalgia to a narrative technique, one that insists on a personal and particularly romantic recounting of the past that, like all rituals, incorporates both memory and forgetting. The film also uses its black and white images for symbolic effect, often juxtaposing light and dark, hidden and seen, imagination and reality, acknowledged and unacknowledged. The light contrasts of the film not only symbolize the overarching theme of race but also are given fullest effect in scenes in which they help convey positive and negative versions of law and community; these lighting effects are most dramatic in the shadowy mob scene and the well-lit courtroom scene, and are replayed again at the end of the film when Boo Radley quite literally emerges from the shadows. In noir style, there are shadows everywhere in Maycomb.

The film in particular tells a complex story about both community and law, and the localism of each. Malcolm Gladwell has compared Atticus Finch to Big Jim Folsom, Alabama's progressive populist governor during the 1950s, arguing that the Alabama that Harper Lee was writing about in the late 1950s was "marked by profound localism."[10] What he means is that politics was more personal than ideological; it was about friends and neighbors. The film version of *To Kill a Mockingbird* is fastidiously local, chronicling a national struggle with racial integration as a story about neighborly inclusion; in other words, it reimagines and ritualizes the national politics of race and class as the politics of county and local community. Like all films, this one exists in and narrates from multiple temporal perspectives: the time in which it is set, the time in which it is made, and the times in which it is viewed.[11] *To Kill a Mockingbird* uses this structure to tell different temporal stories—one about the ways the May-comb County community was unraveling in the 1930s South during the upheavals of the Scottsboro trials and the depression, and another, more redemptive one about how that history might be reconfigured through the discourse of legal equality and social inclusion in 1962. But of course there are also the stories it has told to audiences since 1962 and those still to come, which are informed as much by the culture and politics of the present as by those of the past. In some ways it is ironic that a film which both portrays and helps reimagine civil rights as an issue of local commu-nity has become a ritualized performance of national, and international,[12] racial justice. The film works as ritual, and its popularity persists in part because it continues to redeem us in the face of ongoing racial injustice.

Like many law films, this one tells a deeply conflicted story about the law. As Martha Umphrey and Austin Sarat have argued, films about trials often put the law on trial,[13] and *To Kill a Mockingbird* is a fascinating trial film for a number of reasons. First, the trial is off center in the film, where the legal climax is not the narrative climax. In addition, the verdict on the law in *To Kill a Mockingbird* is deeply unsatisfying. Law utterly fails to vindicate racial equality: Tom Robinson (unambiguously positioned as in-nocent within the film) is found guilty of raping Mayella Ewell, and before Finch can appeal, Robinson is killed by deputies while allegedly trying to escape. So why is it so consistently held up as an example of legal and moral rectitude, of justice triumphing over bigotry? As seen from outside the film's narration, one explanation is dispiriting: the movie elevates the individual local lawyer and his legal rhetoric over national racially charged trials, structural inequalities, and legal outcomes. In the two years between the publication of the novel and the release of the film, the lunch counter sit-ins began, the first Freedom Riders rode into the South, the Student Nonviolent Coordinating Committee was founded, and the beginnings of a more radical version of racial equality were afoot. The film, with its voice-over and noir leanings, can rightfully be seen as an elegy for a less radical vision of racial equality, in which procedural justice stands in for substantive justice and legal equality is fundamentally local rather than na-tional. But within the film's own narration, a sense of racial justice is made available to the viewer precisely because she is allowed to witness racial injustice, recognize and feel Finch's legal rhetoric, and reach an alterna-tive judgment about the outcome. Tom is sacrificed so that the viewer can be redeemed. The film's temporal displacement supports the redemptive experience of its white audience. By placing the trial in the past and the audience in the future (indeed, many futures) and the timeless imaginary space of the courtroom, the film allows the viewer to feel not only capable of enlightened judgment but also absolved of responsibility; the evident failings of the law and the collective sins of racism are displaced onto the past. The structure of the film also supports the viewer's selective memory and forgetting in aid of redemption. By the end, when the story of the rape trial is eclipsed by Ewell's attack on Jem and Boo Radley's symbolic reincorporation into the community, those sins have almost been forgotten.

Memory and Community

The opening credits position the movie as a story about the past, and especially the past as revisited through the personal memory of an adult reimagining her childhood. In close-up we see a child's hand and hear her soft humming as she goes through a box of old-fashioned treasures. The camera tenderly takes in each object as it surveys the contents of the cigar box in extreme close-up: a broken pocket watch, crayons, a rusty harmonica, marbles, jacks, a knife, two carved figures, the style of each item and the dates on the coins literally dating the collection and locating the story at least partly in the past. Each object is made meaningful by the lingering camera and the touch of the child. It is a scene at once nostalgic and elegiac. We don't yet know the significance of the objects for the child, but they have already situated us in another time. While they might be just the relics of childhood, it becomes clear by the end of the film that many of these trinkets are the offerings that were left for Scout and Jem in the knothole of a tree by the unseen Boo Radley. These objects are not just keepsakes but are sanctified by the role they play in Boo's transformation from an unseen but powerfully imagined monster to a neighbor who is reintegrated into the community. The cigar box and the collected objects also frame our understanding of the past in much the same way that the camera frames the scenes and the editing frames the narrative that follows. Some events are left out, offscreen; some things are not fully visible or are allowed to be forgotten. The first images of the movie parallel the images at the end, framing the story as one about Boo Radley and his reincorporation into the community. Before we know what comes between the opening and closing credits, we have already begun the process of framing and forgetting.

The memorialization of the past is one of the central visual subjects of the film, and that past is portrayed as at once personal and local. It is about the very specific community of Maycomb County; the larger history and racial politics of the 1930s are relevant only to the extent that they were unraveling the social balance of Maycomb. These larger historical and political forces, both the Scottsboro trials and the depression, are both unseen and barely articulated in the film. The most we hear is the brief explanation from Atticus of the relative poverty among the people of the county. Instead, the community of Maycomb County, as portrayed in the film, seems to exist apart from other counties and the larger nation of which it is a part. It is conveyed visually and narratively as it seems to be imagined by its members, as a social and political universe unto itself. Like all communities, it is "imaginary" in the sense that the boundaries and membership of the community are imagined by its various participants through a shared understanding of the past, the rules of inclusion, and a shared culture.[14] Communities are distinguished from one another, in Benedict Anderson's famous words, "by the style in which they are imagined."[15] Maycomb, Alabama, is imagined in the film as the coherent community par excellence; the residents all know one another, and they all have a sense of their place in the order. But it is also a community at a moment of disruption, when the accepted understanding of things is unraveling, when the shared sense of the boundaries of the group and the rules of inclusion are less shared and have to be collectively reimagined. In some ways the drama of the film is generated by the knowledge that reimagining the rules of racial inclusion will also shift the social hierarchies and all that flows from them. As Michael Walzer has said: "The primary good that we distribute to one another is membership in some human community. And what we do with regard to membership structures all our other distributive choices."[16]

The very first scene sets the multi-temporal framing and visually establishes the imagined community of Maycomb: a shot of a timeworn middle-class neighborhood and the voice of a woman in 1962 telling a story about Maycomb in 1932, a community of whites marked by fissures of wealth and class, country folk and town folk, but one that understands itself as a community in which all have fallen on hard times. It is in this very first scene that Walter Cunningham comes to pay Atticus Finch in hickory nuts for legal work Finch has done for him. The week before he had paid in collard greens. He comes to the side door as an inferior, not wanting to disturb Finch, but Scout calls for her father so he can thank Mr. Cunningham. When an embarrassed Cunningham leaves, Scout asks Atticus what the payment is for, if the Cunninghams are poor, and she (along with the viewers) is introduced to the complexities of class in this community. The Cunninghams are farmers, Atticus explains, and have been hit harder than others by the crash. The Finches and the Cunninghams are not social or economic equals—indeed it is the strictly observed social distinctions that help hold the community together—but theirs is nonetheless a community of whites forged across class and partly held together by Jim Crow and the stronger social and legal divisions of race. We also learn that Finch has been helping Cunningham with an entailment, a legal impairment on inherited property that runs into the future, which functions as a powerful metaphor for the limitations of the social, legal, and racial inheritance of the community.[17] This community is both held together and torn apart by the inheritance of its racist history.

The temporal gap between the time in which it is set and the making of the film is a significant one for understanding community in the South, as it marks the transition from pervasive white support for racial inequality to demands for inclusion by blacks and tentative support by some whites. If the white community was already an uneasy one in 1932, it was particularly so in 1962, when the most traditional and unspoken distinctions were well frayed; many southern whites were violently resisting desegregation, but some white elites were more forcefully questioning their entailment of racial solidarity and beginning to seek a political alliance with blacks. In the book, we are given a more explicit template of community when Jem, struggling to make sense of how Macomb County is socially structured, decides "there's four kinds of folks in the world. There's the ordinary kind like us and the neighbors, there's the kind like the Cunninghams out in the woods, the kind like the Ewells down at the dump, and the Negroes."[18] Where one fit (or didn't) within that cosmology was a matter of life, injury, and death for community members and outsiders, and the unraveling of the traditional rules of inclusion between the 1930s and the 1960s was a recurring theme taken up by Harper Lee and made vivid by the film's director, Robert Mulligan.

In both the book and the film, the loose coalition of whites includes the three very different sorts of whites articulated by Jem and distinguished by class—elite and middle-class white people who live in town, the country white folks like the Cunninghams, and the poorest whites, those who live by the dump (and on the gleanings of the dump) and whose only claim to social status is that "when scrubbed with lye soap in very hot water, [their] skin was white."[19] It is these poorest whites who have the most to lose from racial equality, and they, rather than the Cunninghams, are eventually imagined out of the community as it is constructed within *To Kill a Mockingbird*. Lee herself explicitly writes them out of the human community early in the book, saying that people like the Ewells "lived like animals" and functioned in the county as guests: "No economic fluctuations changed their status—people like the Ewells lived as guests of the county in prosperity as well as in the depths of a depression."[20] It is clear that "guests" are not the same as "company" in the southern sense that Walter Cunningham's son is company when he comes for lunch. Guests live on the edge geographically, legally, and socially and survive by the goodwill and charity of the community on which they depend. The Ewells not only live near the trash but also are understood by the viewer to *be* trash. Within the world of the film, however, the assessment of where the Ewells fit and the extent to which they deserve to belong is part of the cinematic drama of the trial. Their claim to membership in the community is intimately tied to the charge against Tom Robinson and the status of the blacks in the balcony, and will be determined (differently) by the jury within the film and the viewers of the film.

The different statuses of the Cunninghams and the Ewells are made visually evident in two parallel scenes in the film: the lynch mob and the trial. But even before those dramatic scenes, the Cunninghams are positioned as poor but stable members of the community in more quotidian ways, in both the opening scene and in the schoolyard. Unlike the Ewells, the Cunninghams participate in the civic life of Maycomb County; they seek legal advice, they sit on juries, and their children attend school. The brief schoolyard scene establishes the characteristics of the Cunninghams' membership. They are poor but self-respecting and hostile to charity. The Finches are more socially powerful—a fact manifested physically when Scout beats up the young Walter Cunningham on the first day of school because he makes her "start off on the wrong foot" with the new teacher (who does not yet know the ways of the community or why young Walter has no lunch).[21] As Scout explains, indignant at the social ignorance, the teacher "tried to give Walter Cunningham a quarter when everybody knows no Cunningham will take nothing from nobody. Any fool could have told her that." Indeed, it reinforces a point the audience knows: young Walter's father has already insisted on paying his legal fees in hickory nuts. Much later, in the book, Scout reminds us of the important distinction between the Cunninghams and the Ewells when she comes to young Walter's defense, saying: "That boy's not trash, Jem. He ain't like the Ewells."[22]

Outside the film, outside the script, indeed buried and half forgotten by the story's insistence on temporal and local displacement, are two crucial historical events, and the national anxiety they generated, which deeply inform the interior present of *To Kill a Mockingbird:* the Great Depression and the trials of the Scottsboro Boys. The depression was severe throughout the country and worldwide, with unemployment reaching 25 percent in the United States in 1933,[23] but the economic crisis was even worse in the South, which since the Civil War had remained primarily agricultural and significantly poorer than the rest of the country. In 1938 President Franklin Roosevelt called the American South "the nation's number one economic problem."[24] The economic realities of the country generally and the South particularly are important context for the precariousness of poor whites in the social hierarchy and their intense anxiety about racial hierarchy, but they appear only obliquely in the film—as when Finch explains why the Cunninghams are so poor—and even then they are confined to the enclosed world of Maycomb County. Yet again the national has been made local, and the politics of history has been retold as personal memory.

Like the depression, the Scottsboro case is offscreen, unseen, but haunts the narrative nonetheless. In his book *Remembering Scottsboro,* James Miller argues persuasively that the connected cases of the Scottsboro Boys have become embedded in American memory and were deeply influential for a generation of writers, including Harper Lee.[25] The case began with a rape accusation in 1931 by two working-class white women against nine black boys, the youngest of whom was twelve. With inadequate counsel and on flimsy evidence, eight of the young men were sentenced to death. The case went on for years, generating reversals, important Supreme Court decisions, embarrassing retrials, and enormous media attention, particularly on racial justice in Alabama. Miller argues that not only would the case have been formative for Harper Lee, but also she sets the novel at exactly the time of the Scottsboro case and draws into her characters the very forces and attitudes that shaped Alabama's response to it.[26] Miller finds that while Lee indicts racial intolerance in the novel, she nonetheless insists on understanding it through the local. "By avoiding any references to the intense national and international scrutiny that was trained on Alabama during the 1930s, Lee not only turns the case into a strictly local matter, she strongly suggests, in fact, that it was best understood or treated as such."[27]

The Lynch Mob

As was true in the case of the Scottsboro Boys, a lynch mob comes to the jail where Tom Robinson has been brought the night before his trial. Unlike the Scottsboro mob, which was dispersed when the governor of Alabama called in the National Guard, in Lee's rendition it is handled locally, within the family even, by Atticus and his children.

The scene is visually striking in its darkness, emblematic as it is of the darkest manifestations of community. The scene begins with Atticus searching for a light. Sheriff Tate has warned him there could be trouble, so he takes a lamp from home and sits on the steps of the jail, in his three-piece suit, reading a law book under the glow of the lamp, its extension cord running up to the second-floor window, its thin shadow cast on the dark brick of the jail. The children have sneaked out of the house and come to investigate, and we see Atticus from their perspective, aglow in the darkness, a solitary figure of safety and enlightenment. The mob scene is shot to emphasize what we already intuitively know about mobs: they are formed through collective passion and are threatened by reason and individual differentiation. Thus it is no accident that Atticus, a solitary lawyer with a book and a lamp, visually symbolizes both reason and individuality. The mob has clearly come to defend the right of Bob Ewell to condemn Tom Robinson and less clearly to confront the privilege and pretensions of Atticus Finch. The men arrive in indistinguishable black cars, and they are at first indistinguishable from one another, all wearing overalls and hats, many carrying shotguns. They are here to enforce the law as they understand it, to uphold the soft law of the white community against the hard law of the Fourteenth Amendment, which is embodied in Atticus Finch and his law book.[28]

The men are soft-spoken and polite, asking Mr. Finch to step aside. They know him, he knows them, and everyone knows why they are there. The children run to Atticus and, despite his commands, refuse to leave. In the book, Scout narrates the encounter: "There was a smell of stale whiskey and pig-pen about, and when I glanced around I discovered that these men were *strangers*."[29] She is, for perhaps for the first time in her life, not in the community as she knows it. Unwittingly, it is Scout who defuses the lynch mob, not through courage but by not comprehending it. By not recognizing the norms of the mob, she does not respect the anonymity of its communal existence; when she finally locates the familiar face of Walter Cunningham, she differentiates him by speaking his name and persists in her attempt to be recognized by him:

> Hey, Mr. Cunningham. . . . I said, hey, Mr. Cunningham. How's your entailment getting along? . . . Don't you remember me, Mr. Cunningham? I'm Jean Louise Finch. You brought us some hickory nuts one early morning, remember? We had a talk. I went and got my Daddy to come out and thank you. I go to school with your boy. I go to school with Walter. He's a nice boy. Tell him "Hey" for me, won't you? You know something, Mr. Cunningham, entailments are bad, entailments . . . [there is a long pause as Scout becomes self-conscious and the men shift uncomfortably]. Atticus, I was just saying to Mr. Cunningham that entailments were bad, but not to worry, it takes a long time sometimes. What's the matter? . . . I sure meant no harm, Mr. Cunningham.[30]

In the film Mr. Cunningham is wearing a hat, like the other men, and through most of Scout's speech his head is down and his eyes are not visible. He is still a member of the mob. At the mention of his son's name, he looks up at her for a moment and into the camera, and then ducks his head again in the shadow of his hat. Finally, when Scout apologizes, Mr. Cunningham straightens himself, faces the camera, eyes no longer shaded by his hat. "No harm taken young lady. I'll tell Walter you said 'Hey.' . . . Let's clear out of here. Let's go, boys." Scout undoes the mob by calling Walter Cunningham back into the community as she understands it, a community of neighbors, parents, and children who go to school together, of her father the lawyer and his clients, a community bound together by an entailment of race that is bad and will take a long time to resolve.[31] Scout cannot fully comprehend or even articulate the entailment. It stops her short, delivers her to a moment of self-consciousness, but she performs what she cannot say; the audience sees that it is their (our) dark and shared inheritance.

It might seem that hard law triumphs, at least momentarily, in this scene, but it is only through recourse to the very community whose norms and understandings made the lynch mob possible, even logical. By forcing Cunningham to be acknowledged, Scout brings him back into the norms of the larger community in which she and her father are central and respected. In the white community of the lynch mob, in contrast, the privilege and position of the Finches put them on the periphery, as does Atticus's willingness to defend Tom Robinson. All of Scout's attempts to get Mr. Cunningham to acknowledge her are discomfiting for the group because each at once unravels the community on which a mob depends and is a reminder of how they are bound up in the larger local society of Maycomb County: her father provides them with legal services; she goes to school with their children.

In the lynch mob scene it is not just the Finches and the Cunninghams who are struggling with each other over community definition. There is the unseen black man in the jail over whom the men are arguing and whose existence and defense occasion the larger realignments of community and history. There is, then, a triangulation of claims to inclusion and exclusion in the imagined community of Maycomb County. This triangulation pivots from scene to scene, re-forming among different participants and different claims of belonging, until it assumes the aspect of a religious trinity by the end of the film, when sacrifice and redemption are seemingly complete.

The Courtroom

The courtroom scene is interesting less for what it overtly claims for the law and more for what the discursive space of the law enables. It is a scene that parallels and replays the lynch mob scene, where a triangulation of claims to membership is being made, where variations of hard law and soft law compete with each other, and where the two most despised residents of Maycomb County—Tom Robinson and Mayella Ewell, the black man and the white trash girl—are fully and forcefully seen by the audience of the trial and the film. In the visual and rhetorical space of the courtroom, the community is vividly unraveled, fractured, and reconstituted not by law's triumphs—indeed, the law utterly fails to vindicate or

protect the innocent black defendant, let alone to notice an abused daughter—but simply because it is the law. In effect, the dark lynch mob scene
is reborn in the bright light of legitimation that formal law offers. The
legally authorized jury enacts what the mob could not: it sacrifices Tom
Robinson and the claims of African Americans to ensure the inclusion
of the Ewells and fortify white privilege. But how the courtroom scene
unfolds is important and revelatory, as is the effect of the film's temporal
displacement. The narrative journey within the film is meant to be at odds
with the ritualized emotional and moral journey of its audience thirty
years later, just as it is fifty years further on.

The courtroom—perhaps especially the pre–civil rights southern courtroom—is what the anthropologist Mary Louise Pratt calls a "contact
zone," a social space "where cultures meet, clash, and grapple with each
other, often in contexts of highly asymmetrical relations of power, such
as colonialism, slavery, or their aftermath."[32] In the contact zone of Maycomb's fictional courtroom, the complex but stable community depicted
at the beginning of the film is now a set of multiple, overlapping, and
unstable alliances riven by color, class, and gender. Those intersections and
vulnerabilities are made (literally) visible in the trial scene. The community of whites that had earlier encompassed town and country folk (and
men and women, with women as the sexual symbols of white virtue) allowed wide differences in class to be bridged by white privilege. In the
courtroom scene there is a new triangulation. The Cunninghams were
reintegrated into the legal community in the lynch mob scene, and their
extralegal impulses are further reformed into the legitimate and legal role
of the jury in the trial scene. The new triangulation is composed of those
who mark points along the most extreme boundaries of belonging—the
Finches (white elites), Ewells (the very lowest whites), and blacks (as
mute but visible spectators and the accused), each crucial to the unraveling and reimagining of local and national community, but each with very
different degrees of power and agency. There is also the hard law of the
Constitution, the conflicting hard law of sexual and racial rules, and the
soft law of the hierarchies governing desire, believability, and pity. The
jury, envisioned in the discourse of law as the community itself, mediates
the claims to inclusion.

The way the camera captures the trial and the witnesses is emblematic
of the fractured community, the competing viewpoints of the contact zone,

and the power of the law implicitly to recognize and mediate membership claims. The camera moves around the courtroom; there is no settled perspective or neutral viewpoint. It catches the progression of the trial from the perspective of every audience, but primarily from that of the whites in the gallery and the blacks on the balcony, occasionally from the perspective of Atticus and the prosecutor, only rarely from the viewpoint of the jury, and sometimes from a perspective unique to the film audience. While the trial is shot from many angles to portray the multiple perspectives on what unfolds there, the camera work also appeals to a more universal, moral story about human recognition and redemption. Each witness is treated differently, the camera inching closer to the witness stand as the testimony proceeds. Sheriff Tate begins his testimony in a long shot and concludes it at middle distance. Bob Ewell is shown primarily from a middle distance, though occasionally closer. But by the time Mayella Ewell and Tom Robinson testify, we meet them face-to-face, closer than is comfortable, forcing on the film audience a basic human recognition and even sympathy. If only in the visual legal imaginary of *To Kill a Mockingbird*, the least powerful— a poor white woman and an accused black man—come together not just as adversaries but are made visible as worthy claimants to inclusion in the human community. The camera, following the command of Atticus's moral admonitions to his children, almost forces us to imagine being in their skin. It is not until Atticus's famous summation that the camera becomes stationed in the jury box, where we watch and listen as the community whose judgment counts. In that closing argument Atticus makes a claim for the universal values of liberal legalism, and the camera situates the audience alongside the local community, the jury. But of course we the viewers are not the local community. We come later, and see the action with the eyes of the future and understand it from the perspective of communities long since reimagined, giving us "interpretive adjacency" to the narration of the film.[33] What this interpretive adjacency makes visible and memorable is Atticus's speech while at the same time it allows us to forget what the jury decides, and what the law does.[34]

The temporal displacement and interpretive adjacency are part of the ritual and tension in *To Kill a Mockingbird*—the pull in the courtroom scene between the local, the national, and the universal, between politics and intimacy. The appeals to universal values and the negotiation of local community cannot fully excise the political and the national, which not only descended on local Alabama life during the Scottsboro trials, when the movie is set, but also were even more undeniable in the late 1950s and early 1960s, when the movie was made, as the South resisted desegregation. Like any religion, *To Kill a Mockingbird* appeals to abstract universals of dignity and equality, but the courtroom scene is more striking for the ways in which it depicts a local community realigning itself in the shadow of national politics. The community of whites bound together across class by the white privilege of Jim Crow unravels in the face of the defection of white liberal elites like Atticus Finch, who, in the name of a highly aspirational view of law, claim blacks as de jure equals and cast out the poorest whites as the historical culprits of racism and inequality. The narrative suggests that these whites, who have everything to lose from racial equality, cannot embrace even the minimal and aspirational notion of legal equality in the space of the courtroom. These whites face not just community banishment but displaced blame for the institutionalized racism of a nation. The film constructs a national and legal imaginary in which the white audience is allowed, exhorted even, to identify with Atticus and deflect blame for racism onto others and onto the past. Like a powerful religious ritual, it gives us images with which to make sense of the most difficult aspects of our collective life; it allows us to relive, across the safer distance of time, the sacrifice that bestows the catharsis of our racial redemption.

In the courtroom of *To Kill a Mockingbird,* the blamed and despised whites, the Ewells, fight against their banishment by claiming the scraps of white privilege. Tom Robinson fights for his life and for human dignity, and Atticus Finch fights for a local realignment of community through the discourse of national law, one that will cast out prejudice, in the form of the Ewells, and lay claim to universal legal equality, in the form of Tom Robinson's innocence. The three moments of real passion in the courtroom scene arise from this triangular struggle: Mayella Ewell's testimony, Tom Robinson's testimony, and Atticus Finch's closing argument. Mayella in her testimony is by turns defensive, uncomfortable, ambivalent, and defiant. When Atticus demonstrates that Tom can't use his left arm at all, Mayella looks alarmed and distraught. Atticus challenges her to tell the court what really happened. At that moment she is not just legally cornered by Atticus the lawyer; she knows that this is the crucial moment in her claim to racial privilege and inclusion: if the jury believes Tom over her, she and her family will be pushed to the very bottom, past the outer edges of the community, no longer even tolerated guests. It is here, as she addresses her claim to all the whites above her and challenges them across class, that the camera portrays her abjection, coming so uncomfortably close she is almost blurry: "I got somethin' to say! And then I ain't gonna say no more! He took advantage of me. And if you fine, fancy gentlemen ain't gonna do nothin' about it, then you're just a bunch of lousy, yellow, stinkin' cowards! The whole bunch of you! And your fancy airs don't come to nothin'! Your 'ma'am' and your 'Miss Mayella,' it don't come to nothin' Mr. Finch!" She ends in tears and is rendered inarticulate,[35] unable to speak her complex despair, but we have had to confront her straight on, as a woman virtually powerless but for her whiteness. In telling a lie, however, she is able to articulate a truth about her own injury and the hypocrisy of white elites in laying the blame for racism at her feet.

Tom's testimony is equally passionate but forcefully controlled. We feel his aggrievement keenly and share his knowledge that he is not allowed to articulate it. Whereas the close-up camera blurred Mayella, it is in sharp focus on Tom, showing his deep blackness, the topography of his skin, the sweat on his forehead, his tears, and his despair.[36] He is fighting not for inclusion but for his life, yet in the legal imaginary and civic ritual erected for the viewer, Tom's life is at once a claim for inclusion and equality for African Americans as well as his sacrifice for our sins of racism. For

Mayella in the witness box

Tom in the witness box

the film to be effective as a national ritual of racial redemption, however, its internal logic must be depoliticized and universalized; the political is rendered personal, conveyed as the intimacies of desire and pity. Whereas Mayella's crucial mistake was to "kiss a black man," Tom's mistake was to confess that he had pitied Mayella. This serious breach of Maycomb County norms is, within the logic of the film, another appeal to universal values, the elevation of the human recognition he bestows on Mayella despite the racial protocol that requires him to be only the object of pity.

It is this appeal that Atticus takes up in his closing argument, where he tries to realign the local community in the discursive space of the law and the contact zone of the courtroom. He does so by making Tom Robinson respectable and by making the Ewells not just pitiable but contemptible. While declaring that Tom Robinson is "a quiet, humble, respectable Negro who has had the unmitigated temerity to feel sorry for a white woman," Atticus attacks the Ewells' credibility, accusing them of having represented themselves to the jury "in the cynical confidence that their testimony would not be doubted, confident that you gentlemen would go along with them on the assumption, the evil assumption that all Negroes lie, all Negroes are basically immoral beings, all Negro men are not to be trusted around our women. *An assumption that one associates with minds of their caliber* and which is in itself, gentlemen, a lie which I do not need to point out to you."[37] Atticus, it should be noted, is making not legal arguments but factual and moral arguments about decency, credibility, and inclusion. The Ewells, whom Atticus concedes are the victims of "cruel poverty and ignorance," are nonetheless not worthy members of the May-comb County community in the way that humble and respectable black people are. The law he appeals to is not positive law but a general and universal claim to equality in the sacred space of the courts, which are "the great levelers," where "all men are created equal." In other words, Atticus is not making an argument about law as much as he is reconstituting the community within the discursive ritual of courtroom oratory. "In the name of God," he commands the jury, "do your duty. In the name of God, believe Tom Robinson." In the secular religion of *To Kill a Mockingbird*, Tom Robinson is our martyr. Within the logic of the film it requires only the smallest adjustment to conflate our belief in Tom's testimony with a belief in his power to redeem us. Likewise, Atticus is the high priest and the courtroom the house of worship in the secular religion of the film, a religion fierce enough that the real courtroom of Monroeville, which is as close as we can get to the fictional courtroom of Maycomb County, can serve as a national monument to our faith in legal equality and our redemption from our racist past.

In the space of Tom Robinson's trial, the cleavages of class are not just exposed as fault lines but are held up by Atticus as a marker not merely of difference but of disgust. Racism is laid at the door of poor and ignorant whites rather than friends and neighbors, the nation, or the law. The jury, however, the point of contact between law and community, finds Tom Robinson guilty. It could not be otherwise. It must be heartbreaking for the temporal displacement to do its work. We the future jury must feel and judge differently and feel righteous in that difference, redeemed by it. It is only in the future that the community can be reimagined, and we, the products of that reimagining, know enough to feel awe at what Atticus has said and done. He has not just passionately defended Tom Robin-son; he has made a case that took the jury two hours to reject.[38] We take our cue from silent black folks in the balcony, the idealized community of the future: dressed for church, integrated (having folded in the white children), standing and reverent as Atticus passes out of the courtroom. This scene is the key liturgy of our civic religion, but what knowledge does it promote, and what does it ask us to remember and to forget? It may induct us into liberal legalism by counseling that aspirational procedural justice is enough, that it is what is in our heart that matters most. But if this is right, we must also forget that a commitment to procedural justice (Tom Robinson, unlike the Scottsboro Boys, gets an able and articulate lawyer who believes in him) allows us to live with a substantial amount of substantive injustice.[39] It may allow us to remember the sins of the past at the same time that we forget our responsibility for that past or for the sins of the present. It may—most simply, radically, visually—allow present-day white viewers to disown the past by seeing our idealized future selves in the faces of black people.[40]

Absorbing the Outsider

The trial scene is not the denouement of *To Kill a Mockingbird*. After the trial, the film changes key, the mood shifts, and the end of the film returns to its earlier preoccupation—the children's morbid fascination with the unseen recluse Boo Radley and the stories that circulate about him. In the children's imagination Boo Radley is savage and mythic. Jem describes Boo as having a jagged scar, yellow teeth, and bulging eyes. He tells Dill that Boo comes out only at night, and "judgin' from his tracks, he's six and a half feet tall, eats raw squirrels and all the cats he can catch." Obsessed with his absence, they stalk him, discuss him, and invent ever more elaborate notions of his menace. Then they discover an offering from him in the knothole of the old tree between their houses. He proceeds to leave them a series of gifts: a broken pocket watch, two Indian head pennies, dolls carved out of soap. The objects in the child's box in the opening credits gain meaning: they are the tokens through which Boo Radley comes to be known to the children as something other than a frightening stranger. They are the beginnings of a relationship with his neighbors and his reintegration into the community.

Later that fall, a couple of months after the trial, after Tom Robinson has been killed in an escape attempt, Jem and Scout are attacked by Bob Ewell while they are walking home at night. They are saved by Boo Radley, who stabs Ewell with a kitchen knife. Boo remains unseen by the audience and the children as he carries the unconscious Jem home and Scout struggles out of her ham costume. When Scout arrives home, the pale, awkward stranger comes out from behind the shadow of the door and into the lit room. Scout realizes that this slight and ethereal man is the infamous Boo before Atticus introduces him properly as "Mr. Arthur Radley." Scout takes his hand and befriends him. When she walks him home, she shows him how to bend his arm for her to slip her hand into, so that "if Miss Stephanie Crawford was watching from her upstairs window, she would see Arthur Radley escorting me down the sidewalk, as any gentleman would do."[41] Boo has been not only brought into the community as a friend and neighbor but also restored to a place of social privilege, a southern gentleman. The children's imaginary relationship with Boo Radley has haunted the film and the neighborhood, until he literally emerges from the shadows and is made a neighbor.

Boo at the Finches' house

But if the neighborhood is remade and reimagined, it comes together through another failure of the law, a legal failure common to law films: the law must be subverted in order to do justice.[42] Boo, no longer a monster but an innocent—too innocent to be guilty of killing Ewell—is saved from prosecution by the insistence and authority of Sheriff Tate, who refuses to drag someone with "his shy ways" into the public glare of the law. Tate has both legal and social authority; he's "still the sheriff of Maycomb County," and he is also a central member of the community. For Tate, Ewell's life has repaid Tom's, and he makes his decision as a matter of community justice rather than legal justice: "Lived in this town all my life an' I'm goin' on forty-three years old. Know everything that's happened here since before I was born. There's a black boy dead for no reason, and the man responsible for it's dead. Let the dead bury the dead this time, Mr. Finch."[43] Scout affirms Sheriff Tate's decision and Boo's innocence by likening him to a mockingbird. There is a suggestion that things are as they should be even though Tom, an innocent, was murdered, and Boo, a murderer, is too innocent to be tried. By absorbing the stranger and choosing justice over law, the neighborhood is able to do what the imagined community within the law could not: admit the outsider and maintain stability. The movie ends with the voice-over of Scout grown up, Scout of 1962: "Boo was our neighbor. He gave us two soap dolls, a broken watch and chain, a knife, and our lives." The subtle substitution of Boo for Tom continues. Tom may be the martyr of the civil religion, but Boo gave the children their lives.

The film's conclusion feels religious, as the white audience is redeemed from the sins of the past and given a renewed sense of hope for the future. The possibility of an integrated and just community is the result of the combined effects of the temporal displacement, the shift away from the elegiac conclusion of the trial, and the reintegration of Boo. Tom Robinson and Bob Ewell, the two men who most challenged the community of Maycomb County, are dead. The jury's unwillingness to embrace equality or integration is counteracted by the ability of the neighborhood to embrace the metaphorical stranger, the ghostly white recluse Boo Radley. Memory catches up with time, and the final voice-over pulls us out of the past. We are at the end of the story, in a purified version of the beginning, the same quiet, dusty street but somehow cleansed of the politics of class and race that Tom Robinson and Bob Ewell forced on us. The triangulation has become a symbolic trinity: Ewell, the terrible father, has sacrificed the innocent Tom Robinson, and the spirit-like Boo remains, to save the children's lives, to allow us to forget the past, to reintegrate the community and redeem the nation. Redemption operates in two senses, religious and legal: not only are our sins forgiven, but also the entailment has been bought back, redeemed.

We continue to read the book and watch the movie and feel better for it because they allow us to worship at the altar of racial equality, and they assure us that the sins for which we are still repenting are in the past. *To Kill a Mockingbird* is now one of our cultural rituals for imagining the American national community as inclusive and the law as egalitarian. For all the richness and aspiration of the film, what does it say that over fifty years later we continue to genuflect before the idea that the abstract legal principle of equality by itself can atone for the brutal legacies of the past and be the solution to the problems of injustice in the future?

NOTES

1. Stephen Metcalf, "On First Looking into *To Kill a Mockingbird:* How Sentimental and Nostalgic Is It?" *Slate,* June 9, 2006.

2. See, e.g., www.loc.gov/bookfest/books-that-shaped-america/.

3. "To Kill a Mockingbird Beats Bible in Book Poll," *Telegraph,* April 3, 2009, available ibid.

4. Cathy Newman, "To Kill a Mockingbird," *National Geographic* (January 2006), http://ngm.nationalgeographic.com/ngm/0601/feature8/index.html.

5. Ibid.

6. www.tokillamockingbird.com/index.cfm.

7. www.villageprofile.com/alabama/monroeville/02/topic.html.

8. www.afi.com/100years/handv.aspx. Not surprisingly perhaps, most legal scholarship on *To Kill a Mockingbird,* movie or book, tends to focus on Finch the lawyer. This scholarship takes many forms, including critiques of Finch, defenses of him, and many discussions of his lawyerly tactics. See Monroe Freedman, "Atticus Finch—Right and Wrong," *Alabama Law Review* 45 (1994): 473–82; Abbe Smith, "Defending Atticus Finch," *Legal Ethics* 14 (2011): 143–67; Steven Lubet, "Reconstructing Atticus Finch," *Michigan Law Review* 97 (1999): 1339–62.

9. Metcalf, "On First Looking into *To Kill a Mockingbird.*"

10. Malcolm Gladwell, "The Courthouse Ring," *New Yorker,* August 10, 2009, www .newyorker.com/reporting/2009/08/10/090810fa_fact_gladwell>

11. Marjorie Garber, *Symptoms of Culture* (New York: Routledge, 1998), 116.

12. See Susan Heinzelman, "We Don't Have Mockingbirds in Britain, Do We?" in this volume.

13. Martha Merrill Umphrey and Austin Sarat, "The Justice of Jurisdiction: The Policing and Breaching of Boundaries in Orson Welles' *Touch of Evil*," *English Language Notes* 48.2 (Fall/Winter 2010): 111–28.

14. Benedict Anderson, *Imagined Communities: Reflections on the Origin and Spread of Nationalism* (1983), rev. ed. (London: Verso, 2006).

15. Ibid., 6.

16. Michael Walzer, *Spheres of Justice* (New York: Basic Books, 1983), 31.

17. See Austin Sarat and Martha Merrill Umphrey, "Temporal Horizons: On the Possibilities of Law and Fatherhood in *To Kill a Mockingbird*," in this volume.

18. Harper Lee, *To Kill a Mockingbird* (1960), rev. ed. (London: Arrow Books, 2006), 249.

19. Ibid., 189.

20. Ibid., 34 and 187.

21. *To Kill a Mockingbird* (Universal Studios, 1962). All quotations from the film are my personal transcriptions.

22. Lee, *To Kill a Mockingbird*, 249.

23. www.u-s-history.com/pages/h1528.html.

24. Steve Davis, "The South as 'the Nation's No. 1 Economic Problem': The NEC Report of 1938," *Georgia Historical Quarterly* 62 (1978): 119–32.

25. James A. Miller, *Remembering Scottsboro: The Legacy of an Infamous Trial* (Princeton: Princeton University Press, 2009).

26. Ibid., 230.

27. Ibid.

28. In the novel, Atticus is reading a newspaper as he sits outside the jail. Lee, *To Kill a Mockingbird*, 166.

29. Ibid., 167; emphasis added.

30. Transcribed from the film.

31. Entailments, feudal in nature, not only were used to maintain the privilege and power that came with expanses of landed property but also were about maintaining social status by limiting the inheritance of and to the property as a whole. The gendered effect, which could leave widows and daughters destitute, is evident in the anxiety of many of Jane Austen's women, especially in *Pride and Prejudice*.

32. Mary Louise Pratt, "Arts of the Contact Zone," *Profession* 91 (1991): 33–40.

33. Garber, *Symptoms of Culture*, 125.

34. This point is reinforced by anecdotal experience: among a number of white people I questioned who had not seen the movie or read the book in decades, most had forgotten that Tom is found guilty and finally killed. What they remember is the sense of legal vindication and righteousness that comes from our perception of the closing argument and Atticus's exit from the courtroom.

35. There is a parallel here to the inarticulable moment of loss that Ravit Reichman identifies in the scene of the rabid dog. See Ravit Reichman, "Dead Animals," in this volume.

36. James Miller contends that by casting Brock Peters as Tom, the film flirted "with the very stereotypes, particularly the threat of sexual menace represented by black men, it presumably sought to subvert." Miller, *Remembering Scottsboro*, 233.

37. Transcribed from the film; emphasis added.

38. It is only from the book that we learn it was one of the Cunninghams—chastened, reintegrated, and (almost) enlightened—who nearly hung the jury. Lee, *To Kill a Mockingbird*, 245.

39. Craig Haney, "The Fourteenth Amendment and Symbolic Legality: Let Them Eat Due Process," *Law and Human Behavior* 15 (1991): 183–204.

40. This would be consistent with Carol Greenhouse's contention that after *Brown*, "African American lives were assigned to the semiotics of federal power and, through federal agency, to the nation as a whole." Carol J. Greenhouse, "A Federal Life: *Brown* and the Nationalization of the Life Story," in *Race, Law, and Culture: Reflections on Brown v. Board of Education*, ed. Austin Sarat (New York: Oxford University Press, 1997), 172.

41. Lee, *To Kill a Mockingbird*, 306.

42. Naomi Mezey and Mark Niles, "Screening the Law: Ideology and Law in American Popular Culture," *Columbia Journal of Law and the Arts* 28 (2005): 91.

43. Lee, *To Kill a Mockingbird*, 303–4.

CHAPTER SIX

"We Don't Have Mockingbirds in Britain, Do We?"

Susan Sage Heinzelman

One productive way to examine the hold of *To Kill a Mockingbird* on the American imagination is to address its place in British culture. Long before globalization rendered the distinction between what was American and what was other increasingly difficult to define, America and Britain had a special relationship through which they produced a mutually constructed social imaginary—call it "transatlanticism." Both countries share a triangulation with the Caribbean and Africa through the history of slavery and the flow of military and capitalist ideologies. That shared social reality, constructed in part by their history of affiliation and separation, makes America at once postcolonial (in relationship to Britain and its former empire) and imperial (as a superpower) even as it makes Britain at once, and still, a colonial power (manifest in the Commonwealth) and postimperial. The ideological contradictions produced by these ambiguous political conditions emerge in multiple forms and institutions, from the local to the transnational, and perhaps find their most salient expression in questions of race and class. The August 2011 riots in Britain brought these incoherent articulations of community and national identity sharply into focus. And not surprisingly, British media and politicians once again invoked comparisons with the history of American race riots and civil disorder in their analysis of contemporary social upheaval in Britain, as if some historical necessity bound the two countries to reflect and to represent a mutually agreed-upon narrative of moral and social progress fixated on race. I return to these social disturbances at the end of this essay, but for now I concentrate on the politics of race in immediate post–World War II Britain.

To Kill a Mockingbird was released in the UK in 1963, at a time when the official discourse of immigration was becoming markedly racist. To note that political discourse assumes a specific rhetorical tone is not the equivalent of arguing that the general population is in agreement with its sentiments, but it does indicate that a political consciousness has congealed to produce a set of terms and rhetorical strategies that define the issue—that it has, in fact, become a *political* issue, in addition to being one that might be addressed at the individual or communal level. To situate the reception of the film specifically within postwar Britain, I rely in part on the work of Paul Gilroy, who examines the transnational cultural construction of blackness and the African diaspora in *The Black Atlantic: Modernity and Double Consciousness* (1993). Gilroy invokes W. E. B. Du Bois's term "double consciousness" in his analysis of the relationship between racial oppression and modernity. Gilroy argues: "Striving to be both European and black requires some specific forms of double consciousness. . . [because] where racist, nationalist, or ethnically absolutist discourses orchestrate political relationships, so that these identities appear to be mutually exclusive, occupying the space between them or trying to demonstrate their continuity has been viewed as a provocative and even oppositional act of political insubordination."[1]

For Gilroy, Du Bois's double consciousness is the product of African American encounters with European culture and demands a historical understanding of black culture that is not rigidly marked by cultural nationalisms. But as Rutledge Dennis argues contra Gilroy, this reading of the term seems to counteract the specificity of Du Bois's analysis that double consciousness arises from the social and political inequities experienced by African Americans in the United States.[2] Du Bois's investigation of the condition of a minority group within a majority culture—the condition of the outsider within—was produced, argues Dennis, in a specific sociohistorical context, one in which the racial tension between white citizens and former slaves was exacerbated by the arrival of huge numbers of European immigrants to the United States eager to assert their claims to being "real" Americans. The confusions and contradictions evident in the disposition of racial prerequisite cases from the late nineteenth century to the middle of the twentieth century testify to the pressure on the courts to

settle questions of racial eligibility for American citizenship by naturalization, an option open only to "free white persons" and other specific racial
groups.[3] It is this struggle for status and national identity between what
one might call the involuntary citizens of the United States (those who
came as slaves) and more recent immigrants that contextualizes Du Bois's
account of the peculiar consciousness of the American Negro:

> The Negro is a sort of seventh son, born with a veil, and gifted with second-
> sight in this American world, —a world which yields him no true self-con-
> sciousness but only lets him see himself through the revelation of the other
> world. It is a sensation, this peculiar double-consciousness, this sense of always
> looking at one's self through the eyes of others, of measuring one's soul by the
> tape of a world that looks on in amused contempt and pity. One ever feels his
> twoness, —an American, a Negro; two souls, two thoughts, two unreconciled
> strivings, two warring ideals in one dark body, whose dogged strength alone
> keeps it from being torn asunder.[4]

Du Boisian double consciousness has been read primarily as a psychological and spiritual burden, although later scholars have argued that the
tension between these "two unreconciled strivings" might also be a source
of creative power.[5] As Dennis points out, however, Du Bois's insistence on
the presence of "warring ideals in one dark body" was also accompanied
by a demand that double consciousness be recognized not only as a burden but also as giving rise to a specific political and social identity: that
it be "possible for a man to be both a Negro and an American."[6] In other
words, it ought to be possible to claim both a racial and a national identity.
Gilroy argues, however, that "the modern political and cultural formation"
he names the black Atlantic "can be defined, on one level, through . . . [a]
desire to transcend both the structures of the nation state and the constraints of ethnicity and national particularity."[7]

To these two readings of double consciousness—one of which operates
within national borders, the other of which is diasporic—I would add a
third possibility, one that pushes against the potential of black double
consciousness and attempts its erasure. There exists a form of double consciousness whose consequence is to conceal racial inequality. This consciousness is not that of the racialized other but the consciousness of those
whose individual, cultural, and national identity is synonymous with being white. This kind of double consciousness, then, constitutes a doubling
of whiteness, and as such it is a shape-shifter, morphing as needed into
an imperial and/or postimperial, a colonial and/or postcolonial ideology.

Such a consciousness is informed by an ideology of race that consistently locates people of color against an essentialized, naturalized, and national-ized whiteness. The result of this ideology in political terms is the state's apparent accommodation of the bid for political and legal equality from its formerly enslaved or colonial subjects, while simultaneously preserving its dominant, white, imperial status. Another name for this racialized and nationalized double consciousness is white neoliberalism.

The British response to both the novel and the film of *To Kill a Mock-ingbird* reveals how the cultural and political double consciousness of Britain on issues of race and class—simultaneously racialist and tolerant, class-conscious and egalitarian—mirrors the double consciousness of the American imaginary (and therefore of the novel and its cinematic ver-sion), given that the racial politics and policies of the United States and the UK are a mutually produced, transnational cultural phenomenon. The ongoing popularity of both the novel and the film in the UK helps us understand its persistence in the American imagination as representative of a supposedly utopian, postracial future, as many authors in this volume have argued. I would suggest, however, that the film also elicits as essential to this nationalist narrative of progress a restatement of the racialized and hierarchical binary on which the nation-state is founded. Thus the film may appear to advance the cause of justice even as it conceals the ongoing causes of injustice.

This essay is divided into three parts, each part building toward a better understanding of how *To Kill a Mockingbird* is situated historically and culturally in both the United States and the UK as part of a persistent national agenda that maintains the dominance of a white elite. The coda addresses a recent articulation of the persistence of these class and racial binaries. In part one I situate my own family in the history of empire building and the immediate postwar situation in the UK to illustrate the way in which the idea of Britishness is inextricably entwined with images of exclusion, empire, and whiteness. (Like the novel and film, my narra-tive of history is mediated through the memories of an adult recalling her childhood.) In part two I describe the gradual growth of a restrictive immigration policy for people of color in the UK from the arrival of the first postwar Caribbean immigrants in 1948 through the 1960s. Finally, in part three I explore the complexities of race and class in the film in light

of both Du Bois's theory of double consciousness and the double consciousness that I have suggested exists between postimperial Britain and
imperial America, one that places the audience in alignment with those
who must be "educated" into the morally ambiguous and compromised
condition of white liberals in a racist and classist culture.

Building the Empire

I did not see the movie version of *To Kill a Mockingbird* when it was first
released in 1963 and would certainly have had no opportunity to see such
a film in rural southern England during the 1960s, a very different kind of
"South" from that depicted in the movie. (Ironically, however, BBC Films
announced in 2011 that it planned to produce a "very modern take" on
Harper Lee's 1960 novel, based on Daniel Clay's 2008 novel *Broken,* which
shifts the action from the American Deep South to southern England.)[8] I
do remember seeing *South Pacific* (1958) and *West Side Story* (1960), among
other American movies (mostly westerns), but the distribution of *To Kill
a Mockingbird* was limited to major metropolitan cinemas, and all the reviews of the film refer to screenings in London. My only encounter with
people of color while I was growing up in a homogeneous population
in Hampshire was through the stories my mother and father told about
their wartime experiences. My mother, who was eighteen when the war
broke out, joined the FANYs, the First Aid Nursing Yeomanry, and spent
the next six years driving an ambulance at night and working in a glider
factory by day in Eastleigh, near the port of Southampton. She recalls the
dances organized at the local base for American soldiers and the massing
of troops along the south coast in preparation for the Normandy invasion. In the days before they crossed the channel, those men were fed and
supplied by the women of the home forces. My mother claims she never
thought to treat the colored men, as she called them, any differently from
the white ones, although she was aware of how white American soldiers
treated their black comrades. I suspect she remembers her experiences
correctly rather than in a revisionist mode, but that was wartime, and
those black soldiers were going home, back to the United States, if they
were lucky enough to survive the war.[9]

My father joined the Royal Air Force in 1942 after the Hampshire
Constabulary released him from his police duties. He spent two years on

a training base in what was then Southern Rhodesia (now Zimbabwe), in Bulawayo. He had never witnessed anything like the brutal and dehumanizing racism of the white colonialists toward the Africans, and his experience radicalized his politics and his acceptance of the status quo in England when he returned. He never explicitly voiced the irony of training young white men to fight against fascists and racists over there (in Europe) in a place that was itself the epitome of racism, but his time in Africa unsettled him for the rest of his life, leaving him conflicted about his ascent into the middle class.[10] Such confusion made it difficult for him to return to the police force as a detective after the war, for he recognized in the treatment by police of the poor and immigrants from Europe and former colonies the deep-seated class and race prejudice that lay just below the surface of British tolerance and egalitarianism.

My parents' contribution to the war effort was, of course, a natural continuation of their parents' willingness to die for the empire. Both my parents were from the working class (my father's mother could barely read or write), and both of their fathers had fought in the First World War. Like many young men, my grandfathers had signed up in 1914, responding to the appeal from Lord Kitchener, secretary of state for war, to defend the British way of life, at risk from foreign invaders (from Europe or Asia). While my father's father served in the trenches in France, my mother's father, who was an apprentice railway engineer when the war broke out, joined the Hampshire Territorial Brigade. He was immediately shipped out to India, where he spent three years maintaining peace among Britain's colonial subjects and repairing the railway that opened up the Khyber Pass for the British and Allied troops. I still have the postcards he sent back to his mother from Cawnpore (Kanpur), Allahabad, and the pass.

The point of reviewing my family's history is to indicate that up to the end of the Second World War, almost every family in Britain, whatever its class origins, could claim that it had actively engaged in building the empire; we were, whether willing or no, consciously or not, all engaged in securing, protecting, and solidifying the place of Great Britain as a colonizing power, as so many generations of British citizens had done before us. The first generation that escaped from under this historical burden would not be born until the 1960s, the decade in which *To Kill a Mockingbird* was published and postwar melancholia was replaced with nostalgia for the empire. Nostalgia does not merely recall the past; nostalgia reconstructs the past as a sacred memory that, as Naomi Mezey argues in her essay in this volume, redeems the present. And nostalgia is particularly acute when the present is unsettling.

In 1960s England, the empire was no longer "over there" but increasingly and evidently at home in Britain. Of course, in some ways this had always been the case—Britain had always received travelers and merchants from across the globe, and all those men and women who returned from colonial outposts around the world had already introduced colonial attitudes and cultures into Britain; and this trade of people, goods, and ideologies was itself an extension of the global exchanges of slavery. But after the Second World War there was a change in the geographical and political relationship of the colonizer to the colonized, one that was not immediately comparable to the historical relationship between former slaves and their white masters in the United States. When those who had previously been marked as subservient, uncivilized, and alien, even (and especially) in their own country, now arrived on the shores of the mother country to claim the privileges once reserved for their colonial masters, a relatively homogeneous understanding of class, status, and social hierarchy was ruptured from within. What followed was an effort to exclude those who did not belong, a task made easier when racial difference seems homologous with immigrant status from a former colony. Racial whiteness stood opposed to racial blackness, and immigrants of color became the daily reminder of Britain's lost imperial stature. They came from "white men's countries," as the former colonies in Africa, the Caribbean, and India were called, but they came looking for the equality those very white men had denied them in their own country; what they found was racism fueled by nostalgia for the days of the empire, a nostalgia propelled by recent memories of the war and contemporary representations of the British fighting spirit embodied inevitably in white men and women battling against the threat of invasion from overseas.

Colonizing the Motherland

Britain has always been multiethnic and multicultural, but only since the 1950s has it become multiracial in the sense that permanent settlers, distinguished from other immigrants by the color of their skin, have been officially acknowledged as citizens. Immediate postwar England did not seem to have a race problem—at least, not one of sufficient magnitude to generate sustained public recognition of the need to develop harmonious "race relations" with people of color. Obvious cases of racial prejudice were acknowledged, but there was still no critical mass of immigrants of color to warrant intervention by the state. The outbreak of violence in 1948 against the black residents of Liverpool (approximately eight thousand in number, who came to help in the war effort) was represented not as a racial affair but as a struggle for workers' rights; it coincided, however, with the arrival in the port of Tilbury of almost five hundred Jamaican men on the *Empire Windrush*, many of whom were returning to the motherland, having served there during the war. The Labour government, in power from 1945 to 1951, actively encouraged such immigration to help rebuild the country, and in 1948 Parliament passed the Nationality Act, which conferred UK citizenship on the citizens of Britain's colonies and former colonies, with the right to come to Britain and stay permanently without prerequisites of any kind. Over the next five years, from 1948 to 1953, approximately five thousand men, women, and children immigrated to England from the Caribbean. The numbers increased substantially in the following years, in part as a result of the McCarran-Walter Act, passed by the United States Congress in 1953, specifically limiting immigration from the Caribbean.

The period from 1945 to 1958 has been described as a time of "laissez-faire" immigration control, but closer examination of government policy, especially under the Conservative government, suggests that immigration control was very much part of a concerted effort to preserve the racial purity of the country. After the Conservatives took power in 1951, ministerial discussions began to articulate a "Keep Britain White" policy. The following comment, for example, is taken from a Home Office briefing: "The problem of colonial immigration has not yet aroused public anxiety. On the other hand, if immigration from the colonies . . . were allowed to continue unchecked, there was a real danger that over the years there would be significant change in the racial character of British people."[11] Immigration by people of color increased, and ten years after those five hundred Jamaicans arrived on the *Empire Windrush*, there were about 125,000 West Indians and 55,000 Indians and Pakistanis in Britain, a figure that represented less than 1 percent of the population. (The 2001 census indicated that since the 1950s, the nonwhite population had grown to approximately 7 percent of the total population.) Nevertheless, the immigration of people of color into the UK was perceived as a threat to the very nature of being British, a crucial ingredient of which was that it was free from the kind of racism that plagued the United States. Presumably the logic was that if the British had to deal with "Negroes" in sufficient numbers, they would, of necessity, be forced to become racist! In a March 1954 letter to Lord Swinton, deputy leader of the House of Lords and secretary of state for Commonwealth relations, Lord Salisbury, Lord President of the Privy Council, wrote:

> Before the War the number of coloured people coming into England was a mere trickle—nothing to worry about at all—but now, with each year that passes . . . the flow increases. Indeed, if something is not done to check it now, I should not be at all surprised if the problem became quite unmanageable in 20 to 30 years' time. We might well be faced with very much the same type of appalling issue that is now causing such great difficulty for the United States. . . . I feel that we should recognize that this coloured problem is potentially of a fundamental nature for the future of our Country.[12]

Despite the reality in terms of actual numbers, the perception that black immigrants were overrunning Britain (a perception created in part by the local concentration of immigrants in London and in certain metropolitan communities in the Midlands and the north) generated a progressive accommodation to racism, which manifested itself politically and euphemistically as the "problem" of black immigration. The solution: the smaller the black population, the better for race relations. In 1962 the Commonwealth Immigrants Bill was passed, restricting entry to those with employment vouchers, despite the fact that all holders of British passports had believed they were guaranteed entry to Britain. In an effort to defeat the Conservative immigration agenda, even Labour politicians voiced the immigration mantra, summed up in Roy Hattersley's "without integration, limitation is inexcusable; without limitation, integration is impossible." Labour was returned to power in 1964, but so was a Conservative member of Parliament named Peter Griffiths, who ran on the slogan "If you want a nigger for a neighbour, vote Labour."[13]

That kind of virulent racism found its voice in another Conservative, Enoch Powell, member of Parliament for Wolverhampton (home to a large black population) from 1950 to 1974. In a 1968 speech forever associated with his anti-immigration position, Powell spoke of an "alien element" being introduced into the country, linking the loss of empire and national decline directly to the presence of former colonial citizens of color in Great Britain. He warned his audience against what he believed would be the consequences of continued unchecked immigration from the Commonwealth to Britain: "As I look ahead, I am filled with foreboding. Like the Roman, I seem to see 'the River Tiber foaming with much blood.' That tragic and intractable phenomenon which we watch with horror on the other side of the Atlantic but which there is interwoven with the history and existence of the States itself, is coming upon us here by our own volition and our own neglect. Indeed, it has all but come. In numerical terms, it will be of American proportions long before the end of the century. Only resolute and urgent action will avert it even now." Powell employed the comparison between the United States and Britain to illustrate race horror in its endemic form, as if Britain's racial politics had not also been historically "interwoven with the history and existence of the [nation] itself."[14] Such a distinction between a nation steeped in racial injustice and a nation that cleaves to its narrative of racial tolerance (by practicing historical amnesia) has become fundamental to the discourse of British identity.

In his essay on Michel Foucault's genealogy of racism, Kim Su Rasmussen distinguishes between two kinds of racism: "Hetero-referential racism typically negates the value of the other and follows a logic of domination, whereas auto-referential racism affirms the superior value of the self and follows a logic of exclusion."[15] Another way to distinguish might be between colonial and postcolonial forms of racism, or between the racism that is practiced outside the nation on others and the kind of internal racism manifest in Powell's speech. Internal racism focuses on "the composition, the reproduction, and the development of the population by isolating and excluding the abnormal" and thus is a form of what Foucault would call biopolitical governmentality rather than irrational prejudice.[16] It is in the context, then, of this specific approach to the "race problem" in Britain—as a way of distinguishing Britain's engagement with race from America's and as the articulation of political power made synonymous with the diminishment of white privilege—that we should view the popularity of both the novel and film of *To Kill a Mockingbird*.

The Color Problem in Britain through American Eyes

To Kill a Mockingbird was published simultaneously in 1960 in the United States and the UK and has remained one of the most popular of twentieth-century novels: a poll in England for World Book Day in 2007 placed it fifth, behind *Pride and Prejudice* but ahead of the Bible; a similar BBC poll put it sixth. A survey of British librarians rated it the book they would most recommend, and the novel is taught extensively in secondary education literature and social studies classes. Likewise the film version, released in England in 1963, remains popular for its representation of racial injustice and the ethical heroics of Atticus Finch; most recent commentaries focus on the courtroom scene and Gregory Peck's performance as Atticus.[17]

The contemporary reviews of the film, by contrast, concentrated primarily on the cinematography and on the "brilliantly directed and unsentimentally observed children."[18] One review argued that the trial was "long-winded but suspenseful" and that for "all its gruesome undertones, the film has a gentleness that isn't destroyed by the sudden violence of the attempted lynching and Ewell's attack on the children."[19] Apparently Tom's death while escaping from his jailers does not count as violence, of either the premeditated or the sudden kind, perhaps because its violence is considerably downplayed in the film. One reviewer drew attention to what he considered the bait to lure Oscar voters: the film's "high-toned liberal sentiment," manifest most explicitly in the courtroom scene. It is precisely this "high-toned" liberal response to racial and class prejudice that sits well with the British, with their belief in fair play as one of the nation's essential qualities.

That ideologically powerful construction of national identity as untouched by prejudice finds its novelistic counterpart in the innocence of the children, particularly Scout, through whose perspective the reader encounters the events of the novel. The first-person, retrospective narrative—generically an example of *Bildungsroman*—might be seen as an exemplary narrative of double consciousness, one that moves the child from a clear-eyed, morally uncompromising sense of fairness to one that accommodates the necessary concessions of the adult world. Scout narrates into being the historical double consciousness of her town, Maycomb, whose history is built on blindness to its complicity in racial injustice and its mixed racial heritage, and, by extension, to the American imaginary that cannot align its liberal values with its own history of enslavement. What resonates for America—a nation identified with the idealistic principles of liberal democracy and justice built on a history of oppression and injustice—finds its transatlantic complement in Britain. And just as in the United States, the UK would have to reimagine what Naomi Mezey calls in her contribution to this volume "the rules of racial inclusion" and accommodate the consequent shifting "social hierarchies."

The film opens with the adult Scout poring over a box that contains Boo's gifts to Jem when he was a child. Each gift recalls a moment in the narrative of Boo's redemption from monster to protector and his "coming out" from the isolation and imprisonment imposed on him by his tyrannical father and uncle. This narrative parallels Jem's and Scout's "coming into" the experience of white privilege, class privilege, and racial injustice through the liberty they experience as children of their racially tolerant father. The film foregrounds these two narratives to the exclusion of other complicating narratives that occur in the novel. In so doing, the film symbolically links various manifestations of race and class that reinstate the privilege of certain characters over others, despite the implicit claim that legal and social equality must be imagined now in order to be achieved at some time in the future. Thus the film performs, and thereby invites the audience to embrace, what I have called the morally ambiguous and compromised condition of white liberals in a racist and classist culture: recognizing their privilege sufficiently to attempt to bring about a semblance of equality while not yielding any of the privilege that accompanies their exercise of racial and class power. As Mezey argues in her essay, the "structure of the film . . . supports the viewer's selective memory and forgetting in the aid of redemption." Only Mayella Ewell, the false accuser of Tom Robinson and daughter of the rabid racist Bob Ewell, articulates this insidious and pervasive ambivalence when she accuses Atticus of hypocrisy in his treatment of her in the trial, and she is clearly represented as a totally unreliable moral guide.

Set in the 1930s but released in 1962, the film simplifies the dense and complicit web of race and class relations that the novel narrates. The film veils how these historical and hierarchical relationships produce and maintain a segregated black community and a marginalized, poor white one, both of which serve to promote the interests of the respectable white citizens of Maycomb. In not addressing the structural problems of race and class segregation, the film offers to its American audience a sanitized version of race relations in which the lawyer–father figure Atticus Finch represents resistance and tolerance. The film suggests that it is only through the heroic efforts of individual white citizens like Atticus, and the subsequent passing on of those values of tolerance and equality to his children, that society will be transformed, rather than by systemic and systematic legal and social interventions.

For a British audience, the film's homogenizing version of race as represented by the binary of black versus white confirms their own sense that immigrants of color should be tolerated and treated with dignity, but a historical narrative that articulates how British imperialism actually produced what had not before existed—the hierarchy of racial categories and class—remains out of reach. For the British, the film provides a screen on which to play out their own anxieties about race and class prejudice (just as the American South functions as a scapegoat for national anxieties about race, class, and sexuality); it allows the audience to accept the film's version of race as universal, binary, and determinative of identity (but only if you are "colored," because white is not a color) and, at the same time, to dismiss its relevance to the UK because the film's space-time boundaries appear to seal it off from the British experience. To illustrate the consequences of the film's simplification of the historical and regional narratives of race and class found in the book, I focus on two structurally and symbolically related characters (Boo Radley and Bob Ewell) and events (the killing of the rabid dog and the killing of Tom Robinson).

Boo and Bob

In both book and film Boo Radley is at first demonized by the children as a maniacal monster, a ghostly figure who haunts their street and threatens their lives with his dangerous ways. In the film we hear little of the background story to Boo's eccentricities, but in the book we learn that Boo's father, who "buys cotton," has essentially imprisoned him in his house for adolescent troublemaking with boys from Old Sarum of the Cunningham "tribe."[20] When thirty-three-year-old Boo finally retaliates by stabbing his father with scissors, the sheriff takes him into custody but hasn't "the heart to put him in jail alongside Negroes," so he is locked up in the basement of the courthouse and then, at his father's insistence, once again returned to his home.[21] Although Boo's personal narrative hardly demonstrates what we usually mean by white privilege (especially when contrasted with the "punishment" of the other white boys, who are sent to an industrial school to learn a trade, and one of whom eventually receives an engineering degree from Auburn University), the law's treatment of his case demonstrates a favoritism shown exclusively to white citizens of a certain class in Maycomb. Such favoritism is most fully extended when Heck Tate, the sheriff, refuses to charge Boo with the death of Bob Ewell.

Boo's whiteness, exaggerated in the film by the albino-like appearance of actor Robert Duvall, and the privileges that accompany it are contrasted repeatedly in the book with other forms of whiteness. The complex ways in which race and class produce the social hierarchies of this specific place at this specific time in the history of the South are condensed in the film into a series of binaries, one of which is the opposition between the imagined monster, Boo, and the real monster, Bob Ewell.

Whereas in the book, Boo's physical defense of the children is an extension of the concern he has shown for them over the years, in the film the dichotomies of race and class make it seem inevitable that Boo should kill Bob Ewell. The "whitest" white man, who is aligned in terms of class with the Finches, dispatches that which stains the community. Bob Ewell lives beyond the town boundaries; in the book we learn that the Ewells live in a cabin once occupied by Negroes, occupying a space literally and figuratively between the white and the black citizens of Maycomb. The film, however, leaves his place in the town's geography unspecified. Both book and film suggest that Ewell's vicious racism might flow in part from his recognition that he is, in effect, as marginalized by poverty and ignorance as the African American residents. The film, however, also explicably and repeatedly links Ewell's racism to his condition as the "bad poor." In this way Ewell's racism stands in counterpoint to Atticus's white tolerance, on the one hand, and Tom's black dignity, on the other. Dirty, drunk, impoverished, and sexually perverse, Ewell marks the outermost limits of what it means to be white—so far beyond the pale, as it were, that he is not even referred to as white, just "low grade." And when Heck Tate justifies his refusal to charge Boo with homicide, he acknowledges that Boo is the real white man (one who could not even be jailed with Negroes) while Bob Ewell is not—so much "not white," in fact, that Ewell can metaphorically be buried with a black man. "There's a black boy dead for no reason, and the man responsible for it's dead," says Sheriff Tate. "Let the dead bury the dead this time, Mr. Finch. Let the dead bury the dead" (317). In this case the dead, both those who are black and those who are "low-grade" white, have always been dead to the town—as their abject living conditions near the town dump suggest.

That there is more to the history of race and class in Maycomb County than the film displays is most significantly revealed in a scene in the novel immediately before the trial of Tom for the alleged rape of Mayella. The history of slavery and the cotton trade that establishes the Finches as one of Maycomb's elite families (and related to just about everyone else in town, according to Atticus) has also produced a complex and multiple sense of how individuals, black or white or mixed, belong to the community. In the novel, waiting for the trial to begin, Jem, Scout, and Dill reflect on the exclusion of mixed-race children from both white and black communities. Dill asks how one can tell who is mixed, given that some look black. Jem's response is "You just hafta know who they are" (185). Their conversation turns to their own heritage when Scout tellingly demands, "Well how do you know we ain't Negroes?" (185). That there is no empirical evidence of their race points not only to the fictive nature of racial categories but also, of course, to those often forced sexual interactions between white men and black women that have produced these "in-between" offspring. The irony that the forced sexual submission of so many black women should contextualize the violence done to Tom by a false charge of rape by a white woman is noticeably absent from the film. For the film audience, the injustice of Tom's situation takes place within a universalizable set of moral and ethical representations that secure, once again, race and class privilege at the cost of erasing the local and historically specific nature of race-class relations in the South.

This universalizing of justice and equality is implied in Harper Lee's invocation of the Greco-Roman origins of justice. As in Enoch Powell's summoning of classical antiquity, but to a radically different purpose, Lee names her white father-lawyer Atticus, thus placing him in the context of classical, universal Western values, while his last name, Finch, aligns him with that other songbird in the story, the mockingbird, embodied in the characters of Tom Robinson and Boo, those marginal and vulnerable members of a community that ennobles law and its practitioners.[22] Atticus *requires* the Tom Robinsons and Boos of this world on which to practice, in all senses of the word, his seemingly ungendered and unraced legal sensibility, just as he needs the Ewells to distinguish the worthy from the unworthy. As Colin Dayan suggests later in this volume, Atticus's "goodness . . . depends on . . . the disregard of persons deemed noxious to the community of well-meaning citizens." Even though, as Imani Perry argues in her essay, Atticus is not "normatively male" in the strong sense, he does assume the power to decide who is worth saving and who is disposable. His character functions in the narrative to mark the limits of what abstract liberal law can achieve in the face of apparently natural race, class, and gender hierarchies.

This tale rehearses the oft-repeated narrative of black victimhood and its essentialized relationship to class and sexuality. Despite Atticus's classically liberal noble sentiments, manifest in his plea for equal justice under the law, the film actually inscribes repeated examples of law's failure in the face of a discourse that links class, race, sexuality, and gender into an apparently naturalized and universal social formation. What was true in the 1930s remained true in the 1960s and remains true today.

Rabid Animals

What seems to some a bizarre and arbitrary interruption in the film's narrative—the killing of the rabid dog by Atticus—appears in the book as part of Jem's and Scout's understanding of the worth of their father, even though to them he appears to be feeble ("nearly fifty"), wears glasses, doesn't perform manly physical labor, never goes hunting, and does "not play poker, or fish or drink or smoke" (102). He just reads. For Jem and Scout, such events are part of the narrative of their transition from childhood to adulthood, to seeing their father as something more than just their father, and to grasping the complexities of race, class, and gender that structure their world. And one aspect of this world that they are forced to acknowledge is its violence—not just physical violence but all the kinds that are practiced by the powerful on the powerless: the sexual, the social, the psychological, and the legal, as well as the multiple ways in which the apparently powerless might resist. One of the first occasions for such recognition occurs when Jem, Dill, and Scout spy on the Radley house, and Boo's uncle-caretaker, Nathan Radley, fires a shot at them, believing Jem to be a "Negro in his collard patch" (60). He warns that "he's got the other barrel waitin' for the next sounds he hears in that patch, an' next time he won't aim high, be it dog, nigger, or ..." (61). In the economic calculus of value articulated by Nathan Radley, dogs and certain kinds of humans are disposable when personal property is at stake.

It is not a question of property, however, that causes Atticus to take up a shotgun and kill a dog, unless one considers Jem and Scout Atticus's property. Atticus acts in defense of his children and the town when he fires a single shot at Tim Johnson, the "town pet" that appears to be rabid.[23] The dog has already been claimed as the property of a human by his being given not just a dog's name, Tim, but also a family name, Johnson. In this the dog's identity resembles that of the black residents of Maycomb, who are identified by their slave names, although in the film the dog is anonymous. That Atticus acts without consulting Tim's owner suggests not only his belief that the dog is in fact rabid and not merely sick but also his assumption of the power to dispose of those who are a threat to society. In this he acts as judge and jury, sentences the dog to death, and then carries out the sentence, even as the conventional enforcer of this judicial power, the sheriff, cedes his authority to Atticus, who is the better shot. That Atticus dispatches the dog with a single shot—and thus prevents further threats to the town and further suffering by the dog—attests to his humane sensibility (and his marksmanship); it also allows the dog to die with some degree of dignity, precisely the dignity not afforded to Tom Robinson.[24]

Tom Robinson's death comes as a consequence of his attempt to escape from prison. The account in the film is brief and seems to blame Tom for not trusting Atticus; apparently Tom is less convinced than Atticus that he would receive justice from the courts. We have no firsthand witness to describe what happened, but Atticus reports what he has been told (by the sheriff): "They were taking him to Abbottsville ... for safekeeping. Tom broke loose and ran. The deputy called out to him to stop, and Tom didn't stop. He shot at him to wound him and missed his aim. Killed him. The deputy says ... Tom just ran like a crazy man."[25] A single shot intended, apparently, merely to restrain Tom goes astray, and, like the rabid dog shot by Atticus, he dies, seemingly without suffering. There is no second-guessing of this narrative in the film; we are left with the impression that Tom's guards tried to act humanely in the same way that Atticus has killed the dog but that Tom brought his death upon himself. Indeed, as Imani Perry argues in her essay, one might even be led to believe that Tom stages "southern law" in an act of autonomous agency. Nevertheless, Tom's life ends, in a gesture of either desperation or suicide. The story in the novel, however, is considerably more complex and suggests that Tom's death may have been the result of deliberate murder, or at the very least of a kind of judicial lynching. Atticus tells his housekeeper, Calpurnia: "They fired a few shots in the air, then to kill. They got him just as he went over the fence. . . . [H]e was moving fast. Seventeen bullet holes in him. They didn't have to shoot him that much. . . . [But w]hat was one Negro, more or less, among two hundred of 'em?" (270).

In both novel and film, however, Tom is not mentioned after the reports of his death. He joins Mayella, his accuser, in the silence that marks the futility of their resistance to the status quo. And while we might want to believe that the moment in the courtroom when Atticus pleads for justice redeems the racism and abuse manifest in Tom's and Mayella's lives, the account of Tom's death and the silence about Mayella's fate represents not merely the persistence of individual injustice but the systemic and systematic structures of racism, classism, and sexism against which abstract liberal legality is powerless.

Coda: Dismantling Empire's Home

In the novel, the education of the children into the values of the dominant culture constitutes its narrative teleology. While Scout and Jem react viscerally to the unfairness of the world of adults, those adults spend most of their time shoring up the boundaries between the class and racial categories necessary to secure their white liberal privileges. As Colin Dayan points out in this volume, neither the novel nor the film "perturbs the divisions of class, the fact of privilege." In the film, the distinctly liberal and binary nature of race and class representations offers a point of entry for the British audience into a world that would otherwise seem distinctly American. At the same time, the historical and geographical distance provided by the context of the story—America, the 1930s, the rural South—veils its applicability to contemporary British racial policies and their social consequences, just as the novel and film displace racism in the 1960s in the United States onto the past. Even now, the American South persists in reflecting an essential aspect of the British imaginary, an imaginary that I have suggested is constituted by a kind of national double consciousness, one informed by a tenacious imperial ideology of race operating in the specific context of a postimperial state.

On August 6, 2011, citizens of the predominantly black Caribbean London community of Tottenham marched in a peaceful demonstration to protest the death of one of their own, Mark Duggan, shot on August 4 as he was arrested by the Metropolitan Police. What began as a nonviolent protest against excessive police force erupted into four nights of burning and looting in several boroughs of London and cities in the north and west of England by racially mixed, predominantly unemployed male rioters. Voices from across the political spectrum condemned the violence but assigned very different narratives to explain its cause, from government austerity measures to national moral decline, and from racially charged explanations to class warfare. The government's response, voiced by Prime Minister David Cameron, seemed to embody the call he had made in February for a "muscular liberalism" to counteract religious fundamentalism and terrorism. His speech addressed international security, but it could also be applied to the social unrest in Britain. "Instead of ignoring this extremist ideology, we—as governments and as societies—have got to confront it, in all its forms," argued Cameron. Muscular liberalism, he contended, rejects passive tolerance and state-sponsored multiculturalism (in other words, the failed policies of the Labour Party), and advocates instead a reinforcement of collective national values that define what it means to be British. Cameron insisted that the state must provide a vision of society that does not tolerate separatism and "segregated communities behaving in ways that run completely counter to our values," leaving some feeling a sense of rootlessness, "created by the weakening of a clear collective British cultural identity."[26] The most effective way to counter this rootlessness, he insisted, was by advancing classically liberal political values.

It is, of course, precisely those liberal political values that have constructed and supported a raced class structure in Britain, a country where to be of color is still synonymous with belonging to the underclass, despite individual exceptions. By definition, those classically liberal values, which advance the privilege of individuality and the possession of property as fundamental to the definition of the subject-citizen, cannot engage with questions of race and class (except to insist on abstract notions of equality) and thus have historically enabled empire building and its contemporary, postcolonial, global equivalents. The "values" that Cameron invoked in his vision of what it means to be British are the values he himself embodied—those of the privileged, white, upper-class male who does not need to take into account what others must consider, those who are the very opposite of what Atticus tries to create in Jem and Scout: individuals who can imagine what it means to walk in another's shoes. But as Colin Dayan argues in this volume, these "fictions of sentiment" and tolerance (the privilege of race and class) "are linked in unsettling ways to the social realities of property and possession." For Atticus and his children, it is a matter of *choice* whether they address questions of race and class, not a question of survival—as it is for the Robinsons and the Ewells. The communities that rioted in Britain in the summer of 2011 were not those that espoused religious or political extremism but rather those who, like the disenfranchised "Old Sarum" mob who attempt to lynch Tom Robinson, are forced to occupy a space outside the privileged circles of the elite but who occasionally, and not always in the cause of social justice, rise up against them.

The continued success and popularity of the book and the film in Great Britain are attributable, I would argue, to the powerful need to reconstruct the white father figure as law in the face of what appears to be a loss of an essential Britishness, the loss of an empire and its economic and military might, rather than to a national, innate sense of justice and fairness (which is not to say that many individual citizens do not fervently oppose racism and other forms of social inequality). The admiration of the British for *To Kill a Mockingbird*'s indictment of racial injustice is, for the most part, the admiration of those who have had no real or close contact with black people; surveys attesting to the continued popularity of the novel and film are produced by predominantly white institutions, such as the BBC. The novel's publication and the release of its film version coincided exactly with that period in Britain when the rhetoric of immigration was irreversibly transformed from the rhetoric of citizenship to the rhetoric of race and class. Although the novel and film may have provided their British audience with a way of understanding systematic racial injustice, they would also have indicated that the national immigration crisis was threatening to change irrevocably the nature of what it meant to be British. The British reader and filmgoer would have resonated sympathetically to the portrayal of what is just and fair, given that those values are embodied in Atticus Finch, a stand-in for a certain kind of Englishman (and I do mean here specifically English rather than British, for Englishness remains the central core of British national identity). Atticus struggles mightily against racial prejudice and ignorance as embodied in those white men of a lower class, and it is this inevitable collusion of race and class as a determinant of national identity that is endemic to British culture. While it may be accurate to argue, as Imani Perry does in this volume, that the film is "rich with a great big 'yes' to transgressive humanity, and an overarching admiration for decency above all else," her reading of *To Kill a Mockingbird* does not erase the power of a still-present narrative that aligns law with a specific race, class, and gender, a narrative that, as Ravit Reichman argues in the next essay, skims across the "ways in which the narrative's ethical world is built atop an economic one."

The popularity of *To Kill a Mockingbird* is not a sign that a nation steeped in injustice and racism has come to terms with its imperial history and is now ready to embrace its black citizenry. Rather, the novel's continued success since the 1960s constitutes a way of avoiding the ongoing and deeply held racist beliefs of many in Britain who don't mind rising to the defense of a black man who lived long ago and far away but would not want him living next door. After all, we don't have mockingbirds in Britain, do we?

NOTES

1. Paul Gilroy, *The Black Atlantic: Modernity and Double Consciousness* (Cambridge: Harvard University Press, 1993), 1.

2. See Rutledge Dennis, "W. E. B. Du Bois's Concept of Double Consciousness," in *Race and Ethnicity: Comparative and Theoretical Approaches*, ed. John Stone and Rutledge Dennis (Malden, Mass.: Blackwell, 2003), 13–26, esp. 14.

3. "After persons of African nativity and descent were made eligible for naturalization during Civil War Reconstruction, the statutory classification of 'free white persons,' which had first been predominately used in contrast to African and Native Americans, became contrasted instead with Asians, who because they were considered neither 'white' nor African were often held to be racially ineligible for citizenship. After the turn of the twentieth century the distinction between 'white' and Asian became increasingly difficult to maintain, however, as disputes arose regarding the racial classification

of naturalization petitioners not only from Southeast Asia and the Far East but from central and western Asia, including Hindus, Armenians, Persians, Turks, Syrians, and Arabs, many of whom could trace their biological and cultural descent to pre-modern Indo-European ancestors." Douglas Coulson, "Rhetorical Constructions of Race, Religion, and Nationality in Arguments over the Meaning of 'White Persons' in the U.S. Naturalization Act, 1909–1952" (Ph.D. diss. abstract, University of Texas at Austin, 2012, on file with the author), 1.

4. Dennis, "W. E. B. Du Bois's Concept," 14, quoting W. E. B. Du Bois, *The Souls of Black Folk* (1903; repr., Greenwich, Conn.: Fawcett Publications, 1961), 16–17.

5. See, for example, Robert B. Stepto, *From Behind the Veil: A Study of Afro-American Narrative* (Urbana: University of Illinois Press, 1979); Houston A. Baker Jr., *Blues, Ideology, and Afro-American Literature: A Vernacular Theory* (Chicago: University of Chicago Press, 1984); and Henry Louis Gates Jr., *The Signifying Monkey: A Theory of Afro-American Literary Criticism* (New York: Oxford University Press, 1988), all of which are grounded in the creative possibilities of double consciousness.

6. Dennis "W. E. B. Du Bois's Concept," 15, quoting Du Bois, *Souls of Black Folk*, 17.

7. Gilroy, *Black Atlantic*, 19.

8. The film, which would feature Clay's character Rick Buckley as the equivalent of Lee's Boo Radley, would be an "ultimately uplifting tale" in which "the power of innocence" triumphs. "To Kill a Mockingbird–Inspired Film Announced," *BBC News*, May 17, 2011, www.bbc.co.uk/news/entertainment-arts-13422106.

9. For a fictionalized account of the treatment of Jamaican servicemen who returned to England as civilians after the war and the consequences of familiarity between black servicemen and English women, see Andrea Levy, *Small Island* (London: Headline, 2004).

10. In *The Golden Notebook*, first published in 1962 (repr., New York: HarperPerennial, 1994), Doris Lessing writes: "The mass of Africans up and down the continent were sardonically amused at the sight of their white masters crusading off to fight the racialist devil—those Africans with any education at all. They enjoyed the sight of the white baases so eager to go off and fight on any available battle-front against a creed they would all die to defend on their own soil" (63). A similar irony attended the willingness of white Americans to fight in Europe for freedom and equality while resisting civil rights for African Americans in the United States.

11. From the minutes of a cabinet meeting, November 3, 1955, quoted in Bob Carter, Clive Harris, and Shirley Joshi, "The 1951–1955 Conservative Government and the Racialization of Black Immigration," in *Black British Culture and Society: A Text Reader*, ed. Kwesi Owusu (London: Routledge, 2000), 21.

12. Lord Salisbury to Lord Swinton, March 20, 1954, in *The Conservative Government and the End of Empire, 1951–1957: British Documents on the End of Empire*, ed. David Goldsworthy, ser. A, vol. 3 (London: HMSO, 1994), 394. Lord Salisbury later resigned over colonial affairs.

13. "Looking Back at Race Relations," *BBC News*, October 23, 1999, http://news.bbc.co.uk/2/hi/482565.stm.

14. Enoch Powell, "Rivers of Blood" speech, www.telegraph.co.uk/comment/3643823/Enoch-Powells-Rivers-of-Blood-speech.html.

15. Kim Su Rasmussen, "Foucault's Genealogy of Racism," *Theory, Culture, Society* 28 (2011): 38.

16. Ibid., 40.

17. See, for example, Helen O'Hara, "At Home/Masterpiece: *To Kill A Mockingbird*," *Empire* 243 (2009): 144–45; Angie Errigo, "At Home/Movies: A True American Hero," *Empire* 199 (2006): 188 (review of DVD of *To Kill a Mockingbird*); Raymond Benson, "Benson Turns Back the Clock—1962," *Cinema Retro* 1.3 (2005): 8–10; Geoffrey MacNab, "Homemovies: Reviews," *Sight and Sound* 11.3 (March 2001): 63.

18. John Russell Taylor, "*To Kill a Mockingbird*," *Sight and Sound* 32.3 (July 1963): 147. See also *Daily Cinema* 8741 (March 25, 1963): 7; *Kine Weekly* 2894 (March 21, 1963): 22; *Films in Review* 14.3 (March 1963): 172; *Monthly Film Bulletin* 30, no. 352 (May 1963): 61.

19. *Daily Cinema* 8741 (March 25, 1963): 7.

20. "Old Sarum" is one of the most famously corrupt boroughs in English politics, one of the "rotten" boroughs disenfranchised by the 1832 Reform Act. Interestingly, the borough was owned at one point by the Pitt family, whose money had been made in trading deals in seventeenth-century India, and returned William Pitt the Elder to Parliament in 1735. As prime minister, Pitt led Britain to dominance in world affairs through his advocacy of British expansionism and colonialism. Of course, the MP for Old Sarum in England represented nobody (an irony of which Lee may not have been aware).

21. Harper Lee, *To Kill a Mockingbird* (New York: HarperCollins, 2010), 12, hereafter cited parenthetically in the text.

22. There are several candidates as a model for Atticus Finch: Titus Pomponius Atticus, (112/109–35/32 BC), an ancient Roman philosopher; Atticus, a Platonist philosopher and author of lost Plato commentary; Archbishop Atticus of Constantinople (406–425); Herodes Atticus (ca. 101–177), a Greek rhetorician; and Atticus, a Christian martyr (d. 310).

23. I say "appears to be" because in the novel Jem questions whether he might just have been sick. The film, however, clearly intends the audience to accept the diagnosis of rabies.

24. In the racial economy of the film, it is entirely appropriate that it is Calpurnia's son, Zeebo, who disposes of the dog. For an extended discussion of how the film distinguishes between those who are disposable—human and animal—and those worth preserving, see the essays by Ravit Reichman and Colin Dayan in this volume.

25. Horton Foote, screenplay of *To Kill a Mockingbird*, 125, available at www.screenplaydb.com/film/scripts/To%20Kill%20a%20Mockingbird.pdf. All quotations from the film are taken from this source.

26. "David Cameron's Munich Speech on Multiculturalism," *YouTube*, February 5, 2011, www.youtube.com/watch?v=VsGQvOq8cEs.

CHAPTER SEVEN

Dead Animals

R AVIT R EICHMAN

No cards, no weapons, no property, no rights, no dignity . . .
like a dog.

J. M. Coetzee, *Disgrace*

I do not like your utopia, if there be no dogs.

H. G. Wells, *A Modern Utopia*

In its very title, *To Kill a Mockingbird* announces a broad concern with animal life, and, more precisely, with the human relationship to animals.[1] It
is not yet a fully realized statement—not yet a command about how to kill
or not to kill, nor a description of where or why one might see such killing
or how to prevent it. One has to wait to see this relationship articulated,
and the enigmatic phrase hangs over the film until Atticus Finch explains
to his son, Jem, the proper targets for shooting a gun. Recalling the time
when his father had given him his first gun, Atticus reflects: "He told me
that I should never point at anything in the house, and that he'd rather I
shoot at tin cans in the backyard. But he said that sooner or later, he supposed, the temptation to go after birds'd be too much. And that I could
shoot all of the blue jays I wanted, if I could hit 'em. But to remember it
was a sin to kill a mockingbird." When Jem asks why, Atticus, seeming a
little unsure himself, muses: "Well, I reckon because mockingbirds don't
do anything but make music for us to enjoy. Don't eat people's gardens,
don't nest in the corncribs. They don't do one thing but just sing their
hearts out for us."[2]

The preciousness and precariousness of a being that serves a singularly
ornamental purpose furnishes the film (and the book) with a model for

a life that is sacrosanct, one that must be kept outside the bounds of violence not only because it ushers beauty into the world but also because it
does not figure in any causal chain. It threatens neither livelihood nor life,
and so does not need to be anyone's object of redress or retaliation. And
this retaliation, the question of just deserts and what does or does not
count as just violence, constitutes the film's driving force, a logic under
which it operates and that extends from its depictions of struggles in the
courtroom to those on the playground. Embedded in this logic is that of
cause and effect: every action in the film might be seen as producing its
equally unsettling and tragic reaction. Thus Mayella Ewell's unfounded
charge of rape against Tom Robinson leads to his wrongful conviction in
court; Robinson's attempted escape from prison ends with his being shot
and killed; Atticus's confrontation with Bob Ewell spurs Ewell's attack
on Jem and Scout and precipitates Ewell's own death. For every action, a
reaction.

The novel's opening (in contrast to the film's), too, asserts this logic
as the very basis from which the grown Scout narrates these months of
her childhood. She begins by insisting that everything that happened had
been, first and foremost, the Ewells' fault; Jem objects, locating the cause
in Dill's insistence on seeing the reclusive, terrifying Boo Radley. Sensing
the bottomless search for the story's prime mover, the grown Scout ups
the ante: "I said if he wanted to take a broad view of the thing, it really
began with Andrew Jackson. If General Jackson hadn't run the Creeks
up the creek, Simon Finch would never have paddled up the Alabama,
and where would we be if he hadn't?"[3] The story of these crucial months
in Scout's and Jem's lives thus emerges against the more epic backdrop of
a family's American story, a history of slavery and power (Simon Finch
was a successful fur trader) and the violent elimination of an indigenous
population at the hands of white settlers.

Such causal chains, however, are not always portrayed directly in the
film, where instances of physical brutality—the effects of injustice, the
causes of more injustice—most often occur offscreen. Given this tenden-
cy, the most explicit scene of violence in *To Kill a Mockingbird* is not what
viewers might expect. In a film about racial violence and racial injustice
culminating in the tragic death of Tom Robinson, depictions of violence
remain largely outside the cinematic frame. This is not to say, of course,
that *To Kill a Mockingbird* isn't rent by violence at every turn. On the

contrary: violence always seems to be on the brink of explosion, its force about to break through the surface of encounters like the one between Atticus Finch and Bob Ewell after Tom Robinson's death. Ewell, still seething with rage at what he sees as Atticus's act of racial treason, spits in Atticus's face, and the audience holds its breath in anticipation of a retaliation that never comes. Instead, Atticus produces a handkerchief, wipes his face, and steps around Ewell as one might move aside to avoid a puddle or a pile of rubbish.

If retaliation arrives, its fullest portrayal may well come in the shadowy scene toward the end of the film when Ewell attacks Jem and Scout as they walk home through the woods on Halloween. The children are saved by the uncanny and well-timed appearance of Boo Radley, and Ewell is killed in the ensuing struggle. There is one scene, however, that does not appear to fit into this chain, a scene whose violence seems to have no be-fore and no after. This unassimilable moment occurs about one-third of the way through the film, when Atticus is called home by Calpurnia, the family's housekeeper, to deal with a rabid dog. The mad dog episode im-mediately follows the scene in which Atticus comforts Scout after a less than promising first day at school; everything has gone wrong, she sobs, and she does not want to go back. Ever compassionate, Atticus instructs his daughter on the importance of empathy, urging her to see things from her teacher's perspective. "You never really understand a person until you consider things from his point of view," he counsels. Asking her if she knows what a compromise means ("Bending the law?" Scout asks), he strikes one with her: if she goes back to school, he will continue reading to her before bed each night. Young Scout accepts the deal, and as the scene fades out, her adult voice reflects, "There just didn't seem to be anyone or anything Atticus couldn't explain."

It is from within this context of explanation that I propose to under-stand what happens next. For in what follows, the notion of a rational world, where discussion and compromises prevail, sets the stage for—and is violently shattered by—the mad dog scene. The comfort of a father's gentle reasoning, dispensed in the dim evening glow, dissolves in the harsh exterior light as Jem and Scout catch sight of the dog, and Calpur-nia, quickly appraising the situation, ushers them into the house. Expla-nation gives way to action when Atticus and Sheriff Tate pull up seconds later. It is perhaps the fastest sequence of events in the film, particularly given the pace of life in Maycomb, where, as Scout observes in voice-over in the opening shots, "There was no hurry, for there was nowhere to go." Sheriff Tate implores Atticus ("the best shot in this county," it turns out) to handle the matter; Atticus takes the gun, aims, and fires. The dog, seen from a distance, seems as surprised as the Finch children, his legs shooting out and up from underneath him in clumsy, near-slapstick fashion. His grunts and growls are interrupted by the sound of the gun firing, then replaced by the car engine's metallic rumbling.

One can make a case, to be sure, for this scene's instrumentality: it does, after all, prove the point that Atticus will go to great lengths to protect what is dearest to him, just as it proves that he is a good shot and gains him the admiration of his children, who thought his sole talents lay in his ability to explain things or to draw up an airtight will. But what if we were to think of this scene differently, and to understand it not as a moment that proves a point but as one that is, significantly, pointless? I propose to examine the mad dog episode in this light, as a scene that proves nothing to both viewers and characters and undermines the film's more explicit message of justice. Like the cigar box full of trinkets in the film's opening credits or the mockingbird of its title, it is ornamental, serving no practical purpose other than to adorn—but to do so in ugly, unsettling fashion. What it adorns, and what it mars in doing so, is the *nomos* of *To Kill a Mockingbird*, remaining as an ugly stain or residue that the film's normative and explanatory universe cannot absorb. It is the moment in the film that remains unarticulated. "There just didn't seem to be anyone or anything Atticus couldn't explain"—except this act, in which Atticus, defender of reason and tolerance, is seen for the first and only time shooting to kill.

Consider, in this regard, the moment when Atticus first sets eyes on the dog. Where one might expect a rabid dog to rush at anyone in its path, this one, viewed from a distance, seems to be bounding playfully, making no attempt to approach Atticus or the children. If the dog is indeed dangerous, the film's portrayal of him does little to make this case. The judgment as to whether or not the animal is fit to live, however, has already been made, and at least as far as the adults are concerned, there is no time to waste. The act is quick, very nearly surgical, and accomplished from a safe distance. But from the child's point of view, which is also, in generous measure, the film's, it is less clear that the incident unfolded in just fashion, that what happened is what had to happen. This less convinced point of view takes shape in Jem's expression, which registers not only admiration but also horror and perplexity. Even Atticus cannot help but notice that his son is anything but relieved when Jem asks, "Atticus?" "Yes, son?" Atticus replies. Jem's answer makes plain that there is something inarticulable about this moment of violence, that the feelings or problems it raises for him have not yet risen to the level of a question he can pose cogently. "Nothing," he answers, shuttering the conversation. In the novel, this exchange is twice repeated, as if to underline the urgency of Jem's unasked question and the conversation that never takes place, ebbing instead into the complex stretch of silence between father and son.

There is a lot at stake, I submit, in this "Nothing." What it contains— what we believe it might contain—may begin with an unsettling feeling that perhaps the dog is still, in spite of its fearsome appearance to Calpurnia, less defensible than the gun-wielding person. The book, indeed, makes this explicit in its description of the children's confusion as to whether or not the dog was aggressive or merely "looking for a place to die." Atticus's arrival on the scene is preceded in the novel by discussions about the dog's condition, whether he was sick or dying or confused. Jem's silence figures, too, as a rejoinder to his own loud protests in the film's opening, when he refuses to come down from his tree house because Atticus will not play football for the Methodists. "Every time I want him to do something he's too old. He's too old for anything!" he complains. "He won't let me have a gun, and he'll only play touch football with me—never tackle." If Atticus's killing of the mad dog proves Jem wrong, it does so with a force and cruelty far from the controlled violence of a football game. Jem here gets exactly what he has wanted: a father who is "game," who is not too old after all. It stands to reason, then, that the son cannot help but be in awe of his father after witnessing this feat of marksmanship. Indeed, the book makes this clear when Jem, who "sat in numb confusion" (111) moments after the shooting, finds his words at last. "'D you see him, Scout?" he exclaims. "'D you see him just standin' there? . . . 'n' all of a sudden he just relaxed all over, an' it looked like that gun was part of him . . . an' he did it so quick, like. . . . I hafta aim for ten minutes 'fore I can hit somethin'" (111).

Yet Jem's admiration here, the fact that the too-old father has redeemed himself in his son's eyes, tells only part of the story. For it is hard to discern, at the beginning of this statement, whether Jem refers to the dog or to Atticus: "'D you see him just standin' there? . . . 'n' all of a sudden he just relaxed all over." This confusion becomes all the more plausible when we recall that in the novel, the dog has a name: Tim Johnson. Tim Johnson belonged to one of the town locals, Mr. Harry Johnson, and by the novel's account the dog was "the pet of Maycomb" (105). This is no random, outside threat, in other words, but a familiar animal—and, I would add, an ornamental one. Tim Johnson's value, like the mockingbird's, derives not from any useful contribution to the community around him but from his place as a nonessential, non-instrumental creature in the fabric of life in the town.

And even if the dog, unnamed and ownerless in the film, appears onscreen as both unfamiliar and dangerous, the efficiency with which Atticus dispatches him sets the incident apart from his more common meditative postures. This one, in contrast, is all action—reflexive rather than reflective, guided by external circumstances rather than internal logic. Its muteness, driven home by sounds (the dog's growl, the gunshot, the car's engine) rather than words and punctuated, finally, by Jem's "Nothing," leaves behind a fog of irresolution. Something is missing—a conversation, but also a quality, character, or condition. What we do not find here, as elsewhere, is the condition of self-consciousness, which is necessary for justice but problematic for heroism.

I will have more to say about this missing self-consciousness momentarily, but for now it is enough to note that its absence becomes all the more glaring when we consider it alongside the (foreclosed) possibility of mourning in this scene. For it is not inconceivable that Jem's "Nothing" also contains the possibility of an inexplicable and unrequited need to grieve for the life of this dog, this pet—and the realistic recognition that such grief would not be recognized under the circumstances. In Judith Butler's examination of how we come to value (and recognize) some lives over others, this need might be said to exist beyond the film's frame, and thus cannot be considered a genuine loss. "How do our cultural frames for thinking the human set limits on the kinds of losses we can *avow* as loss?" she asks. "After all, if someone is lost, and that person is not someone, then what and where is the loss, and how does mourning take place?"[4] Butler's focus on human life and the ways it is made not-human and thus ungrievable already sets animal life outside the bounds of its concerns. But the cultural frames through which we come to understand which lives count and which can be expended often turn precisely on finely drawn distinctions between human and animal life, distinctions that can be difficult to maintain and that, if we account for them, reveal to us the animality of human life.

The human animal: that nonverbal but sentient being whose existence marks the spot of *To Kill a Mockingbird*'s ethical core by calling for the protection of a society's most vulnerable members. And by vulnerable, the film's narrative also means ornamental: thus mockingbirds, as Atticus explains, must be protected because "they don't do anything"; they make music, add beauty, but do nothing else. Doing nothing, saying nothing—in a strange and uncanny way, "nothing" comes to designate those occasions in the film that call for an ethical response that has yet to be acknowledged or formulated. "Nothing" tells us that there is something inarticulable, something we can't quite say but that we might reckon—as Atticus puts it in explaining the prohibition against killing mockingbirds ("Well, I reckon because . . .")—demands our moral scrutiny. These moments in the film unfold through speechlessness and sentience, and the pain or perplexity they inflict exists in proportion to how little can be said about that pain or perplexity: the less said, the more suffered. It is thus that the ornamental animal, the film's embodied "nothing"—without speech but with great feeling—exposes how nearly impossible it is to keep *To Kill a Mockingbird*'s ethical core intact, to explain away its arbitrariness (as in the arbitrary injunction against killing beautiful things), and to clarify its constitutive role in a community.

Nothing Happened

The exposure I have described amounts to a falling silent in the face of the problem of who deserves to die, and more specifically the way killing does or does not serve a community. In the case of Tom Robinson's death, such killing is a clear instance of wrong, an example of the law's collusion with racism and of Robinson's own sense of futility before the law; he flees, presumably, because he has no hope that his appeal will reverse his sentence. Atticus's shooting of the mad dog, in contrast, does not trouble the film's moral landscape, both because the dog is presumed to be rabid and because its killer is also the film's agent of justice.

Lest the incident trouble anyone other than Jem, the film frames the scene—or, more accurately, brackets it—in a way that insulates the narrative from its potentially unsettling effect. If the narrative traffics by turns in southern gothic and family romance, the mad dog episode, in odd contrast, stands out as more in line with the western, defined by a stretch of dusty road and dueling opponents. In the face of a perceived threat, the family retreats into the relative safety of the house. (In the novel, the street grinds to a halt as everyone takes shelter indoors, peering out of their windows at the unfolding drama.) The scene boils down to the dirt road separating the hero and his rival, who ambles (or, more precisely, weaves) toward the community that the hero has been charged with protecting.

Staged as a duel, the scene builds its tension not around dialogue but around the silence that precedes a quick draw. And this silence, too, reminds us that what is about to take place is not about seeing but about taking aim: the animal at the other end of the street is neither the "pet of Maycomb" nor a sick animal but a target. What is more, he is a target who can be seen properly only from a distance, a fact underlined (to near-comic effect) in Atticus's adjustment and readjustment of his eyeglasses. Ever the bespectacled thinking man (the ideal citizen, the noble lawyer), he appears not to know what to do with his glasses, pushing them onto his forehead and finally letting them fall to the ground. (In the novel, the point is pressed further when they break at his feet.) The comic potential of such clumsiness does more than counterbalance the sniper's precision that comes into play seconds later. It is as though Atticus does not quite know how he wants to see this moment, cannot reconcile it with the perspective he usually accords the objects of his gaze—the legal case, the ethical dilemma, the human subject.

And then there is the problem of Atticus as himself a human subject, visible from the dog's perspective. If the dog is a target from Atticus's vantage, it is unclear (and indeed questionable) whether the same perception holds true at dog level. Yet the film, in a strange cut, seems for a split second to care about this perspective, reversing the shot to position Atticus in the dog's field of vision. The long shot lasts for little more than a few seconds, just enough to interrupt the scene's flow by installing Atticus, however briefly, as a human figure whose status—friend or foe?—has yet to be determined. He is simply too far away, his face and manner indiscernible, the action he is about to take wholly unpredictable from the dog's point of view. Atticus recognizes the danger posed by the dog because the law, in the person of Sheriff Tate, names it for him ("He's got it all right," Heck

Tate pronounces). This reverse long shot would seem to drive home the fact that no such naming or recognition exists for the dog, raising the possibility that the animal might just be more victim than threat—a doomed creature who cannot, from such a distance, anticipate or defend against his own death. If there is room for pity or regret (or, what is more, empathy) in this sequence, it is here, in the shot that makes literal Atticus's advice to see something from another's view.

This is not, however, a subject position that the film indulges for very long, and the lighthearted, Coplandesque music that closes the scene ushers us out of a darker view of the shooting by marking it as sport. What has just taken place amounts, in effect, to "nothing" when its end is accompanied by buoyant strings and playful flute. In a strangely protective way, the film seems to proceed as though the episode never happened. Severed from the rest of the narrative generically (as a western), its gravitas undercut by the optimism of its closing music (in the spirit of a western), it sinks into cinematic quicksand, a fleeting bubble that goes unrecognized either as a genuine loss or as an experience of ethical or personal struggle. As Butler observes in the context of lives that do not count in a public narrative: "None of this takes place on the order of the event. None of this takes place. In the silence of the newspaper, there was no event, no loss, and this failure of recognition is mandated through an identification with those who identify with the perpetrators of that violence."[5] In the novel, the whole episode is sworn to secrecy, as though swallowed by the novel itself. "Don't say anything about it, Scout," Jem implores (112). The command is his way of respecting and replicating his father's own silence about his distinction as Maycomb's dead shot. One doesn't shoot with such perfect aim, after all, without a good deal of practice, and Miss Maudie reveals to the children that Atticus had been an apt pupil in this regard: "If he shot fifteen times and hit fourteen doves he'd complain about wasting ammunition" (112). What lingers at the end of this scene, then, and what characterizes its silence might be understood as a sense of shame over a past characterized by casual violence, of killing as sport rather than as painful necessity. It makes sense, in this light, that the film does not show the dog's removal and even places the body beyond its frame. In the scene's final shot, Jem, his arms wrapped around a pole as though reaching for support, gazes into the distance to a point outside the frame where the dog's body lies. The field of vision, like the conversation that never takes place, is cut short here—imagined, perhaps, through Jem's eyes but unrealized on the screen.

What lies beyond the frame still lingers, a negative afterimage that *To Kill a Mockingbird*, like Jem, does not assimilate. But if the film cannot assimilate, it can at least dispose. The dialogue briefly notes what will happen to the body when Sheriff Tate remarks that he'll send Zeebo, Maycomb's garbage collector (and Calpurnia's son), to clean up the body. The novel, however, gives this moment slightly more thickness: "We saw Zeebo drive up. He took a pitchfork from the back of the garbage truck and gingerly lifted Tim Johnson. He pitched the dog onto the truck, then poured something from a gallon jug on and around the spot where Tim fell" (112). What moves here seems to be the work of one word, "gingerly," which I read not as a sign of Zeebo's caution, an indication that he fears becoming infected, but in its sense of "gently" or "delicately." It indicates that some measure of care is being taken—for the community (which requires that Zeebo sanitize the "infected" spot) and for the dog, who seems, in an oblique way, to be receiving here a kind of last rite. In its simplicity, Zeebo's gesture manages to evoke the tension that the film sidesteps, a friction between one's actions and one's feelings about those actions. It suggests, in other words, that protecting the community by shooting Tim Johnson is far from incompatible with feeling grief over the death of a loved animal. In the act of disposal, Zeebo pays his respects to this once beloved pet, handling him with care even as he treats his body as toxic. The very act that screenwriter Horton Foote disposes of in his adaptation of the novel turns out to contain the scene's greatest potential for acknowledging the complex ethical nature of killing in the name of community.

Community and Confrontation

What does it mean for this episode, the only shooting we see in the film, both to occur in speechlessness (though, as the mechanized sounds of the car's engine and the gunshot remind us, not in silence) and to be reduced to muteness—to amount, in the end, to nothing? The answer to this question, I have suggested, has to do with the murkier ethical cases, the stories with no clear moral center but with a clear set of moral concerns. In a film replete with conversation and explanation, the pockets of silence—moments of "nothing"—serve as indices of such stories in which inconsistencies or complexities cannot be fully uttered, largely because they cannot be fully grasped. From this craggier ethical terrain, the mad dog scene sets the stage for two pivotal confrontations still to come: the jailhouse standoff between Atticus and the lynch mob, and later, Mayella Ewell's outburst on the stand during Atticus's cross-examination. Both of these moments take shape not in what is spoken but in what is left unsaid, and both expose the nerve endings of an ethical landscape that cannot be neatly fitted into the film's normative contours.

When Atticus faces the lynch mob as he stands guard at the jail where Tom Robinson is being held, he does so not with a shotgun but with a law book (a newspaper in the novel). The men make clear that no amount of law or reason will compel them to disperse; Sheriff Tate is nowhere in sight, and Atticus is but a body in the way of their target. But Atticus's secret weapon, which surprises even him, turns out to be his daughter, who dissolves the scene's tension by addressing the only familiar face in the crowd:

> Hey, Mr. Cunningham. I said, Hey, Mr. Cunningham. How's your entailment gettin' along? Don't you remember me, Mr. Cunningham? I'm Jean Louise Finch. You brought us some hickory nuts one morning. Remember? We had a talk. I went and got my daddy to come out and thank you. I go to school with your boy. I go to school with Walter. He's a nice boy. Tell him "hey" for me, won't you? You know somethin', Mr. Cunningham? Entailments are bad. Entailments . . . Atticus, I was just sayin' to Mr. Cunningham that entailments were bad, but not to worry. It takes a long time sometimes.

If Walter Cunningham Sr. is exposed here for the poor man that he is, his reaction to Scout's address—he orders the men to disperse—suggests something deeper than his own humiliation. It speaks, too, to the delicate interdependence of all the citizens of Maycomb, whatever their politics. The aggressor turns away in this moment because this mutual dependence complicates what he had sought to accomplish, dissolving his affiliation with the mob and its racism by reminding him of another connection to which is he also bound and obligated.

The existence or nature of this connection, however, will remain unspoken, a subject unfit for conversation in any context other than that of a child's naïve attempt at communication. Mr. Cunningham will say nothing about it, for his family's reputation—which Scout had complained of

to Atticus after her unfortunate first day of school—is one of fierce in-
dependence even in the worst of circumstances. "Everybody knows Cunninghams won't take nothin' from nobody," she protests in defense of her
unsuccessful attempt to tell her teacher why young Walter had refused the
woman's offer of a quarter.

Taking nothing, saying nothing: the unspoken here brings us to the
vexed question of class, an issue that shapes the social world of Maycomb
but that should not, ideally, have a hand in determining weightier questions of justice. Pulsing just beneath the surface of the film's racial tensions,
the problem of class lays bare an ethical dimension that the film can't fully
address: that the town's racists also happen to be its poor. This is not to say
that characters like Walter Cunningham or the Ewells should be exoner-
ated for their actions because of their place on the socioeconomic ladder.
But it nonetheless raises the complicated dimension of class in *To Kill a
Mockingbird*, skimming but never settling on the ways in which the narrative's ethical world is built atop an economic one. This experience, in
which Atticus emerges—rightly, but not simply—as the moral superior of
Walter Cunningham and his like, might be understood as a power relation
in which kindness and compassion hover just at the border of condescen-
sion. Thus Atticus graciously accepts Cunningham's offer of hickory nuts
in return for legal services as though he regularly takes his payment in
that form. Yet the gesture of kindness also creates the conditions of moral
indebtedness—and it is this subtler, harder-to-articulate form of debt that
sets the terms for what happens in front of the town's jail.

The power relations that animate the jailhouse standoff hew closer to
the surface of Mayella Ewell's testimony in court. Atticus has just made
short work of her story, exposing it for the lie that it is: the inconsistencies
of her account suggest that it is not Tom Robinson who had beaten her
but her own father. Backed into a corner, Mayella recoils, issuing her last
statement in the form of a seething accusation: "I got somethin' to say an'
then I ain't gonna say no more. He took advantage of me. An' if you fine
fancy gentlemen ain't gonna do nothin' about it then you're just a bunch of
yellow stinkin' cowards, the whole bunch of you. And your fancy airs don't
come to nothin'—your ma'amin' and Miss Mayellin' don't come to nothin',
Mr. Finch—n-n . . ." With the last "nothing" still on her lips, she breaks
down and rushes from the stand, her answer to Atticus's question ("Do you
want to tell us what really happened?") made manifest in her now empty

chair. (In the novel, her silence is underlined further: "She was as good as her word. She answered no more questions, even when Mr. Gilmer tried to get her back on the track" [214].) The many "nothings" of Mayella's reproach to Atticus and the jury, those "fancy gentlemen" who treat her with a studied politeness that smacks of disdain, certainly differ in tone from Jem's "Nothing" in the mad dog episode; they are, after all, not questions but claims lobbed in last-ditch defense. But whether question or curse, these moments reverberate to make a similar point: there are some things that can't be discussed in Maycomb because they can't be fully explained.

In broad strokes, the scenes at the jail and in court might begin to look something like the mad dog shooting: in both, Atticus faces an enemy who threatens the community, and both times he emerges triumphant. But what the lynch mob and courtroom incidents reveal is the imbricated nature of community in Maycomb, where everyone—good or bad, poor or poorer—is bound to one another in ways that make it very difficult, literally or metaphorically, to shoot. Mayella's breakdown in court may be justified, but it is hard not to feel, as Tom Robinson does, some shred of pity for this woman so blinded by hatred, wounded by abuse, and enlisted in the service of her community's racism.

Like Jem's "Nothing," Cunningham's silence and Mayella's repeated "nothin'" open up, in brief but undeniable ways, a parallel itinerary alongside *To Kill a Mockingbird*'s story of racial injustice. The ethical problems raised by these moments of nothing expand but also contort the film's moral universe, forcing it through a palpable if unspoken sense of the power dynamics, class relations, and ultimately shame that underwrite a normative world. If these dimly lit regions remain perpetually in obscurity, it is perhaps because the self-consciousness that could illuminate them is strangely missing—strangely, I suggest, because the narrative's first-person narration, its nostalgic look back, would seem to promise precisely this self-conscious stance. In the final turn of this essay I consider, by way of comparison, how this introspective account, this accounting, might have looked otherwise.

Safe Distance and Close Range: Atticus via Orwell

If the mad dog episode gestures toward *To Kill a Mockingbird*'s blind spots, I want now to bring these shaded regions to light through another

text, George Orwell's "Shooting an Elephant" (1936). Orwell's essay offers a first-person account of an English police officer (arguably Orwell
himself) in Burma who is called to shoot an elephant in a nearby village.
In its structural parallels, the narrative echoes some of the mad dog scene's
signal elements: the summons, the shooting, the dying animal, and the
wider context of race relations. Where it diverges, however, we find the
negative spaces of *To Kill a Mockingbird,* specifically its missing subjectivity—a tremor of equivocation, a hint of regret to temper the efficiency
with which Atticus hits his mark.

The narrator of "Shooting an Elephant," a white official in a colonial
world, knows he is not the most popular man in town—a police officer
rarely is—and hates his work for exposing him on a daily basis to the
seamy underside of empire. When he is summoned to deal with an elephant that has run wild, he finds himself trailed by a large group of villagers, the very people who pay him so little respect and who now follow
him in their eagerness to see the drama unfold. Their presence, rather than
any danger posed by the animal, changes his sense of the situation. "I had
no intention of shooting the elephant," he declares initially, but the more
he becomes aware of his audience, the more his original intention fades
from view.[6] What concerns him above all else—more than his safety, the
security of the village, the sick or healthy state of the elephant—is his
ability to keep up appearances. In a strange rehearsal of Atticus's lesson to
Scout—"You never really understand a person until you consider things
from his point of view"—Orwell's narrator seems to take up his place
in the crowd: "And suddenly I realized that I should have to shoot the
elephant after all. The people expected it of me and I had got to do it; I
could feel their two thousand wills pressing me forward, irresistibly" (239).
The last-minute addition of "irresistibly" feels awkwardly unmoored here:
were the onlookers' wills unable to resist the spectacle, or was it the narrator who could not resist acting under the weight of their gazes? The slippage implies that these subject positions have become one and the same,
that the narrator has become so identified, so irresistibly in league with
the crowd that his own will—the one that would have resisted pulling the
trigger—had become indistinguishable from theirs. His rationalization
here is as much cognitive dissonance and excuse making as it is the honest
appraisal of an individual who wants to maintain his good name (or just
avoid being ridiculed) above all else.

Whether in the form of excuse making or truth telling, we find in Orwell a virtuosic exercise in equivocation. "I knew with perfect certainty that I ought not to shoot him" (238); "I had got to shoot the elephant" (239); "I did not want to shoot the elephant" (239); "I ought to walk up to within, say, twenty-five yards of the elephant and test his behaviour" (240). As the essay unfolds convulsively through such contortions, readers are drawn ever deeper into a portrait of the self-conscious individual as antihero. It is no surprise, given the twisted path toward its foregone conclusion, to find that the killing does not go off in one clean shot. But nothing fully anticipates the protracted, agonizing, messy death that the narrator lays out in lavish detail, from the first bullet to the last:

> He neither stirred nor fell, but every line of his body had altered. He looked suddenly stricken, shrunken, immensely old, as though the frightful impact of the bullet had paralysed him without knocking him down. At last, after what seemed like a long time . . . he sagged flabbily to his knees. His mouth slobbered. An enormous senility seemed to have settled upon him. . . . At the second shot he did not collapse but climbed with desperate slowness to his feet and stood weakly upright, with legs sagging and head drooping. I fired a third time. That was the shot that did it for him. You could see the agony of it jolt his whole body and knock the last remnant of strength from his legs. (241)

What astonishes and haunts about this anthropomorphic description is the loving care the narrator takes in tracing the itinerary of the elephant's death. And this is only the beginning: there are many more shots after the first three; there is an endless stream of crimson blood, the slow, gasping breaths of the wounded animal, the pink inside of his mouth. Yet the irony of this killing, which takes place gradually and at closer and closer range, is that the narrator cannot finish what he started, taking his leave before the elephant is dead and hearing from other witnesses that the animal had gone on dying for another thirty minutes. So far-reaching is the act's impact on him that it exceeds his capacity to see it through—and to see it, period.

The contrast with the dog's quick, clean death in *To Kill a Mockingbird* could not be starker. One shot is all it takes for Atticus to finish the job, and the cleanup is no townwide affair but a one-man task delegated to Zeebo in a scene the film does not show. These surface discrepancies represent more than just incidental points of divergence; taken together, they form interlocking structures of meaning. If, as I have suggested, the mad dog scene functions as the dark, ugly ornament in *To Kill a Mockingbird*, defacing rather than beautifying its normative landscape, then Orwell's text operates as its more robust (and even darker) double. As its negative image, "Shooting an Elephant" depicts in brutal and unremitting vividness the film's counterfactual possibilities, staging the might-have-beens of the brief incident in Maycomb.

Orwell's narrative, an allegory of colonialism, is also—and this is the spirit in which I read it here—an unflinching account of the human-animal relationship as fundamental to any conception of the social or political. Its status as a *literal* story rather than as a purely metaphorical one reminds us of this relationship's violent potential, founded as much on contingency (the human *as* animal or as *not* animal) as it is on vulnerability. If *To Kill a Mockingbird* recognizes this violence in the symbolic universe of its title, it does not acknowledge it in its uglier iteration of the mad dog. The beautiful, ornamental mockingbird works metaphorically; the dog, in unsightly contrast, is not symbolic but instrumental, a matter of character exposition rather than moral acumen.

It is not enough to note that the moral questions do not arise in the film because the killing was legal (not to mention prudent), ratified by the presence of Sheriff Tate and accomplished in the interest of protecting Atticus's children. If anything, the narrator in "Shooting an Elephant" reminds us that legal justification only makes the moral questions more fraught when he invokes the law in an ungainly afterthought. "Besides," he adds in the final paragraph, "legally I had done the right thing, for a mad elephant has to be killed, like a mad dog, if its owner fails to control it" (242). He says this because he needs to say it, needs to shore up the argument against the rising tide of his own intuition, which draws the opposite conclusion when he first sets eyes on the elephant: "I watched him beating his bunch of grass against his knees, with that preoccupied grandmotherly air elephants have. It seemed to me that it would be murder to shoot him" (239–40). The difference between this self-doubt and judgment and Atticus's surefootedness might be grasped as a matter of perspective: Orwell's police officer approaches the elephant, taking him in first as an animal rather than a target. No such proximity figures in the mad dog scene, galvanized as it is by Heck Tate's charge, "Take him, Mr. Finch." Emphasizing the fact that the dog will be "taken" from a distance, Atticus spends a moment adjusting his glasses in explicit reminder that his usual perspective is to view things, whether legal documents or racists, at close range.

It is hard not to feel powerfully the double vision of this moment. For as he focuses, so he is focused on, as Jem, Scout, and Calpurnia watch him nervously from behind the screen door. In this sense he is more like Orwell's police officer than the distance between Burma and Alabama would admit, bearing some resemblance to the narrator who, by his own admission, shoots the elephant "solely to avoid looking a fool" (242). This is not to say that Atticus kills the dog simply to prove to his children that he can do more than explicate the law. But it does call to mind the British police officer's unsettling feeling of being looked at, the painful relationship between self-consciousness and brutality that frames Orwell's account. And what is Atticus Finch, indeed, if not the object of so many gazes throughout *To Kill a Mockingbird?* From the eyes that fix him in the courtroom to the curious or bewildered expressions of his children, who look to him to explain the vicissitudes of the world around them, he is perpetually being looked at. If Orwell's narrator shoots the elephant because he would become the villagers' laughingstock if he demurred, Atticus, too, has something to prove or maintain. But if there is anything beneath or behind his deft handling of the gun, it too remains at a safe distance. As his cerebral posture falls away to reveal the man of action, we come to understand that reflective or reflexive, Atticus Finch will never trip over the loose ends of his self-consciousness or ambivalence.

And this, I would venture, is hard to countenance. For it is not easy to relinquish the feeling (or is it the hope?) that someone who is looked at so often and so hard can't help but bend, like Orwell's narrator, irresistibly under the weight of scrutiny. There are certainly hints of this ambivalence in Atticus, whose first impulse, when Heck Tate asks him to shoot the dog, is to refuse ("I haven't shot a gun in years"). But when he takes the gun, his resolve is as unwavering as when he takes Tom Robinson's case: his determination is steadfast, and his aim is true. The ambivalence that warps the text of "Shooting an Elephant" but is curiously absent here is passed, it would seem, from actor to spectator, father to son, hovering like a shadow over Jem's face. Like the watch that Atticus will one day bequeath to him ("It's customary," he tells Scout earlier, "for the boy to have his father's watch"), this too is Jem's inheritance. The question remains whether he will ultimately claim it.

Undisposed Remains

"A mad elephant has to be killed, like a mad dog, if its owner fails to control it." In bringing the two animals in question together, yoking them to each other through madness and law, "Shooting an Elephant" speaks to the unresolved questions of *To Kill a Mockingbird:* How to draw the line between disposable and sacrosanct lives? How to grieve for lives—the mad dog's, Tom Robinson's, Bob Ewell's—that the law does not deem worthy of protection? The unanswerability of these questions designates the film's residue, the excess that Wai Chee Dimock finds in encounters of law and life and that gives rise to "the abiding presence—the desolation as well as the consolation—of what remains unredressed, unrecovered, non-corresponding."[7] What remains of this encounter is a scene that cannot be subsumed into the film's explanatory universe and remains, in Walter Benjamin's understanding, on the level of story rather than information. For even as it fills out Atticus's character sketch, its force issues from its inability to be fully interpreted by the narrative and moral universe that contains it. As Benjamin writes in "The Storyteller," "it is half the art of storytelling to keep a story free from explanation as one reproduces it."[8]

It should not surprise us, then, that this unresolved moment haunts the film in its final scenes. As Jem and Scout walk through the woods on Halloween night, just before they are attacked by Bob Ewell, we hear the piercing howl of a dog somewhere in the distance—an uncanny return, the unarticulated question recurring as similarly inarticulate but all too familiar animal sound. And when Jem is brought home by Boo Radley after the children are attacked in the woods, Scout speaks of him as though he were a dog himself. As Jem lies in bed, she tells Boo: "You can pet him if you want to, Mr. Arthur. He's asleep. If he was awake, he wouldn't let you."

The human animal surfaces powerfully in this moment as a figure that the film engages here as elsewhere, in the figure of the mad dog as in Tom Robinson, who, like Tim Johnson, will be shot with little ceremony or solace. In a work that imagines responsibility, precariousness, and preciousness through dead animals and also depicts our human animality, it is fitting that the final revelation concerns the humanity of its most animal-like character, Boo Radley. Boo, of course, has functioned very much like the film's rabid dog: he is the man everyone has taken to be dangerous and who, significantly, is nearly mute—a creature whose silence sets him apart from the social world. Yet he emerges in the end as *To Kill a Mockingbird*'s gentlest soul, a person of kindness and loyalty so profound that it needs no language. And emerging as such, he serves as a stark emblem, a poignant reminder, of what might be possible when judgment remains suspended and when no trigger is pulled.

In *The Open* (2004), Giorgio Agamben claims that "the decisive political conflict, which governs every other conflict, is that between the animality and the humanity of man."[9] I would suggest that this conflict animates and problematizes the *nomos* of *To Kill a Mockingbird*, pushing its ethical and normative ideals and adumbrating a political landscape in which even the most just judges cannot survive on heroics alone. Atticus Finch, in this understanding, cannot rise above—at least not for long—the violence he works so hard to temper. He is an agent of justice, but also a source of violence.[10] It is tempting, and indeed necessary, to uncouple his violence from his justice, as Atticus himself seems to want to do when he tells his children not to go near the dead dog ("He's just as dangerous dead as alive"). I read this injunction as a stark reminder of what the film won't touch, the dead animal it hopes to take out of circulation. And nothing, on the level of plot, of cause and effect, does indeed seem to follow from this scene, not even an explanation from the man who has the remarkable gift of being able to explain everything.

The Ugly Ornament

In a strange but apt resonance, *To Kill a Mockingbird*'s depiction of animal life calls to mind Josef K.'s last words in Kafka's *The Trial* (1925), uttered as he is being killed by two unnamed men: "Like a dog!" Like a dog, Josef K. receives a trial that is no trial at all: "Where was the judge he'd never seen?" he thinks moments before his murder. "Where was the high court he'd never reached?" From the strength of these piercing questions, the novel closes on a resounding note that falls simultaneously sharp and flat: "It seemed as though the shame was to outlive him."[11] The surprise element of shame where one might expect indignation or disbelief tells us something about the potential of the animal to arouse feelings that run counter to our better judgment. For even as Josef K. knows that a terrible wrong has been done to him, he nonetheless feels, quite implausibly, that he has somehow received his just deserts. Like a dog who has succumbed to a stronger master, he will slink away in disgrace. And just as implausibly, he will believe—or rather he will *make* believe (witness the clumsy contortions of the final sentence)—that the afterlife of his experience will be suffused with this shame in perpetuity.

Like *The Trial,* the mad dog episode sows the seeds of both senselessness and shame, which speak to the unsustainability of justice and, more pointedly, to the demise of language and communication. Later in the film, the indignity of unfairness will be writ large in the faces of the black spectators in court following the guilty verdict for Tom Robinson. In the mad dog scene, it is inscribed with contorted complexity in Jem's perspective alone. It thus falls in line with the irrationality, the sin, of killing the purely ornamental mockingbird, intimating that perhaps something in Jem dies too in this moment: the part of him that, as his own last name suggests, bears an affinity to the mockingbird he has been warned not to shoot. This Finch, his father's son in so many ways, marks in this instant his radical distinction from Atticus in the question that he cannot formulate. I am arguing, in other words, not that the dog operates as a figure for the mockingbird, but that the scene itself does: that it is the dark, ugly refraction of the beautiful ornament, the fine line that instructs a person to shoot this, not that.

"It seemed as though the shame was to outlive him." Kafka's closing line, I submit, echoes in unsettling fashion through the frames of *To Kill a Mockingbird.* The film's afterlife may well be this shame, made visible in the distant body of a mad dog whose killing is both deliberate and acceptable, whose killer has honed his skill over many years of shooting "acceptable" prey, and whose death cannot be narrated as anything more than an unformulated question and its heavy, perplexed afterthought: "Nothing."

NOTES

1. For treatments of the human-animal relationship, see Jacques Derrida, *The Animal That Therefore I Am,* trans. David Wills, ed. Marie-Louise Mallet (New York: Fordham University Press, 2008); Gary Steiner, *Animals and the Moral Community: Mental Life, Moral Status, and Kinship* (New York: Columbia University Press, 2008); Gary L. Francione, *Animals as Persons: Essays on the Abolition of Animal Exploitation* (New York: Columbia University Press, 2008); and Kelly Oliver, *Animal Lessons: How They Teach Us to Be Human* (New York: Columbia University Press, 2009).

2. All quotations from the film are from my own transcription.

3. Harper Lee, *To Kill a Mockingbird* (1960; New York: HarperCollins, 2006), 3, here-after cited parenthetically in the text.

4. Judith Butler, *Precarious Life: The Powers of Mourning and Violence* (London: Verso, 2004), 32.

5. Ibid., 36.

6. George Orwell, "Shooting an Elephant," in *An Age Like This, 1920–1940,* vol. 1: *Essays, Journalism, and Letters,* ed. Sonia Orwell and Ian Angus (Jaffrey, NH: David R. Godine, 2000), hereafter cited parenthetically in the text.

7. Wai Chee Dimock, *Residues of Justice: Literature, Law, Philosophy* (Berkeley: University of California Press, 1996), 6.

8. Walter Benjamin, "The Storyteller: Reflections on the Works of Nikolai Leskov," in *Illuminations,* trans. Harry Zohn, ed. and intro. Hannah Arendt (New York: Schocken, 1968), 89.

9. Giorgio Agamben, *The Open: Man and Animal* (Palo Alto: Stanford University Press, 2003), 80.

10. See in this regard Robert Cover's seminal "Violence and the Word," in *Narrative, Violence, and the Law: The Essays of Robert Cover,* ed. Martha Minow, Michael Ryan, and Austin Sarat (Ann Arbor: University of Michigan Press, 1993), 203–38.

11. Franz Kafka, *The Trial* (New York: Schocken, 1999), 231.

CHAPTER EIGHT

Humans, Animals, and Boundary Objects in Maycomb

Colin Dayan

A black dog suffered on a summer's day.
Harper Lee, *To Kill a Mockingbird*

What is an animal? What is human? What is good? What is evil? It might seem that these questions are easily answered in *To Kill a Mockingbird*, even when the bounds are permeable, when such distinctions are most threatened. There is something equivocal in Harper Lee's assumptions about human and animal, about the role of reason in making us who we are. The easy, comfortable stance granted to those who are elite, hereditarily and historically accepted members of the Maycomb County community and who quite naturally claim it as "home" is not granted to those who live on the southern edge of town, near the dump, or in "the quarters."

Although the taxonomies of the novel seem clear and its hierarchy appears obvious, there are moments in the film when the viewer becomes uncomfortably aware that the boundaries of humanity are being tested. The mad dog carries a great deal of weight in the film, even though he remains unnamed (in the book he is called Tim Johnson), is present for only a few minutes, and is seen only far in the distance, never close up. In the book Tim is described as "a liver-colored bird dog, the pet of Maycomb."[1] But the film strips the dog of belonging and identification. It also deprives him of his status as property. For who owns the dog? In the book we learn nothing about the owner, Mr. Harry Johnson, except that he drives the bus and lives somewhere on the border of town. But in the film the dog appears as a stray, not a pet. He is *res nullius;* he belongs to no one.

Here I examine how the making and management of human boundary objects, whether human or nonhuman animals, ensure the liberal beneficence of Atticus Finch and the civilized values he represents. The courtroom scenes are at the center of numerous rituals of exclusion that enforce the division between the worthy and the worthless, those put in proximity with pigs and those who live "clean" and do "right." The goodness of Atticus Finch, I suggest, depends on the project of dumping, the disregarding of persons deemed noxious to the community of well-meaning citizens— those outside the precincts of law. To be made superfluous is to be outside the pale of human empathy, and this movie frames the waste products of society in peculiarly salient ways.

Why a Dog

Only two creatures in *To Kill a Mockingbird* are disposable. Objects of disregard, they can be killed without provoking the concern of the community, without due process of law. It is as if they occupy a special terrain, doomed to be delivered to subjection or disposal without recourse. Their deaths seem necessary, legitimate, and reasonable. The unnamed dog and Bob Ewell are both killed. In a sense, they are both nuisances—and ferocious: the dog maddened by rabies and Ewell rabid with hatred.

In the novel Scout's words raise the unsettling possibility that the dog might not be "mad" but just a threat, not suffering from rabies but "sick," not foaming from the mouth, not leaping or lunging, but just, in Jem's words, "lookin' for a place to die."[2] In the film the dog appears out of nowhere, barking, moving down the street in a bizarre combination of wobbling and bounding. Thin and scruffy, his ribs noticeable even though the camera (like the gun that will kill him) keeps far away, the dog remains forever in the distance, even as he comes closer, causing terror to Calpurnia, Scout, and Jem. But Atticus is not afraid, and though Sheriff Heck Tate knows what must be done, he cannot do it. So Atticus raises his rifle, looks through the scope, takes off his glasses, and shoots the dog dead. Although what I call the dog fable takes up nearly seven pages in the book, in the film only a couple of minutes are needed to make the points required: Atticus is not feeble but strong; the police power when accompanied by legal nobility (in the person of Atticus) can exterminate any threat to communal health and safety. So the mad dog is not only a metaphor for unreasoning race hatred, an incurable disease, but also a warning of what *can* be done away with by the man *too good* to miss a shot, who is also *so good* that he will shoot only when necessary.

But there is more. The dog fable is presented in the film as nothing less than a ritual encounter, a ceremony nearly sacred in its controlled violence. The formal killing scene and the jaunty music that follows it press upon us a question: Why does Heck Tate refuse to shoot the dog? The explicit reason is that he fears missing, since he is not as good a shot as Atticus. But why did Harper Lee put the responsibility for exterminating an allegedly mad dog not in the hands of the law but in the hands of a citizen who happens to be a lawyer? Would it be too overstated to urge our recognition of this scene as a frank confrontation with the notoriety of white privilege and its entwinement with the law? I grant this killing representation a materiality, an ethnographic intensity. Once violence is authorized, it can never be impermissible or illegal. I want to stake a lot on the survival of law in and as ritual. The dogged insistence on the *already done that must be redone* accounts for the legal ritual's power, both sacred and civil. Ritual, after all, in its repetitions and apparently intense ordinariness can make the exceptional commonplace. Here, the killing ritual is about power, and is itself to be read as more or less political.[3]

Once the job is done, Atticus warns his children: "Don't go near that dog. . . . [H]e's just as dangerous dead as alive."[4] When I was younger, years ago, I wondered after seeing this film for the first time what Atticus meant. How could a dead dog be dangerous? But I'm getting ahead of my story. For now, to put this crudely but precisely: the threat of contagion does not die with the dog. That night Atticus takes a trip to the edge of town, out to the black quarters, to talk to Helen Robinson about her husband, Tom, who will be tried for the rape of a white woman, Mayella Ewell, the next day. Scout and Jem stay in the car as he walks into Helen Robinson's cabin. Out of the dark woods comes another image of viciousness, the stooped figure and glowering face of Bob Ewell, who presses close up to the car, looking in at the children. A black boy stands on the other side. He has come to see and perhaps talk to Jem. Their greeting is implicit though never spoken, and Jem asks him to tell Atticus to come outside. At the sight of Atticus, Ewell speaks, this time with hate and disdain: "Nigger lover" is all he says.[5] He has said it before, the first time that he confronted Atticus in the courthouse. In the novel, these words are repeated by schoolchildren and respectable ladies, as well as those considered "white trash," since racism seems to be a disease endemic to Maycomb. But in the film, Ewell, like the dog, is singled out for disposal.

Regulatory policies and the police power that accompanies them always resurface. If a dog is a stray, the state has the right to unleash familiar practices of discrimination and violence.[6] The summary disposal of dogs branded as "dangerous," "vicious," "offensive," or a "threat" to the public can be traced to early common law and later to the range of police measures instituted ostensibly to protect community interests. Dogs are liable to extermination if their presence signals disturbance or danger, even if they themselves are not dangerous. A dog without a license faced death by gunshot or beating not just from the officials entitled to destroy any threat to the public welfare but from anyone.[7] Let us take dogs, then, to stand in for a bridge—the bridge that joins persons to things, both in our law and legal concepts and in the real world of our daily lives. The continuity is there, and dogs form the bridge. The bridge is what matters, the connectivity between gradations of personhood.

Law was always influential in shaping a new understanding of the relation between dogs and humans. Judges were called upon to pass judgment on dogs, as well as on fugitive slaves and civilly dead prisoners. As I describe in *The Law Is a White Dog*, by the 1890s tort cases began to describe, evaluate, and judge the limits of canine injury and death. When can a dog offensive to humankind be legally killed? And what is the nature of the offense? In *Brown v. Carpenter* (1854), the Supreme Court of Vermont decided that there was no remedy for killing a dog if it was known to growl and jump on people, for "such a dog is *hostis communis,* the common enemy, and may be killed by any one." Other cases were cited to demonstrate that such a dog must be treated "as an outlaw and a common nuisance, liable to destruction." An appellate case in Kentucky did not spare even harmless dogs that wandered into a neighbor's yard without their master: "Even though it be for the propagation of his species, his innocence is no protection to him. . . . [H]is life is forfeited, if the owner of the premises on which he is found will exact the penalty, and chooses to execute the sentence."[8]

What is at stake here? Let me stress that the language of threat and re-moval, used to warn against vicious dogs, also applied to humans deemed offensive or harmful: vagrants, criminals, or fight-crazy, lecherous, and dirty outcasts like Ewell. After the dog fable, Ewell's appearance leads us into the terrain of the degraded, but this personality composed of bad hygiene and immorality is in the fiction of *To Kill a Mockingbird* noth-ing more than a stray. We watch how this stray becomes criminal, and fully human: filled with intent and with a look in his eyes that gives him the fullness of malice, a vessel replete with *mens rea*. After the trial of Tom Robinson, Ewell is out of control, and out of bounds. In the film, he leaves his defined area out there behind the dump in Old Sarum and twice comes to town, first when he comes to court, and, ultimately, when he attempts to kill Scout and Jem as they walk home from the Halloween pageant at the school auditorium. Crossing the dark woods right past the schoolyard, they hear sounds; a dog howls—"an old dog"[9]—and Ewell tries to kill them. They are saved by Boo Radley, who kills Ewell, though they don't know that at the time. Atticus wants to be honest, to turn Boo over to the authorities. After all, he just murdered a man. But the sheriff persuades him to lie, to say that Ewell was responsible for his own death: "Bob Ewell fell on his knife. He killed himself."[10]

No one will care enough to doubt the story, and Heck Tate and Atticus Finch, even Scout, know this. When we watch the film, we are relieved that a crazed attacker has been killed. But we are also complicit in another kind of relief, and our acceptance of the story is unnerving, even sad. We are glad that a vengeful racist gets his comeuppance, especially when he stands in for the white southerners who threatened, tortured, and lynched blacks or anyone else who fought for their rights in the Jim Crow South. We feel that the death of the innocent Tom Robinson, shot dead by pris-on guards as he allegedly tried to escape, has been redeemed by the death of the man responsible for the whole sordid drama of lies, accusation, and undeserved punishment. As Heck Tate puts it: "There's a black man dead for no reason, and now the man responsible for it is dead. Let the dead bury the dead."[11]

But once we put the mad dog slaying in proximity with the quiet dis-patch of this evil human entity, we understand that the logic of elimi-nation, brute or refined, also tells a history of value and disregard. This history crosses species. It reshuffles our conceptual schemes, the paired

paradigmatic sets that usually oppose each other: necessity and sponta-
neity, body and mind, animality and humanity. The killing of animals, as
Reviel Netz reminds us in his remarkable *Barbed Wire: An Ecology of Modernity*, is never without effects on the life of humans.[12] And in this film,
the shooting of the dog prepares us, both figuratively and literally, for the
knifing of the man. The dog, like the man—acceptable when domesticated
but cast out when wild—is sacrificed to a social picture that depends for
its meaning on the division between a polite, rational world and a violent,
savage one. Yet the division does not hold, since the violence of reason,
though masked, is equal in its effects to that of unreason. This becomes
a question of ethics as well as of politics. Dog and human are killed as
threats. But we know now in the twenty-first century that entitlement to
destroy and permission to disregard are not always acceptable or desirable.
The engines of control, once systematized and embedded in human affairs, can be applied anywhere and to anyone. No matter if the destruction
is "humane" or "enlightened." Where do we draw the line? What Jacques
Derrida famously called the "sacrificial current in the Cartesian *cogito*"
and Giorgio Agamben recognized as *homo sacer*, he who can be killed
with impunity, "who may be killed and yet not sacrificed," becomes in the
moral discrimination of Maycomb County the legitimate, even desirable
ostracism of the useless.[13]

Right before he shoots the dog, Atticus gives Scout and Jem a lesson
in firearms that his father taught him when he gave Atticus his first gun.
The lesson is really about who or what can be rightfully or rightly or rationally killed. Just like a mad dog or a crazed, no-good Tom Ewell, blue
jays could be freely eliminated—"I could shoot all the blue jays I wanted,
if I could hit them," says Atticus—but never a mockingbird: "It is a sin to
kill a mockingbird." He explains the distinction: "Well, I reckon because
mockingbirds don't do anything but make music for us to enjoy. They
don't eat people's gardens, don't nest in the corncribs, they don't do one
thing but sing their hearts out for us."[14] The ethical life for Atticus is one
of control, exclusion, choice, and status. So blue jays are entitled to no
regard and protection, while mockingbirds are valuable. They are worthwhile and hence superior to blue jays because they do nothing but serve
humans, pleasuring us with their song.

If we take the shooting of the dog as central to the meaning, to the
scope of violence and civility in the film, then we can understand why

the screenwriter, Horton Foote, put this conversation right before that scene. The stigma associated with certain breeds of dogs demands legal fictions that recall an older, enchanted world where voiceless and pre-sumably mindless things were first personified and then surrendered, for-feited, exterminated. The indeterminate breed of dog in this film helps us to understand how old forms of brutality can be transfigured. As I have argued more than once, only with dogs before us and beside us can we understand the making and unmaking of persons—and certify what kinds of creatures are too diseased to live.

Throughout the film, while we assume we're watching a good and he-roic Atticus Finch stand tall for equality in a racist and class-bound Ala-bama town, we are also shown, again and again, how to judge, when to ignore, and whom or what to loathe. We are prompted, again and again, to distinguish between the valuable and the worthless. Our safe assumptions about such distinctions become an invitation to act as if there is—or could be—a place of moral purity. The film does not merely celebrate privilege or whiteness. Rather, it makes its drama work in homage to the confines of the civil, or, more precisely, to the meaning of belonging to the polite society of Maycomb.

Social acceptance and valuation are the tools of damage. This is, sur-prisingly, a cruel world, though its inhabitants—whether old ladies, black maids, curious children, or the forces of law and order—do not intend to be cruel. Harper Lee insisted on the good intentions of those blinded by tradition, snobbery, or flat-out racial prejudice. Although the unlettered country folk, like the poor but respectable farmer Walter Cunningham, are never given the same centrality in the film as the varied assortment of humans in town, there is a sweet tolerance for them, almost as if they were members of another species. Even in the case of a mean, shiftless drunk like Bob Ewell, cruelty is not explicit. In fact it is so natural, so much a part of the lovely Scout's coming of age, that we do not see it. What we do remark in the film—even with the older Scout's retrospective voice-over—is the silence, the failure of speech between characters like Atticus and Ewell or the tight-lipped dialogue between Scout and Cunningham.

But cruelty is there, even when not reasoned or thought out. The dulcet mockingbird is the flip side of the mad dog. Both generally do noth-ing, but what distinguishes mockingbirds is their natural care for human property and possessions: no eating people's gardens, no nesting in corncribs. They live the life of endearment in that they do nothing *except* make music for people; they're natural servants who naturally delight and gratify. The dog in question is useless, beyond the bounds of the human community, not guarding, not gratifying in any way. Dog and mockingbird are, however, joined in their subordination to humans—quite predictably, of course, since human control over nature, whether domesticated or wild, is commonplace. That is our history, after all, from the biblical admonition to name and control to our contemporary acceptance of factory farms. But what matters here is the threat of extermination. For that threat undergirds the performance of justice. The familiar argument of reasonableness and necessity is made whenever the object is a risk to society. Then it would be put outside society's protection, for justice must always guard against depredation, ordaining the disregard of the superfluous, the ugly, the unfit.

Beneath the tenderness and humor, the seasonal shifts of the film, lies the constant pull of that violence which permits every kindness and indulgence for whatever is of service to or enhances the lives of humans but prescribes certain death and contempt for the worthless. The film's compression of the novel forces us to see how intertwined are the control and elimination of animals and humans. In the logic of disregard, both humans and dogs become insignificant once judged dangerous or, more ominously, simply not worthwhile: too old, too poor, too grubby to matter.

It is striking that the killing of the dog, though melodramatic, and the covering up of the murder of Bob Ewell, though cause for debate, are expected, accommodated, and not at all a matter for concern. Somehow the mad dog and the mad man have simply ceased to matter. But what about Tom Robinson? Where does he fit in this hierarchy of value and waste, threat and removal? When *To Kill a Mockingbird* became a Hollywood film, the evil in the world became visible as something more than the rabid racism of the Ewells and the unlettered country folk. Something harmful, bad, and shocking happens in this film, though it is overlaid with sentiment, goodwill, and right diction. Its continued popularity proves a resistant strain of racism. And it is not surprising that reviews in the film's trailer announce: "It gets close to the heart"; "It's heart-warming and poignantly real."[15] Yet the damage done to persons that is seamless with the everyday disregard of animals becomes clear in cinematic representation. One has only to look at the scream in the eyes of the actor playing Tom

Robinson to know how terrible are the misrecognized but commonplace gestures of white beneficence, which keep blacks forever in their place: if not invisible then stilled, frozen as objects of regard—a regard that is as destructive as and actually analogous to the disregard I have described. No sentimental magnanimity must be allowed to conceal from us that violence.[16]

The Courtroom

Dogs are always barking in Maycomb County. Along with Elmer Bernstein's haunting music, there is the sound of dogs. They are there, stray dogs or pet dogs, along with the shade trees and sweet tea, and they form a backdrop to the daily lives, the pretensions and love of this remembered southern town. Who gets to walk the streets of Maycomb? Not a dog that appears rabid, and if we take seriously the random comments of the ladies, not a "nigger lover," not even little Dill, who can also be called a "stray," since "he gets passed around from relative to relative."[17] But there are other creatures besides dogs, other entities suggestively contained, quarantined, or eliminated, who live outside the normative narratives of citizenship.

Despite repeated claims to universality, humanity and rights are not shared. When persons are deemed anomalous and extraneous to community, they do not have rights as the term is normally used. Furthermore, at the moment when one gives most, seems most beneficent in the largess of recognizing rights—in the person of Atticus, for example—one is following most closely the feeling toward, the sentimentality for animals. Hence the maudlin promise of that mockingbird song and its power to mask the question of cruelty, the presumption of knowledge, and the hidden pathologies of the social. Perhaps the radical intervention called for by this film is to force us to see how exclusion and depersonalization are everywhere, even, or most of all, when we mean well.

The courtroom becomes the stage for the human need to categorize, to dominate, for disfiguration and degradation lurk and even thrive in the scaffolding of the quotidian. In the site of justice making we observe not the undoing of racism but the making of stigma. Nonetheless, the film successfully presses cinematic artifice into the service of legal mystification. In scenes of Atticus standing tall in confrontation with his seated interlocutors, viewers in turn are given their comfortable positions out-side the arena of the dispossessed. The violence of the law's inhabitation of persons, and its dispelling of them, becomes in these scenes a cruelty that annuls the possibility of resistance and leads to humiliation and pain. When the pressure is on to construct, legally and socially, degradation and inferiority, the law toys with the perils of hierarchical thinking even as it perpetuates its effects.

If, as I have argued, the dead dog and the other dogs heard in the film come off as interstitial, mysterious, and undetermined, that is because *animality* is what we should be thinking about instead of any claims for the *humane*.[18] Watching Bob and Mayella Ewell perform their outrage, tell their lies, and comport themselves before an audience of whites around them and blacks up in the gallery is a painful, even appalling experience. Stooped, like cornered or trapped animals, they perform the imperative of subjugation even as their eyes flash with anger or, in the case of Mayella when she is questioned by Atticus Finch, with terror. They are uncomfort-able in their bodies, as if the move from the natural into the severity of a culture that is not theirs to have has forced the lies out of their mouths like pus squeezed out of a wound.

One of the intriguing things about this interpretation is that it gives us the specific landscape for judicial cruelty.[19] That cruelty appears kind. Atticus has the calm, and he owns the field of speech and language. And his questions, even though polite—or, as his rough interlocutors under-stand, because of such politeness—are regulatory. I see the look in his eyes, and instead of feeling empathy, I too begin to squirm, assessing its consequences. The Ewells are destroying Tom Robinson, but they are also disquieted and rendered powerless. Morally outrageous and of no social value, both Bob and Mayella are sacrificed—and they know it—to the agreeable, officially sanctioned personal growth that is allowed characters like Atticus, Jem, and of course Scout.[20]

What we witness during their interrogation by Atticus is not only their lying selves but also the violence the film at once conceals and exposes. The cross-examination feeds on and cultivates an unequal struggle, a war waged between compassion and meanness, visceral repugnance and strict gentility. But where does Mayella figure in these dualisms? That is the question. To look at, to think about the poverty and darkness out of which she comes, only to be exposed to the light of the court, leads us into an ordeal that makes us see the vulnerability shared by no one else in the film. The scandal of her deed, the kiss desired and the lie fabricated, diminish before the abuse she has suffered, her struggle to conjure an appearance of dignity out of inestimable loss.

Maycomb is a very feminine place. Although Aunt Alexandra and her tea-drinking missionary ladies are gone from the film, along with other specimens of prejudicial, genteel vanity, the sensation of female care abounds. Calpurnia and Miss Maudie Atkinson provide the contours of domesticity for Jem and Scout. Although Scout wants nothing more than to continue wearing her overalls, she puts on that dress; and although she squirms, we know that she will become accustomed to putting on the veneer of refinement. But Mayella is outside any possible care. The dress she wears hangs lightly and somewhat askew on her frame. The hat she holds takes on the appearance of frailty that is as much a part of her as strength. In her tangled, painful, and perplexed way, she gives more flesh to real passion than any other person. I am claiming for her a singular place, even though we will not see her (or her sensory experience) develop or grow in any way. Indeed, stasis and entrapment define her status. After her testimony and her appearance in court, she is never seen or heard from again. She vanishes.

But she never really existed for anyone who counts in Maycomb. Not only does she seem to exist outside the scope of law, but she actually exists beyond any legal claims as well. Her calamity is to be condemned to non-relation, though encompassed in a murky zone of affect. The circle of pity extends from Tom Robinson, who dares to say, "I felt right sorry for her," to Atticus Finch, who excuses her—not because of her neglect and abuse, but for her debasement, which seems God-given and natural: "I have nothing but pity in my heart for the chief witness for the State. She is a victim of cruel poverty and ignorance." When Heck thinks about all the town ladies bringing food to Boo Radley and his discomfiture, he never once considers Mayella's reaction to the death of the man who just happens to be her father. Untethered to the world that matters to the inner circle of this film, she is rendered as somehow blurred or broken, a remnant of non-relation in spite of the care we know she gives to a brood of children. In the end, then, even after her defiant "I ain't gonna say no more," her tears strikingly underscore a defeat that is fully expressed in her crumpling to the floor like a rag doll.[21]

A Ghost Story Is Born

Narrow notions of the visible and the empirical, reasonable domination, and social propriety are overtaken by the haunt that is the character of Boo Radley. What about Boo, kept near death in the damp basement of the courthouse, and now, so it is said, "chained to a bed in that house"?[22] He is an extraordinary presence in the film, a person at the threshold of animality, watchful and prescient. Warned away from his house by Dill's nervous aunt, "There's a maniac living there and he's dangerous," the children are obsessed with him.[23] And we learn that he, too, is compelled by them: leaving them a broken watch, chewing gum, a couple of carved dolls, and other tokens of his affection in a hole in an oak tree. His shadow across the porch is invested with a corporeality that lingers, even though he is mostly invisible. Again, what are we to make of the apparition that is Boo Radley, more formally known as Mr. Arthur Radley, a fact we do not learn until the final scene, after he has saved Scout's and Jem's lives, when he stands behind the door of the room where the injured Jem lies in bed?

The scene in the bedroom with the physical contact between Boo and Jem, urged on by Scout, helps us to recognize how inhuman we are for opposing humans to animals. In this tangled segment of the film, Boo Radley is nothing more and simultaneously everything more than a dead man. We watch in his eyes the move from the bruised and broken neighborhood relic to an enhanced, terribly sentient body. That this body is very close to a phantom presence is the point: matter and spirit are in this frame unthinkable apart from each other. His eyes are limpid, beautiful in his witnessing of the events, experiencing pleasure as well as a kind of cognition. How do we understand this spectral vitality?

The end of the film is a new kind of ghost story that redefines the ghostly, for Boo is a figure that is neither clearly vital nor clearly spectral but somehow in between. And we are mesmerized by this aura that is not quite human, not quite animal, and not quite phantasmal. Perhaps we are forced now, with this finale, to move beyond the false hierarchy of race and class and the assumptions about status, value, and damage to a new terrain. This novel ground takes the making of monsters—whether called "mad dogs," "niggers," or "strays"—and shows that fabrication for what it is. We see in full form Boo, once called the crazed idiot. Now, in this congruence between animal, human, and, ultimately, spectral embodiment, he challenges the brutality of discrimination and the rules of law. In this frame, with Boo no longer hovering behind the door but moving radiantly into the light, the question of what it means to be human—and even what we mean by human treatment—becomes moot. Boo is marginalized but not physically annihilated. What we are to imagine happens to his mind and spirit after he returns to his home is not the book's or the film's concern.

Boo Radley's fascination with the sleeping Jem, a gaze that seems to be modeled by animals, becomes the prelude to Scout's invitation that he "pet" the creature that sleeps, who takes on a nature alien to the waking human who would reject that gesture. Boo's saving appearance takes away, in some way consumes the fact of Tom's death. For instead of being, as Sheriff Tate puts it, "with his shy ways, [dragged] into the limelight," he is left alone, spared a fate that, as Scout tells Atticus, "would be sort of like shooting a mockingbird."[24] After the bedroom mystery, the slippage between human, animal, and saving apparition, we now return to the song of the mockingbird, purely and simply a transfer of focus. The film ends with the move from bedroom to swing to the street, where Boo, his hand in Scout's, goes home again, into the place that is also his cage.

The empty swing moving on the porch, a leitmotif in the film, for a moment is vibrant with the seated Scout and Boo, two living creatures who experience an intimacy that is visceral. Perhaps there is nothing wrong with the world envisioned here—and what is nothing less than a glimpse of grace—but the question remains whether this world has been rendered meaningful to viewers. What seems to matter most here, apart from the victims (and they can be good or evil)—Tom Robinson, the dog, Bob Ewell, Mayella Ewell, and Boo Radley—is that claims of sentiment and the ruses of piety saturate the film to such an extent that we are left with only the illusion of benevolent possibility. Nothing more than the fade-out and a lingering sense of violence done. We have relived it, knowing all the while that it is not to be redressed. That is not the point of this film.

Let us recall *Uncle Tom's Cabin*. The comparisons to be made are many: the kind and generous if obeisant Tom (not the Uncle but Tom Robinson); the maternal and food-making Calpurnia; the villainous, immoral, and dirty Ewell (a latter-day Legree). As I said, Boo Radley in his whiteness radiates a saving quality, and although he does not die, he serves the fiction of scrupulously redemptive integrity, much like Little Eva. And so *To Kill a Mockingbird* remains popular: it is high-minded and decent.

But neither Harriet Beecher Stowe nor Lee challenges the moral order of things. While they make us encounter the wayward logic of degradation and the disgrace of servility, neither writer resists the reality of what Emmanuel Levinas has called "the servile soul," gathering into itself particular kinds of oppression or pieces of injustice.[25] Neither writer perturbs the divisions of class, the fact of privilege, or the species-specific bias that form the backdrop to their stories. The relation between those inside and those outside the fantasy of the upright does not concern them. But Lee's fantasy of amelioration succeeds because she knows which kinds of human and nonhuman materials must remain tainted with the same brush of disregard and extinction—a death that is either spiritual or bodily, that blurs the distinction between animal and human.

Even at the lyrical end of the film, in the shadows of the porch and in the sweep of the trees, we are living in the wake of the dead. As long as Scout's voice sustains and concludes the film, we decorously forget the rituals of exclusivity so necessary to the romance of the South. Privilege is a funny thing: it is kind; it can cast a tantalizing safety net around those who are ready to acquiesce in the so-called "natural order" of things. Fictions of sentiment and idealizations of love—the special realm of right-minded women, reasonable men, and domesticated blacks, are linked in unsettling ways to the social realities of property and possession. Lurking in every effusion of ennobling care is the terror of literal dehumanization: things dirtied, bodies forgotten. What remains outside the circle of civilized promise—and the myths of humanity that still beset us—are the characters who are easily eliminated, those who die like dogs: whether shot in the back like Tom Robinson or knifed in the dirt like Bob Ewell. And then, of course, there remains Mayella, not granted the ghostly resonance that hovers over Boo Radley, but forgotten, a nuisance easily dismissed and potentially expendable.

NOTES

1. Harper Lee, *To Kill a Mockingbird* (Philadelphia: Lippincott, 1960), 100.
2. Ibid., 104.
3. I take my application of ritual from Roy Rappaport, "The Obvious Aspects of Ritual," in *Ecology, Meaning, and Religion* (Berkeley: North Atlantic Books, 1979), 175. In his examination of what he describes as "the entailments of the *ritual form,*" he shows

how the interpretation and application of rules—whether legal or behavioral—become ritual, by which he means a "performativeness" that leads to an understanding not only of "the social contract" but also of the "morality intrinsic to its structure."

4. Unless otherwise noted, quotations are from the screenplay of the film published in Horton Foote, *Three Screenplays: To Kill a Mockingbird, Tender Mercies, and The Trip to Bountiful* (New York: Grove Press, 1994), 1–80; quotation, 38.

5. Ibid., 41.

6. For my extensive discussion of dog law, see Colin Dayan, "Skin of the Dog," in *The Law Is a White Dog: How Legal Rituals Make and Unmake Persons* (Princeton: Princeton University Press, 2011), 209–53.

7. The modern conception of dogs as personal property has done very little to advance their position. They remain subject to the same repressive treatment as others targeted for coercion and control. They take their place alongside vagrants and criminals. Out of the maimed right of property in dogs has come a familiar deprivation of persons considered either too servile or too poor to count.

8. *Brown v. Carpenter,* 26 Vt. 638, 642, 643 (1854); *Bradford v. McKibben,* 67 Ky. 545 (1868).

9. Foote, *To Kill a Mockingbird,* 74.

10. Ibid., 78.

11. Ibid.

12. Reviel Netz, *Barbed Wire: An Ecology of Modernity* (Middletown: Wesleyan University Press, 2004).

13. Jacques Derrida, *The Animal That Therefore I Am,* ed. Marie-Louise Mallet, trans. David Willis (New York: Fordham University Press, 2008), 91; Giorgio Agamben: *Homo Sacer: Sovereign Power and Bare Life,* trans. Daniel Heller-Roazen (Stanford: Stanford University Press, 1998), 8. For the only response I know to the marginalization so crucial to the mythology of Maycomb, see Teresa Godwin Phelps, "The Margins of Maycomb: A Rereading of *To Kill a Mockingbird,*" *Alabama Law Review* 45 (1994): 511–30.

14. Foote, *To Kill a Mockingbird,* 33.

15. These quotations are my personal transcriptions.

16. I do not emphasize the treatment of Tom Robinson, arguably the most maligned and injured character in the film, but instead focus on Mayella, the origin of the "lie" that kills him; but she is also the one who lies forever outside the claims of legality. At least Tom's story is known by everyone to be true, and he stands upright in his rightness even though the final judgment fails him. But Mayella has no purchase on justice; there is never an expectation that her voice can be heard. She lives in an unmoored time, a place where even her anger and her shrill final speech cannot remove her from a bestiality condemned as disgraceful. Tom is no disgrace, even in death. I thank Imani Perry for pushing me to ponder Mayella's place in a film ostensibly about the sheer horror of a black man sacrificed to white supremacy.

17. Lee, *To Kill a Mockingbird,* 91.

18. Perhaps no author has fought as strongly against the ruses of sentiment as J. M. Coetzee. In stressing the rather seamless posture of animality as a cure for the lure of liberal beneficence, characters as distinct as David Lurie or his daughter Lucy in *Disgrace* (1999) and Elizabeth Costello in *The Lives of Animals* (1999) or in *Elizabeth Costello* (2003) deliberately put themselves outside the bounds of both propriety and civil life. In that passage they find a different impetus for care, and an ordinary but also dazzling

intimacy with the animal. For a stunning reflection on the "border-boundary between humans and beasts"—and its unsettling—see Jean-Christophe Bailly, *The Animal Side*, trans. Catherine Porter (New York: Fordham University Press, 2011), 5.

19. Claudia Johnson argues that *To Kill a Mockingbird* has received more critical attention from legal scholars than from literary critics. See Claudia Johnson, "Without Tradition and Within Reason: Judge Horton and Atticus Finch in Court," *Alabama Law Review* 45 (1995): 483–510. What is intriguing about legal commentary on *Mockingbird* is the hyperidealization of the courtroom scenes. There have been some attempts to question the iconic Atticus Finch and his presence as force of reason and necessity in confrontation with the lawless or "primitive" unreason in the midst of his community. See Steven Lubet, "Reconstructing Atticus Finch," *Michigan Law Review* 19 (1999): 1339–62; Teresa Godwin Phelps, "Propter Honoris Respectum: Atticus, Thomas, and the Meaning of Justice," *Notre Dame Law Review* 77 (2002): 925–36; Tim Dare, "Lawyers, Ethics, and *To Kill a Mockingbird*," *Philosophy and Literature* 25 (2001): 127–41; Christopher Metress, "The Rise and Fall of Atticus Finch," *Chattahoochee Review* 24 (2003): 95–102. But old myths—and the legal attachment to ruses of beneficence—die hard. See Ann Althouse, "Reconstructing Atticus Finch? A Response to Professor Lubet," *Michigan Law Review* 97 (1999): 1363–69; Rob Atkinson, "Comment on Steven Lubet Reconstructing Atticus Finch," *Michigan Law Review* 97 (1999): 1370–72; Burnele V. Powell, "A Reaction: 'Stand Up, Your Father [a Lawyer] Is Passing,'" *Michigan Law Review* 97 (1999): 1373–75; Randolph N. Stone, "Atticus Finch, in Context," *Michigan Law Review* 97 (1999): 1378–81.

20. As I have argued elsewhere (see, e.g., *The Law Is a White Dog*), the mark of infamy is a threat to certain individuals no matter their color or the abstract claims for individual rights. The forms of law that perpetuate a servile order are sometimes anchored in but most often unmoored from a racialized episteme in order to resurface under the guise of criminal agency, the socially excluded and civilly dead.

21. Foote, *To Kill a Mockingbird*, 65, 66, 61.

22. Ibid., 11.

23. Ibid., 12.

24. Ibid., 79.

25. Emmanuel Levinas, "Freedom and Command," in *Collected Philosophical Papers* (Dordrecht: Martinus Nijhoff, 1987), 16.

CONTRIBUTORS

COLIN DAYAN is Robert Penn Warren Professor in the Humanities, Vanderbilt University.

THOMAS L. DUMM is William H. Hastie '25 Professor of Political Science, Amherst College.

SUSAN SAGE HEINZELMAN is associate professor of English, University of Texas.

LINDA ROSS MEYER is professor of law, Quinnipiac Law School.

NAOMI MEZEY is professor of law, Georgetown Law Center.

IMANI PERRY is professor of African American studies, Princeton University.

RAVIT REICHMAN is associate professor of English, Brown University.

AUSTIN SARAT is William Nelson Cromwell Professor of Jurisprudence and Political Science and Professor of Law, Jurisprudence, and Social Thought and Political Science, Amherst College.

MARTHA MERRILL Umphrey is professor of law, jurisprudence, and social thought, Amherst College.

INDEX

Page numbers in *italics* refer to illustrations.